His Name
Is Jesus

Yacov A. Rambsel

Frontier Research Publications, Inc.
P.O. Box 129, Station "U", Toronto, Ontario M8Z 5M4

His Name Is Jesus

Copyright © 1997 by Yacov A. Rambsel

Library of Congress Cataloging in Publication Data:

Yacov A. Rambsel
His Name Is Jesus

1. Eschatology   2. Apologetics   3. Messianic
1. Title

July 1997 Frontier Research Publications, Inc.
Second printing, November 1997

ISBN 0-921714-00-9

Unless otherwise indicated, Scripture quotations are from the Authorized King James Version.

Cover design: The Riordan Design Group
Printed in Canada: Harmony Printing Limited

Table of Contents

Foreword

Yacov A. Rambsel has spent many years searching the phenomenon of hidden Hebrew codes within the Scriptures. He has found many significant codes through his diligent examination of the Hebrew text of the Scriptures without the aid of a computer program for such studies. Yacov's level of concentration amazes me, even after many years of observing him virtually every day as he painstakingly examines the marvelous discoveries encoded within the Hebrew. Yacov's passion for the truths of God's Word motivates his careful checking and rechecking to verify these insights (the hidden encoded words). The guidance of the Holy Spirit (*Rauch ha'Kodesh*), however, is the most indispensable ingredient of Yacov's work, "Howbeit when He, the Spirit of truth, is come, He will guide you into all truth. . . ." (John 16:14 KJV)

At times, Yacov simultaneously analyzes numerous combinations of coded insights. He copies each Hebrew letter — placing each a certain distance from the next — until he reaches the seventh or ninth row. After analyzing and calculating these letters, he then underlines a Hebrew word or phrase that he has discovered. These words or phrases that he finds reveal that no human mind could have written them or created such a complex pattern. As part of his daily research into these biblical truths, Yacov often experiences a profound thrill of discovery as another insight almost leaps off the pages of Scripture.

Occasionally, Yacov will find that God uses the same encoded insight again and again in order to emphasize some deep truth from the depths of the Hebrew text. As you read *His Name Is Jesus*, you will sometimes encounter what appears to be a redundant use of a particular verse of Scripture. As you read, however, you will find new and glorious truths from God's Holy Word.

Many people have asked about these Hebrew codes. The evidence is overwhelming that God inspired the human authors of the Hebrew Scriptures to write the text in a very precise pattern of letters to convey His truths to humankind. Jesus Himself referred to the importance of the precise lettering when He declared, "For verily I say unto you, until heaven and earth pass, one jot or one tittle shall in no wise pass from the law, till all be fulfilled" (Matthew 5:18). By examining a wide range of interval distances (i.e., every fifth, twentieth, or forty-ninth letter) between the Hebrew letters (and sometimes between Hebrew words), Yacov analyzes a variety of calculations to verify the existence and meaning of these encoded insights.

The code technique known as "equidistant-letter sequence" (ELS) is the one that he most frequently uses. In addition, he has found fascinating insights at equidistant-word sequences in which the first letter of a series of words, spaced at equal intervals (i.e., every tenth word), reveals significant Hebrew words. Yet another technique involves examining the Hebrew letters by using sequential progression (1, 2, 3, 4) and sequential digression (4, 3, 2, 1).

Yacov has discovered that these codes can overlap from

one biblical book to the next. Some of the codes that reveal the name *Yeshua*/Jesus, begin in the last chapter of a book, such as Genesis, and continue in the first chapters of the next book, Exodus. It appears that the inspired Word of God is an inexhaustible mine of deeply embedded words and phrases that continually glow beneath the surface of the printed text. Without the guidance of God's precious Holy Spirit, Yacov's intriguing research would not have progressed this far. In fact, it would have been impossible. The next section reveals some helpful information about the beautiful language of Hebrew that will assist you in gaining the most benefit from this study.

Yaphah Rambsel

April 9, 1997—1 Nissan 5757

A Word to the Reader

Hebrew . . . What is it about this language that beckons us to it as though Someone from beyond its spoken or written letters is calling to us? "O Lord, how great are Thy works! Thy thoughts are very deep" (Psalms 92:5). Well, speaking for myself, as I listen to its melodious and precise sounds flowing over the tongue of a fluent speaker . . . like clear, sparkling water . . . like the sound of a babbling brook gushing from a faraway, timeless realm . . . I feel a deep sense of awe as the Living Water (*Mayim Chayim*) of *Ruach haKodesh* (the Holy Spirit) washes over my heart, reminding me that I am in the very presence of my Yeshua HaMashiach, whose precious Name is the Word of God (Revelation 19:13).

As I observe the Hebrew aleph-bet in huge, blue letters flowing across our computer's screen-saver, I get a sense of the calligrapher's art. I promise myself that I must write the twenty-two letters of Hebrew עברית with more graceful precision. I take a special delight in the fact that Hebrew is written and read from right to left. I also have found it somewhat easier to learn than my native tongue of English, which I speak with a Texas drawl. I have learned to appreciate the English language even more for the following reason: "The English agreeth one thousand times more with the Hebrew than the Latin or the Greek" (William Tyndale).

Do you want to experience a new kind of adventure? Do you want to know why you sometimes get a wistful, nostalgic feeling as you learn to speak one or more foreign languages? Then I suggest that you buy or borrow a copy of *The Word: The Dictionary That Reveals the Hebrew Sources of English* by Isaac E. Mozeson. Let us get back to the roots of our spiritual heritage articulated in the dazzling light of Hebrew: "Our eyes are holden that we cannot see things that stare us in the face until the hour arrives when the mind is ripened. Then we behold them, and the time when we saw them not is like a dream" (Ralph Waldo Emerson). And another very special word: "It is the glory of God to conceal a thing; but the honor of kings is to search out a matter" (Proverbs 25:2).

Yaphah Rambsel

April 9, 1997—1 Nissan 5757

The Hebrew Aleph-bet

Sefardi Pronunciation

Numerical Value	Phonetics	Letters	Associated Meanings
1	aleph	א	beginning, first, teach, Jehovah (Adonai), thousand
2	bet, vet	ב ב	house, dwelling place
3	gimmel	ג	bridge, camel
4	dalet	ד	pivotal door, lifting up, elevation, poor
5	hey	ה	revelation, word, promise, Spirit, wind, covenant
6	vav	ו	hook, pillars
7	zayin	ז	weapon, sword, number of spiritual perfection
8	chet	ח	life, fear of the Lord, circumcision
9	tet	ט	good, goodness, humanity
10	yod	י	hand, thrust, strength
20	kaf	כ ך	palm, power to suppress, lift up
30	lamed	ל	to learn, to teach
40	mem	מ ם	water
50	nun	נ ן	Heir to the Throne, faithfulness
60	samek	ס	endless cycle, support, wedding ring
70	ayin	ע	eye, color, fountain
80	pey feh	פ ף	mouth, here, present
90	tzadi	צ ץ	righteous, to hunt (for insights)
100	qof	ק	to surround, great strength, monkey
200	resh	ר	head, chief, poor man
300	shin sin	שׁ שׂ	full cycle, tooth, El Shaddai
400	tav	ת	sign, mark, more, end, last

Hebrew is written and read from right to left.

Acknowledgments

I thank all my friends and relatives for their encouragement of my writing this second volume concerning the insights of Yeshua HaMashiach. My wife, Yaphah, and I personally thank Grant and Kaye Jeffrey of Frontier Research Publications, Inc. in Toronto, Canada, for their support and friendship. James and Alene Rambsel, our son and daughter, whom we love very much, have given us undying encouragement. My father-in-law and mother-in-law contributed their ceaseless love and prayers. Paul, my father-in-law, went to be with the Lord in September 1996, at the age of ninety. The patience and spiritual daily support that I receive from my wife, Yaphah, have made this work possible. I personally thank my friend Donald F. Shomody, a student of Hebrew from Toledo, Ohio, for his contribution of intricate research of the insights, part of which is in this book. I also acknowledge my dear friend and companion, Dr. Joel Young from Richardson, Texas. His life-long study of the Hebrew Scriptures has enhanced my research and the quality of this book. Last, but not least, I thank my wonderful Savior, Yeshua HaMashiach, for strengthening me, and I give Him all the glory for this work and His guidance by the Holy Spirit. Without Him, there would be no purpose in life.

Yacov A. Rambsel

Introduction
by Grant R. Jeffrey, author of
The Signature of God

Introduction: The Mysterious Hebrew Bible Codes

Recently, researchers in Israel rediscovered and validated a staggering phenomenon. Underneath the Hebrew text of the Old Testament are hidden codes that reveal an astonishing knowledge of future events and personalities that cannot be explained unless God inspired the writers to record His precise words.

Rabbi Weissmandl's Astonishing Discovery

Rabbi Michael Dov Weissmandl, a brilliant Czechoslovakian Jewish scholar in astronomy, mathematics, and Judaic studies, found an obscure reference in a book by a fourteenth-century rabbi known as Rabbeynu Bachayah that described a pattern of letters encoded within the Torah — the first five books of the Bible. This discovery, made during the years before World War I, inspired Rabbi Weissmandl to begin exploring other examples of codes hidden within the Torah. During the war years he found that he could locate certain meaningful words, phrases, and word pairs (e.g., hammer and anvil) if he found the first letter and then counted a certain number of letters to find the second one, and then counted the same number again to find the third one, and so on. In other words, if he found the first letter of *Torah* somewhere in the Hebrew text and then, by skipping forward seven letters, he found the second letter, he would continue to skip forward seven letters to see whether or not the complete word *Torah* was spelled out in the text at equally spaced intervals. The rabbi was astonished to find that an incredible number of significant words were hidden within the text of the Torah at equally spaced intervals. These intervals varied from every five letters up to intervals of hundreds of letters. In one place the letters of the word *Torah* might be found at seven-letter intervals, in another at sixty-seven-letter intervals.

Although Rabbi Weissmandl found many coded names simply by manually counting the letters in the text, he did not record his discoveries in writing. Fortunately, some of his students did record several examples of his discoveries. Over the following decades, students in Israel who had heard about his research began searching the Torah for themselves to ascertain whether or not such codes actually existed. Their discoveries ultimately resulted in research studies at Hebrew University that have proven the validity of the codes, which are now known as *Equidistant Letter Sequences* (ESL). The introduction of sophisticated high-speed computers allowed Jewish scholars at Hebrew University to explore the text of the Torah in ways that previous generations could only dream about.

Scientific Proof for Weissmandl's Discovery

In 1988, Doron Witztum, Yoav Rosenberg, and Eliyahu Rips at Hebrew University and the Jerusalem College of Technology completed a research project that followed up on Rabbi Weismandl's research. In August, 1994, they published a paper called "Equidistant Letter Sequences in the Book of Genesis" in one of the most prominent scientific mathematics journals in the world, the American mathematics journal *Statistical Science*.

In their experiment, the scientists arbitrarily chose three hundred Hebrew word-pairs that were logically related in meaning, such as *hammer* and *anvil*, or *tree* and *leaf*, or *man* and *woman*. They asked the computer program to locate any such word pairs in the Genesis text. Once the computer found the first Hebrew letter in the word *hammer*, it would look for the second letter at various intervals or spaces between letters. If the program could not locate the second letter of the target word *hammer* following the first letter at a two-letter interval, it would then search at a three-letter interval, then a four-letter interval, and so forth. Once it located the second letter at, say, the twelve-letter interval, it would then look for the third letter at the same twelve-letter interval, and so on through all 78,064 Hebrew letters in Genesis. The computer also looked for coded words by checking in reverse order.

After the program had examined the text for each of the three hundred word-pairs, the researchers were astonished to realize that every single word-pair had been located in Genesis in close proximity to each other. As mathematicians and statisticians, they were naturally astounded because they knew it was humanly impossible to construct such an intricate and complicated pattern beneath a surface text, such as Genesis, which told the history of the Jewish people. The odds against the three hundred word-pairs occurring by chance in the text of Genesis are simply staggering! The bottom line is that only a supernatural intelligence, far beyond our human capacity, could have produced the pattern of secretly coded words found in the Bible.

Hebrew Codes Speak of the Future

But that was only the beginning of the story. In a 1994 follow-up paper, the team of researchers recorded the results of their search for pairs of encoded words that relate to *events that occurred long after the time when Moses wrote the Torah*. They selected the names of thirty-four of the most prominent rabbis and Jewish sages who lived during the last two thousand years. The process was simple. The researchers simply selected the thirty-four sages with the longest biographies in the *Encyclopedia of Great Men in Israel*, a well-respected Hebrew reference book. They asked the computer program to search the text of the Torah for close word pairs coded at equally spaced intervals that contained the names of the famous rabbis paired with the dates of their birth or death (using the Hebrew month and day). The Jewish people celebrate the memory of their famous sages by commemorating the dates of their deaths. Incredibly, the computer program found every single one of the thirty-four names of these famous rabbis embedded in the text of Genesis, paired at significantly close proximity with the actual date of birth or the date of death. The odds against these particular names and dates occurring by chance were calculated by the Israeli mathematicians as only one chance in 775,000,000!

The scientists and editors at the *Statistical Science* journal who reviewed the experimental data were naturally astonished. They demanded that the Israeli scientists run the computer test program again on a second sample. This time they searched for the next thirty-two most prominent Jewish sages listed in the encyclopedia. To the astonishment of the skeptical reviewers, the results were equally successful with the second set of famous sages. The staggering result of the combined test revealed that the names and dates of the birth or death of every one of the sixty-six most famous Jewish sages were coded in close proximity within the text of Genesis.

Despite the fact that all of the reviewers held previous beliefs against the inspiration of the Scriptures, the overwhelming evidence and the integrity of the data were such that the journal reluctantly agreed to publish the article in its August 1994 issue under the title "Equidistant Letter Sequences in the Book of Genesis." Robert Kass, the editor of *Statistical Science*, wrote this comment about the study:

> Our referees were baffled: their prior beliefs made them think the Book of Genesis could not possibly contain meaningful references to modern day individuals, yet when the authors carried out additional analyses and checks the effect persisted. The paper is thus offered to *Statistical Science* readers as a challenging puzzle.

An article in *Bible Review* magazine by Dr. Jeffrey Satinover, in October 1995, reported that the mathematical probability of these sixty-six names of Jewish sages and their dates of birth or death occurring by chance in an ancient text like Genesis was less than one chance in two and a half billion! Interestingly, the researchers attempted to reproduce these results by running the computer program on other religious Hebrew texts outside the Bible, including the Samaritan Pentateuch. The Samaritans developed their own variant text of the five books of Moses, called the Samaritan Pentateuch, which differs in many very small textual details from the standard Hebrew Bible (known as the Masoretic text). Despite the surface similarity of the two texts, the researchers could not detect word pairs in the Samaritan Pentateuch or any other Hebrew text outside the Bible.

The *Bible Review* article provoked an onslaught of letters (mostly critical) to the editor. Dr. Satinover responded to his critics as follows:

> The robustness of the Torah codes findings derives from the rigor of the research. To be published in a journal such as *Statistical Science*, it had to run, without stumbling, an unusually long gauntlet manned by some of the world's most eminent statisticians. The results were thus triply unusual: in the extraordinariness of what was found; in the strict scrutiny the findings had to hold up under; and in the unusually small odds (less than 1 in 62,500) that they were due to chance. Other amazing claims about the Bible, Shakespeare, and so forth, have never even remotely approached this kind of rigor, and have therefore never come at all close to publication in a peer-reviewed, hard science venue. The editor of *Statistical Science*, himself a skeptic, has challenged readers to find a flaw; though many have tried, none has succeeded. All the [basic] questions asked by *Bible Review* readers — and many more sophisticated ones — have therefore already been asked by professional critics and exhaustively answered by the research. Complete and convincing responses to even these initial criticisms can get fairly technical.   (*Bible Review*, November 1995)

The Purpose of *His Name Is Jesus*

The discovery of complex Hebrew codes that reveal supernatural and prophetic knowledge about the future has caused tremendous consternation in the academic community because it challenges the long-held beliefs of liberal scholars who generally reject verbal inspiration of the Bible.

The discovery has also been used for more

sensationalistic purposes. A recent article in *Newsweek* (June 9, 1997) reviews a book by journalist Michael Drosnin entitled *The Bible Code*. The headline of the article was "Seek and Ye Shall Find: A controversial new book claims that buried within the Bible is a secret guide to all that was, is and shall be."

Yacov Rambsel's purpose in this book is not to pander to a search for the sensational nor to convince antagonistic scholars. Yacov, as a Messianic Jew, seeks to express his love for Yeshua, his Messiah, through his work. By bringing to light the pervasive presence of Yeshua in the very words of the Old Testament, he wants others, Jews and Christians, to find that same love. The findings he presents in this book are marvelous and appeal to the mind — but it is his love for Yeshua shining from every page that can transform our hearts.

After Yacov's first book, *YESHUA,* was released last year it quickly became an international bestseller. However, some scholars challenged his discovery of the name *Yeshua* in every major messianic prophecy in the Old Testament. They claimed that the name *Yeshua* was a short name with only four Hebrew letters that could be found by random chance everywhere. However, they could not explain why the name *Yeshua* would appear encoded within so many major messianic prophecies. We have not found any other significant names appearing in small ELS (equidisant-letter sequences) intervals within these significant messianic passages.

However, these skeptics dismissed Yacov's discovery of the Yeshua Codes and declared that the word *Yeshua* did not refer to Jesus of Nazareth. They acknowledged that the word *Yeshua* appeared repeatedly within these messianic passages, as Yacov's book claimed, but they rejected Yacov's claim that these codes were "significant." The skeptical scholars claimed that you could find *Yeshua* encoded in ELS in almost any portion of Hebrew literature, including the Israeli phone book or Woody Allen's writings translated into the Hebrew language. During the last few months, in discussions with Yacov, I asked him to complete an exhaustive analysis of the "Suffering Servant" prophecy in Isaiah 52:13 through Isaiah 53 that predicts many incredible details about Jesus Christ's death on the cross that were fulfilled centuries later.

Yacov has made an astonishing discovery that God has encoded the names of Jesus and virtually everyone else that was involved in the tragic crucifixion of Christ over seven hundred years before the event. He found the encoded names of Jesus, the Nazarene, Messiah, the three Marys, the two high priests, Herod, Pilate, and many of Christ's disciples in one small prophetic passage — Isaiah 53 — the greatest messianic prophecy in the Old Testament. Furthermore, these names were encoded in Isaiah's prophecy in 740 B.C., more than seven centuries before Jesus was born. Can any unbiased observer of this evidence honestly claim that these codes refer to anyone other than Jesus of Nazareth?

A Word of Caution

1. *These codes have been found only in the Hebrew Masoretic text of the Old Testament.*

No one has been able to locate detailed, meaningful Bible codes in any other Hebrew literature outside the Bible. Experimenters have carefully examined other Hebrew writings for the existence of codes including the Jewish *Talmud*, the *Mishnah*, the Apocryphal writings of *Tobit* and the *Maccabees*. They even examined modern Hebrew literature, such as translations of *War and Peace*. However, the scientists found no pattern of codes in any literature other than the Old Testament. Several researchers have told me they found indications of codes in the Greek of the New

Testament, but no detailed research has been published to date.

2. *No one can search the Bible using these codes to foretell future events.*

It is impossible to extract the encoded information unless you already know what the future facts are. The encoded information about a future event cannot be pulled out of the biblical text in advance of the event because you wouldn't know what to tell the computer to look for. It is only after a historical event has occurred that you can have the computer program look for the name of the person or event and check to see if the codes contain the information confirming the event. In other words, this method confirms that the Bible contains encoded data about events that occurred centuries after it was written. However, the method cannot be used to foretell the future. The Bible prohibits us from engaging in foretelling the future. Agnostic writer Michael Drosnin, in a recent book called *Bible Code*, has claimed that he discovered codes that allowed him to predict future events. However, a close examination of his claims reveals that the encoded information is insufficient to allow anyone to confidently predict any future event. The information encoded in the Bible can only be accurately interpreted after an event, such as the coming of the Messiah, has actually occurred. Then we can compare the historical event with the encoded information to determine whether or not God has revealed these prophetic details centuries before they occurred. Therefore, the codes give God the glory, not the human researcher.

3. *These Hebrew codes do not contain any hidden theological or doctrinal messages.*

The phenomenon of the Hebrew codes has nothing to do

with numerology. Numerology has been defined by the authoritative *Webster's Dictionary* as "the study of the occult significance of numbers." There are no secret sentences, detailed messages, or sentences about theology in the encoded words. God's message of salvation and His commandments for holy living to humankind are found only in the open words of the Scriptures.

4. Why then did God place these hidden Hebrew codes in the text of the Bible?

For almost seventeen centuries, from the time of Emperor Constantine's conversion in A.D. 300 until 1900, the Bible has been generally accepted by Western culture as the inspired and authoritative Word of God. However, the last ninety years have witnessed an unrelenting assault on the authority of the Bible by the intellectual elite, the academic community, and the media. Most people in our culture have been exposed to countless attacks on the authority and accuracy of the Scriptures throughout their lives in educational institutions and from the mass media. I believe that God has provided this extraordinary evidence in the form of the Hebrew Codes to prove to this generation of skeptics that the Bible is truly the Word of God.

The discovery in the last decade of these incredible codes provides powerful evidence to our skeptical generation that God truly inspired the writers of the Bible to record His message to mankind. These encoded words describing the names of people, places, and dates provide powerful evidence to any unbiased inquirer that they can trust the message of the Bible that promises salvation to all those who will accept Jesus the Messiah as their personal Savior and Lord.

Grant R. Jeffrey
July, 1997—Toronto, Canada

1

Isaiah: The Messianic Chapters

The central theme of this book, *His Name Is Jesus*, is the Bible's inspired revelation of the Lord Jesus the Messiah *Jehovah Yeshua HaMashiach* יהוה ישוע המשיח.

Special Note

The insights that reveal significant Hebrew words (*Yeshua, Jehovah*) never detract, modify, or add to the basic, foundational doctrines of the Scripture. Our recently discovered encoded words provide overwhelming evidence that all of Scripture, both in its surface reading and in the encoded insights, glorifies God. This phenomenon has nothing to do with numerology or divination. Webster's dictionary defines numerology as the "study of the occult significance of numbers." This phenomenon of the Hebrew Codes has nothing to do with the occult. In addition, this phenomenon does not allow one to know anything about future events. God clearly forbids fortune-telling. Until an event has occurred, we cannot know what word(s) to look for, and, therefore, we cannot use the codes to find out anything about future events. However, after an event, such as the life, death, or resurrection of Yeshua, has occurred, we can examine the Hebrew text to see whether or not there are coded words that reveal God's foreknowledge of that event. In this way, only God receives the glory from our examination of these fascinating codes.

A powerful indication of the validity of these encoded insights is found in the fact that these codes glorify Jesus of Nazareth repeatedly as the Messiah, Adonai, Jehovah, and Lord. The First Epistle of John clearly teaches that those who declare that Jesus Christ has come in the flesh are of God: "Hereby know ye the Spirit of God: Every spirit that confesseth that Jesus Christ is come in the flesh is of God" (1 John 4:2). I believe that the fact that these coded words glorify Jesus Christ as the Son of God is the strong proof that God placed these insights into the ancient scriptural text.

We translate the Hebrew word signifying the personal name of God, *Jehovah* יהוה, with the word "Adonai," which means "Lord" — a traditional practice followed by the Jewish people in reverence for the ineffable holy name of God, which they believe is too sacred to pronounce.

Within the book of Isaiah, there are three famous messianic chapters known as the Suffering Servant passage. Isaiah 52 shows us a promise of a blessing. Isaiah 53 reveals the sacrificial price of the blessing, and Isaiah 54 offers us the wonderful blessings of the Lord because of the sacrifice of the Lamb of God. These three chapters in Isaiah should be read together as one unit. Beginning with Isaiah 52:13 and continuing through Isaiah 53:12, the Scripture gives a dynamic description of the Messiah as the Lamb of God and a sin offering unto His death, His burial, and His resurrection to life.

Throughout these three chapters, the Lord has hidden many astonishing insights composed of equidistant-letter sequences called ELS Bible Codes. The events associated with these codes were precisely fulfilled seven centuries later in the life of Jesus, as recorded in the New Testament. Within these prophetic Scriptures, the Lord God of Israel has encoded the name of the Messiah, who is Yeshua (Jesus), and the names of almost every single participant in the crucifixion of Jesus the Messiah. In addition, the Scriptures reveal the names of the chief priests at the time of the crucifixion, as well as Herod, Pilate, Caesar, and many others that lived during this terrible time of Christ's prophetic fulfillment of the Passover sacrifice.

The Lord God of Heaven is exact and perfect in all that He does. Our God never makes a mistake and His timing is impeccable. He has meticulously placed, in its proper position, every word and letter throughout all the Bible. Not one jot or tittle is misplaced, but most importantly, all His word will be fulfilled to the letter.

First Thessalonians 5:21 tells us to "prove all things; hold fast that which is good," and 1 Peter 3:15 admonishes us to "sanctify the Lord God in your hearts: and be ready always to give an answer to every man that asketh you a reason of the hope that is in you with meekness and fear." The disciple Thomas needed proof of Jesus' resurrection. Despite the fact that Jesus had predicted His crucifixion and resurrection on the third day, Thomas would not believe the reports of the women that Jesus had indeed risen from the dead. However, the Lord personally appeared to Thomas in the Upper Room to give him the proof he needed in spite of his doubt. Many people today are like Thomas; they need additional verification of the truth of the Bible and the deeper things of God. In our skeptical generation, God is using the discovery of the Bible Codes, including the astonishing insights in this book about Yeshua, to provide overwhelming scientific proof of the authority and inspiration of the infallible Word of God.

Yeshua is My Name יִשׁרע שׁמי

One of the most astonishing discoveries mentioned in my first book *YESHUA* was that the name *Yeshua* (Jesus) was encoded within the Hebrew text of virtually all of the messianic passages of the Old Testament. The name "Jesus" in Hebrew is *Yeshua* יִשׁרע. It is spelled with four Hebrew letters (right to left) as follows: yod (יִ); shin (שׁ); vav (ו) and ayin (ע). I was thrilled when I found the name *Yeshua* encoded in Isaiah 53:10. This famous prophecy foretold the grief of the suffering Messiah and His atoning sacrifice when He offered Himself as the Lamb of God, a perfect sacrifice, on the cross. "Yet it pleased the Lord to bruise him; he hath put him to grief: when thou shalt make his soul an offering for sin, he shall see his seed, he shall prolong his days, and the pleasure of the Lord shall prosper in his hand" (Isaiah 53:10). The words *Yeshua Shmi* "Yeshua [Jesus] is My Name" יִשׁרע שׁמי are encoded in this messianic verse beginning with the second Hebrew letter yod (יִ) in the phrase "He shall prolong" *ya'arik* יאריך and counting every 20th letter from left to right. This discovery, together with the finding of *Yeshua* encoded in dozens of other well-known messianic prophecies in the Old Testament has thrilled hundreds of thousands of readers.

However, my friend Grant Jeffrey challenged me to complete my in-depth investigation for additional codes related to the life of Jesus Christ in Isaiah 53. As a result of hundreds of hours of detailed research, I would like to share my recent discovery. Over forty names of individuals and places associated with the crucifixion of Jesus of Nazareth were encoded within this Suffering Servant messianic passage centuries before the birth of Jesus. I trust that my readers will be as thrilled with this unprecedented discovery as I am.

The Names of Jesus and His Disciples

God has secretly encoded within these chapters of Isaiah many names of people, places, and events in the life of Jesus Christ that are recorded in the New Testament. It is as though the history of Christ's crucifixion was written centuries before the events took place. All things are known to God, and He is revealing these wonderful truths to His servants.

Let us examine the information about those in power at the time of the crucifixion. In Isaiah 52:15, starting with the third letter in the seventh word and counting every forty-first letter from right to left spells "Caiaphas" *Kayafa* כיפה. In Isaiah 53:3, starting with the fifth letter in the sixth word and counting every forty-fifth letter from left to right spells "Annas" *Ahnan* ענן. In Isaiah 53:11, starting with the first letter of the second word and counting every fourteenth letter from left to right spells "the desperate (despairing)" *Levis noash Levim* נואש לוים. In addition, in Isaiah 53:9, starting with the second letter in the thirteenth word and counting every seventh letter from left to right spells "the evil Roman city" *rah eer Romi* רע עיר רומי. The New Testament confirms the names of the high priests of that day in Luke 3:2: "Annas and Caiaphas being the high priests, the word of God came unto John the son of Zacharias in the wilderness." That the high (chief) priests were involved in the crucifixion is evident from John 19:15: "But they cried out, Away with Him, away with Him, crucify Him. Pilate

The Names of Israel's Two High Priests

Caiaphas *Kayafa* כיפה (every 41 letters forward)

Annas *Ahnan* ענן (every 42 letters forward)

15. כן יזה גוים רבים עליו יקפצו מלכים פיהם כי אשר

לא-ספר להם ראו ואשר לא-שמעו התבוננו.

1. מי האמין לשמעתנו וזרוע יהוה על-מי נגלתה.

2. ויעל כיונק לפניו וכשרש מארץ ציה לא-תאר

לו ולא הדר ונראהו ולא-מראה ונחמדהו.

3. נבזה וחדל אישים איש מכאבות וידוע

חלי וכמסתר פנים ממנו נבזה ולא חשבנהו.

4. אכן חלינו הוא נשא ומכאבינו סבלם

ואנחנו חשבנהו נגוע מכה אלהים ומענה.

Isaiah 52:15 to 53:4

saith unto them, Shall I crucify your King? The chief priests answered, We have no king but Caesar [the Roman]."

In Isaiah 53:12, starting with the third letter in the second word and counting every fifty-fifth letter from left to right spells "the disciples" למדים. Sometimes, the tav (ת) precedes this word.

The Names of the Disciples

The disciples names and their meanings are encoded as follows:

1. *Peter*. Simon *Shimon* שמעון אהפער כפה; Peter *Petros* פטרוס.

In Isaiah 53:10, starting with the fifth letter in the

eleventh word and counting every fourteenth letter from left to right spells "Peter" כפה.

2. *James, son of Zabbadee. Ya'akov ben Zabedai* בן זבדי יעקב.

In Isaiah 52:2, starting with the third letter in the ninth word and counting every thirty-fourth letter from left to right spells "James" *Ya'akov* יעקב.

3. *John (James' brother). Yochanan* יוחנן.

In Isaiah 53:10, starting with the fourth letter in the eleventh word and counting every twenty-eighth letter from left to right spells "John" *Yochanan* יוחנן.

4. *Andrew (Peter's brother). And'drai* אנדרי

In Isaiah 53:4, starting with the first letter in the eleventh word, which is "God" *Elohim* אלהים and counting every forty-eighth letter from left to right spells "Andrew fears God" *And'drahi yirel* אנדרי. Also, the adjacent letters spell "the one finding My Spirit" *ruchi metz'mayi* רוחי מצמאי. The name "Zion" *Tziyon* ציון shows up in this same area at ninty-six-letter intervals. Note that John 1:40–41 says, "One of the two which heard John speak, and followed him, was Andrew, Simon Peter's brother. He first findeth his own brother Simon, and saith unto him, We have found the Messias, which is being interpreted, The Christ [*HaMashiach* המשיח]."

5. *Philip. Pilip* פילך; *Pilipos* פילפוס.

In Isaiah 53:5, starting with the third letter in the tenth word and counting every 133rd letter from left to right spells "Philip" פילך.

6. *Thomas. Toma* תומא.

In Isaiah 53:2, starting with the first letter in the eighth word and counting every thirty-fifth letter from right to left spells "Thomas" *Toma* תומא.

7. *Matthew*. There are three ways to spell Matthew: *Mati, Mattai, Mattiyahu* מתי מתתי מתתיהו. *Mattai* מתתי is an abbreviated form of *Mattiyahu* מתתיהו.

In Isaiah 53:8, starting with the first letter in the twelfth word and counting every 295th letter from left to right spells "Matthew" *Mattai* מתתי.

8. *James, son of Alphaeus. Ben Chalipi Ya'akov* בן חלפי יעקב.

In Isaiah 52:2, starting with the fourth letter in the third word and counting every twentieth letter from left to right spells *Ya'akov* יעקב. The adjacent letters spell "the Levites" הלוים. Also, in Isaiah 53:1, starting with the second letter in the first word and counting every 188th letter from right to left spells "James" *Ya'akov* יעקב. Two of Christ's disciples were named James.

9. *Simon*. (Zelotes), the Canaanite. *Shimon hakanai* שמעון הקני.

In Isaiah 52:14, starting with the first letter in the second word and counting every forty-seventh letter from right to left spells "Simon" *Shimon* שמעון.

10. *Thaddaeus. Taddai* תדי, and *Lebbaeus* לבי.

In Isaiah 53:12, starting with the first letter of the eighth word and counting every fiftieth letter from left to right spells "Thaddaeus" תדי.

11. *Matthias. Mattiyah* מתיה.

In Isaiah 53:5, starting with the fourth letter in the seventh word and counting every eleventh letter from left to right spells "Matthias" מתיה. This is the name of the disciple who was chosen by lot to replace the traitor Judas

Thomas *Toma* תומא (every 35 letters in reverse)

Peter *Kepha* כפה (every 19 letters)

Andrew And'drahi אנדרי (every 48 letters)

1. מן האמין לשמעתנו וזרוע יהוה על-מי נגלתה.

2. ויעל כיונק לפניו וכשרש מארץ ציה צ'ה לא-תאר
לו ולא הדר ונראהו ולא-מראה ונחמדהו.

3. נבזה וחדל אישים איש מכאבות וידוע
חלי וכמסתר פנים ממנו נבזה ולא חשבנהו.

4. אכן חלינו הוא נשא ומכאבינו סבלם
ואנחנו חשבנהו נגוע מכה אלהים ומענה.

Isaiah 53:1-4

Iscariot. Acts 1:26 tells us how Matthias was chosen: "And they gave forth their lots; and the lot fell upon Matthias (מתיה); and he was numbered with the eleven apostles." One of the criteria for choosing a replacement disciple was that he had to have been a personal witness to the complete ministry and resurrection of Jesus Christ so that he could present an eyewitness account to those he would teach about the Christian faith.

Yeshua the Nazarene

Christ was called Jesus of Nazareth because He was brought up in Nazareth with His family until commencing His ministry. "And He [Jesus] came and dwelt in a city called Nazareth: that it might be fulfilled which was spoken by the prophets, He shall be called a Nazarene" (Matthew 2:23). Some of the critics of the Yeshua Codes discovery have challenged our judgment that the name *Yeshua* found encoded in Isaiah 53 actually refers to the historical Jesus of Nazareth.

In Isaiah 53:6, starting with the third letter in the eleventh word and counting every forty-seventh letter from right to left spells "Nazarene" נזיר. Throughout Isaiah 53, the word "Nazarene" is encoded several times. This discovery of the name "Nazarene" נזיר near the name "Yeshua" ישוע in the same messianic passage, together with the names of His disciples, is overwhelming evidence that these codes refer to the historical Jesus. A Nazarene was a special person who was chosen for a special purpose. The dedication of a Nazarite is quite compelling, to say the least. Yeshua is called the Nazarene because of His total commitment to His calling. One must be totally dedicated to the Lord to fulfill the vow of the Nazarene. The prophet Samuel was given to the Lord by his mother when she took the Nazarene vow for him.

> And she vowed a vow, and said, O Lord of hosts, if Thou wilt indeed look on the affliction of Thine handmaid, and remember me, and not forget Thine handmaid, but wilt give unto Thine handmaid a man child, then I will give him unto the Lord all the days of his life, and there shall no razor come upon his head. (1 Samuel 1:11)

We see, however, a greater fulfillment of the Nazarene vow in the Messiah:

> And he [Jesus] came and dwelt in a city called Nazareth: that it might be fulfilled which was spoken by the prophets, He shall be called a Nazarene נזיר.
> (Matthew 2:23)

Nazarene נזיר (every 47 letters forward) ⬡

6. כלנו כצאן תעינו איש לדרכו

פנינו ויהוה הפגיע בו את עוֹן כלנו.

7. נגש והוא נענה ולא יפתח-פיו כשה לטבח

יובל וכרחל לפני גֹזיה נאלמה ולא יפתח פיו.

8. מעצר וממשפט לקח ואת-דורו מי ישוחח

כֹֹ נגזר מארץ מיים מפשע עמי נגע למו.

9. ויתן את-רשעים קברו ואת-עשיֹֹ במתיו

על לא-חמס עשה ולא מרמה בפיו.

Isaiah 53:6-9

In 1 Samuel 1:11, starting with the second letter in the fourth word, which is "Adonai" *Jehovah* יהוה and counting every thirty-ninth letter from left to right spells "the Messiah" *HaMashiach* המשיח. Also, in verses 27 and 28 of 1 Samuel, the name *Yeshua* ישוע is encoded twice, one at twenty-two-letter intervals and the other at twelve-letter intervals.

In Isaiah 53:7, starting with the second letter in the first word and counting every thirty-second letter from left to right spells "Galilee" גליל. There are two ways to spell Galilee. The first is with the heh (ה) at the end of the word, and the second is without the heh letter. Jesus came out of Nazareth in the region of northern Israel called Galilee, as confirmed in Matthew 21:11: "And the multitude said, this is Jesus [Yeshua] the prophet of Nazareth of Galilee."

The Three Marys Who Witnessed the Crucifixion

While Jesus was on the cross, He made seven statements. The third statement is recorded in John 19:25–27. Three women named "Mary" *Miryam* מרים were present at the crucifixion together with the beloved disciple, "John" *Yochanan* יוחנן. John 19:25–27 says, "Now there stood by the cross of Jesus His mother, and His mother's sister, Mary the wife of Cleophas, and Mary Magdalene. When Jesus therefore saw His mother, and the disciple [John] standing by, whom He loved, He saith unto His mother, Woman, behold thy son! Then saith He to the disciple [John], Behold thy mother! And from that hour that disciple took her unto his own home."

The names of the three Marys and the disciple John are encoded in the book of Isaiah. I am including the full passage from Isaiah 52:13 through chapter 53 as follows:

Behold, My Servant shall deal prudently, He shall be exalted and extolled, and be very high. As many were astonied at Thee; His visage was so marred more than any man, and His form more than the sons of men: So shall He sprinkle many nations; the kings shall shut their mouths at Him: for that which had not been told them shall they see; and that which they had not heard shall they consider.

(Isaiah 52:13–15)

Who hath believed our report? and to whom is the arm of the Lord revealed? For he shall grow up before him as a tender plant, and as a root out of a dry ground: he hath no form nor comeliness; and when we shall see him, there is no beauty that we should desire him. He is despised and rejected of men; a man of sorrows, and acquainted with grief: and we hid as it were our faces from him; he was despised, and we esteemed him not. Surely he hath borne our griefs, and carried our sorrows: yet we did esteem him stricken, smitten of God, and afflicted. But he was wounded for our transgressions, he was bruised for our iniquities: the chastisement of our peace was upon him; and with his stripes we are healed. All we like sheep have gone astray; we have turned every one to his own way; and the Lord hath laid on him the iniquity of us all. He was oppressed, and he was afflicted, yet he opened not his mouth: he is brought as a lamb to the slaughter, and as a sheep before her shearers is dumb, so he openeth not his mouth. He was taken from prison and from judgment: and who shall declare his generation? for he was cut off out of the land of the living: for the transgression of my people was he stricken. And he made his grave with the wicked, and with the rich in his death; because he had done no violence, neither was any deceit in his mouth. Yet it pleased the Lord to bruise him; he hath put him to grief: when thou shalt make his soul an offering for sin, he shall see his seed, he shall prolong his days, and the pleasure of the Lord shall prosper in his hand. He shall see of the travail of his soul, and shall be satisfied: by his knowledge shall my righteous servant justify many; for he shall bear their iniquites. Therefore will I divide him a portion with the great, and he shall divide the spoil with the strong; because he hath poured out his soul unto death: and he was numbered with the transgressors; and he bare the sin of many, and made intercession for the trans-gressors.   (Isaiah 53:1–12)

Isaiah ישעיהו 52:13–15

13. הנה ישכיל עבדי ירום ונשא וגבה מאד.

14. כאשר שממו עליך רבים כן משחת מאיש מראהו ותארו מבני ארם:

15. כן יזה גוים רבים עליו יקפצו מלכים פיהם כי אשר
לא-ספר להם ראו ואשר לא-שמעו התבוננו.

Isaiah ישעיהו 53:1–12

1. מי האמין לשמעתנו וזרוע יהוה על-מי נגלתה.

2. ויעל כיונק לפניו וכשרש מארץ ציה לא-תאר
לו ולא הדר ונראהו ולא-מראה ונחמדהו.

3. נבזה וחדל אישים איש מכאנות וידוע
חלי וכמסתר פנים ממנו נבזה ולא חשבנהו.

4. אכן חלינו הוא נשא ומכאבינו סבלם
ואנחנו חשבנהו נגוע מכה אלהים ומענה.

5. והוא מחלל מפשעינו מדכא מעונתינו
מוסר שלומנו עליו ובחברתו נרפא-לנו.

6. כלנו כצאן תעינו איש לדרכו
פנינו ויהוה הפגיע בו את עון כלנו.

7. נגש והוא נענה ולא-יפתח-פיו כשה לטבח
יובל וכרחל לפני גזזיה נאלמה ולא יפתח פיו.

8. מעצר וממשפט לקח ואת-דורו מי ישוחח
כי נגזר מארץ חיים מפשע עמי נגע למו.

9. ויתן את-רשעים קברו ואת-עשיר במתיו
על לא-חמס עשה ולא מרמה בפיו.

10. ויהוה חפץ דכאו החלי אם-תשים אשם נפשו
יראה זרע יאריך ימים וחפץ יהוה בידו יצלח.

11. מעמל נפשו יראה ישבע בדעתו יצדיק
צדיק עבדי לרבים ועונתם הוא יסבל.

12. לכן אחלק-לו ברבים ואת-עצומים יחלק
שלל תחת אשר הערה למות נפשו ואת-
פשעים נמנה והוא חטא-רבים נשא ולפשעים יפגיע.

The names of the three Marys and the disciple John are encoded with the name of Jesus (Yeshua) in Isaiah 53:10. These are phenomenal insights that were precisely fulfilled over seven hundred years after the book of Isaiah was written.

The Messiah

In Isaiah 53:11, starting with the fifth letter in the ninth word and counting every twentieth letter from left to right spells *Ma 'al Yeshua Shmee ohz* מעל ישרע שמי עז, which means "exceedingly high, Yeshua is my strong (powerful) name." From the yod (י) in Yeshua's name and counting in reverse every twenty-eighth letter spells "John" יוחנן. Isaiah 52:13 says, "Behold, my Servant [Yeshua] shall deal prudently, He shall be exalted and extolled, and be very high." In Isaiah 53:11, starting with the first letter in the first word and counting every forty-second letter from left to

John   יוחנן   **(every 28 letters in reverse)**

[note: the final two letters נן both represent the letter N]

Two Marys   מרים   **(every 6th letter in reverse and every 44th letter forward)**

8.   מעצר וממשפט לקח ואת־דורו מי ישוחח
כי נגזר מארץ חיים מפשע עמי נגע למו.

9.   ויתן את־רשעים קברו ואת־עשיר במתיו
על לא־חמס עשה ולא מרמה בפיו.

10.   ו
יהוה חפץ דכאו החלי אם־תשים אשם נפשו
יראה זרע יאריך ימים וחפץ יהוה בידו יצלח.

11.   מעמל נפשו יראה ישבע בדעתו יצדיק
צדיק עבדי לרבים ועונתם הוא יסבל.

12.   לכן אחלק־לו ברבים ואת־ עצומים יחלק
שלל תחת אשר הערה למות נפשו ואת־פשעים
נמנה והוא חטא־רבים נשא ולפשעים יפגיע.

Isaiah 53:9-12

right spells "Messiah" *Mashiach* מָשִׁיחַ. From the mem (מ) in Messiah's name and counting every twenty-third letter from left to right spells "Mary" מרים. In Isaiah 53:10, all three of the names of Mary use the word *ya'arik* יַאֲרִיךְ, where the yod (י) in Yeshua's and John's names are found for their beginnings. In Isaiah 53:10, starting with the third letter in the seventh word and counting every sixth letter from right to left spells "Mary" מרים. In Isaiah 53:12, starting with the fifth letter in the fourth word and counting every forty-fourth letter from left to right again spells "Mary" מרים. It is surely no coincidence that we find three Marys encoded in these verses surrounding the name Yeshua and John in light of the Gospel's description that these four individuals were present at the crucifixion of Jesus Christ.

In Isaiah 53:5, starting with the seventh letter in the fifth word and counting every twentieth letter from right to left spells "lamp of the Lord" *ner Jehovah* נר יהוה. This count is adjacent to *Yeshua* ישוע at the twenty-letter interval. That Jesus is the light is confirmed in John 8:12: "Then spake Jesus again unto them, saying, I am the Light of the world: he that followeth Me shall not walk in darkness, but shall have the Light of life."

Shiloh

In Isaiah 53:9, starting with the second letter in the eleventh word and counting every fifty-fourth letter from right to left spells *Shiloh* שׁילה. Both Jewish and Christian scholars acknowledge this word *Shiloh* is a clear prophetic title of the coming Messiah. Genesis 49:10 states, "The sceptre shall not depart from Judah, nor a lawgiver from between his feet, until Shiloh come; and unto Him [Yeshua] shall the gathering of the people be."

Jesus - Yeshua ישוע (every 20 letters in reverse)

Shiloh שילה (every 54 letters forward)

9. ויתן את-רשעים קברו ואת-עשיר במתיו

על לא-חמס עשה ולא מרמה בפיו.

10. ויהוה חפץ דכאו החלי אם-תשים אשם נפשו

יראה זרע יאריך ימים וחפץ יהוה בידו יצלח.

11. מעמל נפשו יראה ישבע בדעתו יצדיק

צדיק עבדי לרבים ועונתם הוא יסבל.

12. לכן אחלק-לו ברבים ואת- עצומים יחלק

שלל תחת אשר הערה למות נפשו ואת-פשעים

נמנה והוא חטא-רבים נשא ולפשעים יפגיע.

Isaiah 53:9-12

Caesar, Herod, Pharisee

Also, it is known that, in addition to the chief priests, the three Marys, John, and the other disciples, another major player in the crucifixion was Caesar. In Isaiah 53:11, starting with the fourth letter in the seventh word and counting every 194th letter from left to right spells "Kaisar" *ahmail ovaid* קיסר עמל אבר which means "wicked (labor, toil) Caesar wretched (perish)," or better stated, "wicked Caesar to perish." Now we have not only the evil Roman city but also the wicked wretched Caesar. Adjacent to the above, but in 388-letter increments (2 × 194) we find the letters that spell out the phrase "for My people trouble," *ki'ami eeyov* כעמי איוב.

The Pharisees and Herod were also involved in the crucifixion, and their names are encoded in Isaiah 53. In verse 9, starting with the second letter in the fourteenth word and counting every sixty-fourth letter from left to right spells "Pharisee," *pahrush* פרוש. In Isaiah 53:6, starting with the first letter in the fourth word and counting every twenty-ninth letter from left to right spells "the man Herod" *ish Herod* איש הורד. That the Pharisees and Herod show up in this chapter is no coincidence.

We also find the word Messiah encoded in this passage. In Isaiah 53:8, starting with the third letter in the second word and counting every sixty-fifth letter from left to right spells "Messiah" משיח. In this same count, but starting with the third letter in the tenth word of verse 10, which is the ayin (ע), and counting every sixty-fifth letter from left to right spells *Yeshua* ישוע. This is an awesome insight. We have the words "Jesus" and "Messiah" in the same area with the same ELS. In Isaiah 53:2, starting with the second letter in the first word and counting every 210th letter from right to left spells "Joseph" *Yoseph* יוסף, the husband of Mary, the mother of Jesus. The adjacent letters in Isaiah 53:1, starting with the fifth letter in the eighth word and counting every 210th letter from right to left spell "the bread" *ha'lachem* הלחם, possibly referring to the symbol of bread that Jesus used at the Last Supper to refer to His body broken for our sins. It was fascinating to find another group of letters at the same 210-letter interval that spell the word "wine" *yeyin* יין, which was another symbol used by Jesus at the Passover Supper in the Upper Room to symbolize His blood, which was shed for our sins. The word "wine" is spelled out in reverse at a 210-letter interval by starting with the second letter in the eleventh word and counting from right to left. The wine and bread clearly represent the body and blood of Jesus, as presented to His disciples at the last Passover of Yeshua, the son of Joseph. The Old Testament personality Joseph was obviously a type of the Messiah, as he supplied food (bread) for the starving Egyptians and his family.

Mark 15:40 says,"There were also women looking on afar off: among whom was Mary Magdalene, and Mary the mother of James the less and of Joses, and Salome." In Isaiah 52:15, starting with the third letter in the sixteenth word and counting every 113th letter from right to left spells "Salome" *Shalomit* שלמית. In verse 13, starting with the fourth letter in the second word and counting every 149th letter from right to left spells "Joses" *Yosai* יוסי. The man Joses was a half brother of Jesus. Both Marys described in Mark 15:40 were wailing at the crucifixion of Jesus. Encoded in Isaiah 52:15, starting with the fifth letter in the eighteenth word and counting every thirteenth letter from left to right spells *na'ar Miryam be'ku* "abhor weep bitterly" נאר מרים בכו. This type of wailing, *be'ku* בכו, is also found in Jeremiah 22:10. In Isaiah 53:9, starting with the first letter in the third word and counting every twenty-eighth letter from right to left spells *rahal Miryam* רעל מרים, which means "tremble (shake, reel) Mary." The adjacent letters to the above spell "the blessed" *habarucha* הברוכה. Mary was called blessed, as we see in Luke 1:28: "And the angel came in unto her [Mary], and said, Hail, thou that art highly favoured, the Lord is with thee: blessed (ברוכה) art thou among women."

Thus far, we have found encoded words in the Old Testament for virtually all the people involved with the crucifixion who are named in the New Testament. We now turn to other insights surrounding the crucifixion of the Messiah. In Psalm 22:21, starting with the second letter in the first word and counting every twenty-second letter from left to right spells *tzelbi lemoot* צלבי למת, which means "My cross of death." In Psalm 22:9, starting with the third letter in the seventh word and counting every 265th letter spells "cross" צלב. In Psalm 41:11, starting with the second letter in the fourth word and counting every forty-fourth letter from left to right spells "cross" צלב. In Psalm 41:13, starting with the third letter in the fifth word and counting every fifty-first letter spells "His cross" צלבו, as does Isaiah 5:36. Starting with the second letter in the second word and counting every eighth letter from left to right spells "His cross" צלבו.

Passover — Cross

In Isaiah 53:10, starting with the third letter in the second word and counting every fifty-second letter from right to left spells "cross" צלב. From the same word, taking the first letter and counting every 104th letter from right to left spells "Passover" פסח. In Isaiah 52:11, starting with the bet (ב) in the word for "purify yourself" *hibahru* הברו, which is the second letter in the tenth word, and counting every 262nd letter from right to left spells "in My cross" *be'tze'lahvi* בצלבי. In the previous verse, verse 10, starting with the third letter in the twelfth word and counting every thirty-second letter from right to left spells "My cross" צלבי. The book of Daniel also has encoded references to the cross. In Daniel 9:24, starting with the first letter in the sixteenth word and counting every fifty-eighth letter from right to left spells "cross, blood" צלב דם. Daniel 9:26a says, "And after threescore and two weeks shall Messiah be cut off, but not for himself."

References to the Passover are encoded in Psalm 22:11. Starting with the second letter of the fourth word and counting every forty-fourth letter from left to right spells "in the cross, overflowing bullock," *be'tzelahv bahlal shur* בצלב בלל שור. The adjacent letters, starting with the first letter in the tenth word of verse 15 and counting every forty-fourth letter from left to right spells "in My Passover forever" *be'pesachi ohlam* בפסחי עולם.

The Father knew of the crucifixion because it was His will. Encoded in Psalm 20:5, starting with the third letter in the third word and counting every forty-fourth letter from right to left spells "in Yeshua and the Father" בישוע והאב. The yod in Yeshua's name is taken from the yod in *Jehovah* יהוה. It was the Father's will that humankind should be saved from hell. In Psalm 22:14, starting with the first letter in the fourth word and counting every forty-fourth letter from left to right spells "the ram of His cross, bitterly cursed" *ail tzelahvo ahrar* איל צלבו ארר. The adjacent letter spells "the great hades (hell)" *sheol ha'rav* שאול הרב. In Isaiah 52:15, starting with the second letter in the tenth word and counting every 338th letter from right to left spells *shoht haim said* שרט הם שר, which means "whip (scourge), they, demon, (devil)." Counting the same 338-letter count in both directions spells "alas (woe), the whip of destruction" אי שרט המשר. The adjacent letters spell *sheol ve'moot* שאול רמת, which means "hell and death." Revelation 1:18 says, "I am he that liveth, and was dead; and, behold, I am alive for evermore, Amen; and have the keys of hell and of death."

Not only does the Father want to save us from hell, but he also wants to save us from Satan. In Isaiah 53:10, starting with the third letter in the eighth word and counting every sixtieth letter from left to right spells *shoht* שרט. The adjacent letters spell *rashah* רשע, which means "wicked." Other adjacent letters spell *tekal* תקל, which means "weighed in the balances." In Isaiah 53:4, starting with the second letter in the eighth word and counting every ninety-seventh letter in both directions spells "fullness of the whip" המלו שרט. The adjacent letters spell "the serpent" נחש. Continue counting every ninety-seventh letter to the right spells "ravage, destroy" שדר.

Isaiah 53:8, starting with the sixth letter in the second word and counting every forty-eighth letter from right to left spells "Satan" שׂטן. The adjacent letters spell "bind up" כפת and "weighed" תקל. In Psalm 22:1, starting with the third letter in the fourth word and counting every forty-first letter from right to left spells "from the great scourge (whip)" מגדל שׂוט. Yeshua Messiah died on a tree to save us from being bound and destroyed by Satan.

Encoded in Exodus 12:7, starting with the third letter in the ninth word and counting every seventeenth letter from right to left spells "crucify three" *shalosh tzahlav* שׁלשׁ צלב. Three men were crucified on the day of fulfillment of the Passover: two thieves on the outside crosses and Jesus, the perfect Lamb, on the middle cross. In reference to the Passover, we read in Exodus 12:7,"And they shall take of the blood, and strike it on the two side posts and on the upper door post of the houses, wherein they shall eat it."

We find insights to Jesus' death in the Torah as well as in Isaiah. In Exodus 12:29, starting with the fourth letter in the third word and counting every nineteenth letter from right to left spells "crucify" לצלב. The adjacent letters, but at thirty-eight-letter intervals spell *Chanukkah* חנכה. Also, "His Holiness" קדושׁ is found at nineteen-letter intervals. In Genesis 27:33, starting with the second letter in the eighth word and counting every ninth letter from right to left spells "crucify Him" יצלב. Starting with the fifth letter of the fifth word of Genesis 27:38 and counting every ninth letter from right to left spells "behold, Messiah" הא משׁיח. Jesus died at the ninth hour, but Barabbas was released in His stead. In Genesis 27:35, starting with the first letter in the second word and counting in sequential digression the sixteenth, fourteenth, twelfth, and tenth letters from right to left spells "Barabbas" *Bar'aba* בר אבא. In verse 38 of chapter 27, starting with the third letter in the fourth word and counting every sixth letter from left to right spells *Yeshua* ישׁוע. Jesus was on the cross for six hours.

In Genesis 22:1, starting with the third letter in the first word and counting every seventeenth letter from left to right spells "the cross of captivity" *ha'tzelahv le'shahvah* הצלב לשבה. Genesis 22:1–2 says, "And it came to pass after these things, that God did tempt Abraham, and said unto him, Abraham, and he said, Behold, here I am. And he said, Take now thy son, thine only son Isaac, whom thou lovest, and get thee into the land of Moriah; and offer him there for a burnt offering upon one of the mountains which I will tell thee of." This event foreshadowed the final sacrifice for our sins that would be fulfilled in Yeshua the Messiah. The purpose of the crucifixion was to bring salvation to all and to destroy the works of the Devil (Satan, Lucifer). They are one and the same Enemy of the Cross. The Cross neutralizes or destroys Satan. In Isaiah 53:3, starting with the first letter in the eleventh word and counting every twentieth letter from right to left spells "neutralize Lucifer" *noo heylel* נוא הילל. The Hebrew word *noo* נוא can also mean "make of none effect." 1 John 3:8 says, "He that committeth sin is of the devil; for the devil sinneth from the beginning. For this purpose the Son of God was manifested, that he might destroy the works of the devil."

> How art thou fallen from heaven, O Lucifer הילל, son of the morning! how art thou cut down to the ground, which didst weaken the nations!
>
> (Isaiah 14:12)

The Messiah: The One Whom They Crucified

> As Moses lifted up the serpent in the wilderness, even so must the Son of man be lifted up: That whosoever believeth in him should not perish, but have eternal life. (John 3:14–15)

> Who, being in the form of God, thought it not robbery to be equal with God: But made himself of no reputation, and took upon him the form of a

servant, and was made in the likeness of men: And being found in fashion as a man, he humbled himself, and became obedient unto death, even the death of the cross.   (Philippians 2:6–8)

There are numerous additional codes and insights that are found at nineteen-letter intervals, some of which are presented below.

1. In Isaiah 53:12, starting with the third letter in the eighteenth word, which is "sin" חטא, and counting every nineteenth letter from left to right (reverse) spells *uhl be'nod nahchash* אול בנד נחש, which means "to twist (a body rolled up together), to wander (roam), the serpent."

2. In Isaiah 53:2, starting with the second letter in the fifth word and counting every nineteenth letter from left to right spells "Job" *Eeyov* איוב. The name Job means "trouble."

3. In Isaiah 53:6, starting with the second letter in the tenth word and counting every nineteenth letter from left to right spells *tola* תולע, which means "worm." This was the worm from which the priest extracted the crimson red for use in the Tabernacle and both Temples. It also represents the sins of humankind and the blood of the Lamb.

4. In Isaiah 53:7, starting with the second letter in the third word for "was afflicted" נענה and counting every nineteenth letter from left to right spells "Obed" *Oved* עבד. "Obed" means "servant" and was the name of the son of Ruth and Boaz, the ancestor of King David. Jesus was the suffering Servant [Obed].

5. In Isaiah 52:9 Starting with the first letter in the third word, which is "together" יחדו, and counting every nineteenth letter from left to right spells "Jesse" *Yishai* ישי, the son of Obed and the father of King David. The name "Jesse" means "wealthy" or "gift."

6. In Isaiah 53:5, starting with the second letter in the

second word and counting every nineteenth letter from right to left (forward) spells "life of grace of Noah" *chai chahn ve'Noach* חי חן ונח. This is a picture of the grace of God in our lives.

7. In Isaiah 52:14, starting with the second letter of the third word and counting every nineteenth letter from right to left spells "Leah" לאה. She was the first wife of Jacob and the mother of Judah, from whom would come the royal seed of the Messiah.

8. In Isaiah 52:14, starting with the first letter in the third word (same word as above) and counting every nineteenth letter from right to left spells "seed" זרע. This word is spelled in reverse. This coded word "seed" זרע reminds us of the first prophecy in the Bible that predicted the virgin birth of Jesus in God's prophecy to Eve that "her seed" — the future Messiah — would defeat Satan (Genesis 3:15).

9. In Isaiah 52:14, starting with the second letter in the first word and counting every nineteenth letter from right to left spells "my brother" אחי.

10. In Isaiah 53:12, starting with the fourth letter in the twenty-first word and counting every nineteenth letter from right to left spells "Shiloh" שלה. Shiloh is another title, recognized by both Jewish and Christian scholars, for the Messiah, who would come out of the tribe of Judah. Genesis 49:10 says, "The sceptre shall not depart from Judah, nor a lawgiver from between his feet, until Shiloh come and unto him [Messiah] shall the gathering of the people be."

11. In Isaiah 53:11, starting with the second letter in the fourth word and counting every nineteenth letter from left to right spells "the Almighty" שדי.

12. Isaiah 52:8 says, "Thy watchmen shall lift up the voice with the voice together shall they sing: for they shall see eye to eye, when the Lord shall bring again Zion." Starting with the second letter in the sixth word and counting every nineteenth letter from right to left spells "My

Spirit" *ruachi* רוחי. A very interesting insight is associated with the phrase "eye to eye" *ayin b'ayin* עין בעין. Starting with the ayin (ע) to the far right and counting every 129th letter from left to right spells *ohnah* ערנה, which means "to dwell together." From the same ayin and counting every 129th letter from right to left spells *Yeshua* ישרע. Yes! Those who love Jesus Christ shall dwell with Him in complete unity in the not-too-distant future.

13. In Isaiah 52:4, starting with the fourth letter in the sixth word and counting every nineteenth letter from left to right spells "Jonah" יונה.

14. In Isaiah 52:7, starting with the first letter in the ninth word and counting every nineteenth letter from left to right spells "water" מים. Remember, Jonah was in the bitter waters of rebellion. These codes revealing "Jonah" and "water" in the same passage reminds us of the history of the prophet Jonah, who was "three days and three nights in the whale's belly" as a prophetic symbol of the death and resurrection of Jesus.

15. In Isaiah 52:15, starting with the second letter in the fourth word and counting every nineteenth letter from left to right spells "exalted in the name" *berahm ha'shem* ברם השם.

16. In Isaiah 52:12, starting with the second letter in the first word and counting every nineteenth letter from left to right spells *Yoash* יואש, which was the name of a prophet and means "the fire of the Lord."

17. In Isaiah 54:3, starting with the sixth letter in the third word and counting every nineteenth letter from right to left spells "Levites" לוים.

18. In Isaiah 53:10, starting with the second letter in the twelfth word and counting every nineteenth letter from left to right spells "Moses" משה. Moses was from the tribe of Levi. The apostle Peter declared that Jesus of Nazareth fulfilled the prophecy of Moses (Deuteronomy 18:15) that

God would "raise up" a prophet like himself who would be Israel's true Messiah (Acts 3:12–24).

19. In Isaiah 53:10, starting with the second letter in the sixth word and counting every nineteenth letter from right to left spells "my prince" שׂרִי.

20. In Isaiah 53:9, starting with the first letter in the third word spells "the Syrian" *Rammi* רמִי.

21. In Isaiah 53:4, starting with the third letter in the twelfth word and counting every nineteenth letter from left to right spells "Esau" עשׂו.

22. In Isaiah 53:10, starting with the first letter in the fifteenth word and counting every nineteenth letter from left to right spells "Beri" ברִי. He was a son of Asher.

23. In Isaiah 54:2, starting with the second letter in the second word and counting every nineteenth letter from left to right and extending into the fifty-third chapter gives us sixteen letters in sequence. This spells *kubah l'shanah m'kol eer shul* קבה לשנה מכל עיר שׂול, which translates "tent (pavilion) of the year, from all the city, the skirt (train)." Another way to say this is, "the year of the pavilion from all the city of shul." Shul is another term for "the assembly" and is the item that Isaiah saw when the Lord revealed Himself to the prophet in Isaiah, chapter 1.

24. In Isaiah 52:9, starting with the second letter in the tenth word and counting every nineteenth letter from right to left spells "light" אור.

25. In Isaiah 52:8, starting with the fourth letter in the second word and counting every nineteenth letter from left to right spells "Caleb" כלב.

26. In Isaiah 53:12, starting with the second letter in the eighth word and counting every nineteenth letter from left to right spells "Leban" לבן. Leban was Jacob's father-in-law.

27. In Isaiah 54:3, starting with the sixth letter in the third

word and counting every nineteenth letter from right to left spells "the Levites" לוים.

28. In Isaiah 52:10, starting with the second letter in the ninth word and counting every nineteenth letter from right to left spells "to loath (abhor) the wild bull" *re'aim bah'chal* ראם בטל. The messianic Psalm 22 refers to the bulls of Bashan. Psalm 22:12 says, "Many bulls have compassed me [Yeshua]: strong bulls of Bashan have beset me round." In Psalm 22:15, starting with the second letter in the sixth word and counting every twenty-sixth letter spells *Yeshua* ישוע. From the same verse, starting from the first letter in the eleventh word and counting every ninth letter spells "Messiah" משיח. Also, from the chet (ח) in Messiah's name and counting in reverse every thirty-second letter spells "the Passover" פסח. It is fascinating to observe these codes showing "Yeshua," "Messiah," and "Passover" found in the prophecy of King David that predicted the crucifixion of the Messiah (Psalm 22:16).

29. In Isaiah 52:12, starting with the fourth letter in the eleventh word, which is *Jehovah* יהוה, and counting every nineteenth letter from left to right spells "the ark" *ha'taibah* התבה. This is the same word used in Genesis 7:1 when the Lord commanded Noah to come into the ark התבה.

30. In Isaiah 52:12, starting with the second letter in the twelfth word and counting every nineteenth letter from left to right spells "from the Atonement Lamb (varigated)" *me'kippur tela* מכפר טלא.

31. In Isaiah 52:7, starting with the first letter in the tenth word and counting every nineteenth letter from left to right spells *taleh* טלה, which means "a lamb." There are at least two ways to spell this word: the way that it is spelled in number 30 above and the way it is spelled here. In Isaiah 53:7, the phrase "and not did he open his mouth, as a lamb to the slaughter he was led" ולא יפתח-פיו כשה לטבח יובל gives us an awesome

insight. Starting with the second chet (ח), the reverse of the ten letters above translates "bosom lamb to be observant of a hole (pit, snare)" חב טלה שכוי פחת. Yeshua was God's bosom Lamb who was sent to the cross for our sakes.

32. In Isaiah 52:12, starting with the sixth letter in the tenth word and counting every nineteenth letter from left to right spells "from the tabernacles (*Sukkot*)" מסכת. The Feasts of Atonement and Tabernacles are only five days apart. We see the final scenario in Zechariah 14, which suggests the return of our Lord Jesus may occur on the Day of Atonement (Yom Kippur). The great battle of Armageddon, the judging of the nations and the setting up of the thousand-year reign of Messiah on earth may occur on the Feast of Tabernacles (*Sukkot* סכת). The year and exact time that this will occur is not known to us, but we see all the signs of the end time being fulfilled before our eyes. Zechariah 14:16 says, "And it shall come to pass, that every one that is left of all the nations which came against Jerusalem shall even go up from year to year to worship the King, the Lord of hosts, and to keep the feast of tabernacles."

33. In Isaiah 52:2, starting with the fifth letter (ל) in the fifth word, which is "Jerusalem" ירושלם, and counting every nineteenth letter from right to left spells "the heart of My treasured people" *li'bah etzer ha'am* לבה אצר העם.

Yeshua, the One Who Was Pierced

But one of the soldiers with a spear pierced his side, and forthwith came there out blood and water. And he that saw it bare record, and his record is true: and he knoweth that he saith true, that ye might believe. For these things were done, that the scripture should be fulfilled, A bone of him shall not be broken. And again another scripture saith, They shall look on him whom they pierced.   (John 19:34–37)

And I will pour upon the house of David, and upon the inhabitants of Jerusalem, the spirit of grace and of supplications: and they shall look upon me [Yeshua] whom they have pierced, and they shall mourn for him, as one mourneth for his only son, and shall be in bitterness for him, as one that is in bitterness for his firstborn.   (Zechariah 12:10)

As many were astonished at thee [Yeshua]; his visage was so marred [disfigurement מִשְׁחַת] more than any man, and his form more than the sons of men.   (Isaiah 52:14)

At this point, I need to mention several ninety-two-letter combinations that require our careful consideration. The Word of God is in complete harmony from beginning to end. There are no flaws found throughout His Word. The apparent mistakes that we encounter from the Scriptures are man-made, either from printing errors or human interpretation. In Zechariah 12:10, starting with the second letter in the fifteenth word, which is the qoph (ק) in the word "pierce" דקר, and counting every ninety-two letters from right to left spells "His Holiness" קדשׁ. In Isaiah 52:10, starting with the third letter in the fifteenth word, which is "in His hands" בידו, and counting every ninety-two letters from left to right spells "pierce" *dahkar* דקר in reverse. Continue counting from the dalet (ד) to the right, and you will have a shin (שׁ) then the vav (ו). Now we have, at ninety-two-letter intervals, the word for "His Holiness" קדשׁו. In Psalms 22:16, starting with the second letter in the fifth word and counting every ninety-second letter from right to left also spells "pierce" *dahkar* דקר. Continual counting to the ninety-second letter in reverse from the dalet (ד) spells "holy" *kodesh* קדשׁ.

What are the odds of these three combinations from the messianic Scriptures having the same letter count with a complementary likeness? The probability of these combinations appearing by chance are astronomical. These three areas of Scripture were written by three different men hundreds of years apart. The Holy Spirit guided their hands while they penned the Word of God. Revelation 1:7 says, "Behold, he cometh with clouds; and every eye shall see him, and they also which pierced him: and all kindreds of the earth shall wail because of him. Even so, Amen." Evil men did evil things to Yeshua, but He allowed this to happen for our justification, salvation, and peace. However, it was our sin that caused the sacrifice.

There are many additional insights encoded at twenty-six-letter intervals. Twenty-two of them are presented here.

1. In Isaiah 52:14, starting with the third letter in the sixth word, which is "marred" מָשְׁחַת and counting every twenty-sixth letter from right to left spells *chazah* חָזָה, which means "to gaze, behold, or look." Psalm 22:17 says, "I may tell all my bones: they look and stare upon me [Yeshua]."

2. In Psalm 22:15, starting with the second letter in the sixth word and counting every twenty-sixth letter from right to left spells *Yeshua* יֵשׁוּעַ.

3. In Isaiah 52:15, starting with the third letter in the seventeenth word and counting every twenty-sixth letter from right to left spells "evil" *ahvan* עָוֶן.

4. In Zechariah 12:10, starting with the first letter in the twenty-second word and counting every twenty-sixth letter spells "evil" עָוֶן. Zechariah 12:10b says, "And they shall look upon me whom they have pierced (דָקָר), and they shall mourn for him, as one mourneth for his only son, and shall be in bitterness for him, as one that is in bitterness for his firstborn."

5. In Isaiah 52:14, starting with the third letter in the sixth word and counting every twenty-sixth letter from left to right spells "My Feast (sacrifice)" *Chaggai* חַגִּי.

6. In Isaiah 52:10, starting with the fourth letter in the

fifteenth word for "our God" אלהינו and counting every twenty-sixth letter from right to left spells *yotzai Shabbattah* יצאי שבתה, which means "coming out of (begotten of) the Sabbath." This is an unusual way of spelling the *Shabbat*; nevertheless, the insights reflect the pure Word of God.

7. The word for "coming out of (begotten)" is found in Judges 8:30. In Judges 8:31, starting with the first letter in the fourth word and counting every twenty-sixth letter from left to right spells *Yeshua* ישׁע.

8. In Judges 8:29, starting with the fourth letter in the second word and counting every twenty-sixth letter from left to right spells *ohtzer* עצר, which means "prison." This same word is used in Isaiah 53:8.

9. In Isaiah 53:12, starting with the fourth letter in the second word and counting every twenty-sixth letter from left to right spells "My Holiness" *kahdshi* קדשׁי.

10. In Isaiah 53:5, starting with the fourth letter in the ninth word and counting every twenty-sixth letter from left to right spells "enter into our salvation" *bo hoshi'ahnu* בא הושׁענו.

11. In Isaiah 53:12, starting with the first letter in the tenth word and counting every twenty-sixth letter from left to right spells "my God" *Alai* אלי.

12. In Isaiah 53:8, starting with the second letter in the first word for "from prison" מעצר, and counting every twenty-sixth letter from left to right spells "burnt offering" *ohlah* עלה.

13. In Isaiah 53:2, starting with the second letter in the seventh word and counting every twenty-sixth letter from left to right spells *ayal* איל, which means "ram (of sacrifice)."

14. In Isaiah 53:12, starting with the third letter in the second word and counting every twenty-sixth letter from right to left spells "bread" *lachem* לחם. Yeshua is the Bread of Life.

15. In Isaiah 53:7, starting with the fourth letter in the ninth word and counting every twenty-sixth letter from right to left spells "to life" *lechai* לחי.

16. In Isaiah 53:7, starting with the first letter in the seventh word and counting every twenty-sixth letter from right to left spells "for My brothers" *ke'achim* כאחים.

17. In Isaiah 53:10, starting with the fifth letter in the eleventh word and counting every twenty-sixth letter from left to right spells "bride" *kala* כלה.

18. In Isaiah 53:12, starting with the second letter in the second word and counting every twenty-sixth letter from right to left spells "Bridegroom" *chah'tahn* חתן.

19. In Isaiah 52:14, starting with the first letter in the thirteenth word and counting every 130th letter (5 × 26) from right to left spells *Jehovah* יהוה.

20. In Isaiah 54:16, starting with the third letter in the ninth word and counting every 260th (10 × 26), from left to right spells *Yeshua anem* ישוע ענם, which means "Yeshua, the twin springs of water." This combination goes through chapters 54, 53, and 52. I would say that Yeshua covers all things.

21. In the Hebrew phrase "for our iniquities" *mai'aonitai'yenu* מעונתינו we see two magnificent insights in the twenty-six-letter interval. Starting with the second letter in the fifth word, which is מעונתינו, and counting every 156th letter (6 × 26) from right to left spells, in reverse, "Father Jesus" אב ישוע. Starting with the sixth letter in the fifth word and counting every 156th letter from right to left spells "Joel" *Yoel* יואל, which means "Lord God." The words "forever," עולם, "Joel" יואל, and "Jonah" יונה show up at 468-letter intervals (18 × 26) in the same areas where *Yeshua* is encoded.

I will greatly rejoice in the Lord, my soul shall be joyful in my God; for he hath clothed me with the garments of salvation [Yeshua], he hath covered me with the robes of righteousness, as a bridegroom [Chah'tahn] decketh himself with ornaments, and as a bride [kalah] adorneth herself with her jewels.

(Isaiah 61:10)

The Signature of God in Jerusalem, the Holy City.

Him that overcometh will I make a pillar in the temple of my God, and he shall go no more out: and I will write upon him the name of my God, and the name of the city of my God, which is new Jerusalem, which cometh down out of heaven from my God: and I will write upon him my new name.

(Revelation 3:12)

And they shall see his face; and his name shall be in their foreheads.   (Revelation 22:4)

Awake, awake; put on thy strength, O Zion; put on thy beautiful garments, O Jerusalem, the holy city: for henceforth there shall no more come into thee the uncircumcised and the unclean.   (Isaiah 52:1)

The Hebrew phrase "O Jerusalem, the Holy City" *Yerushalayim eer ha'kodesh* ירושלם עיר הקדש starts us on a trek through His Word at forty-nine-letter intervals that baffle the mind.

There are ten such passages that contain these insights:

1. In Isaiah 52:1, starting with the third letter in the tenth word, the resh (ר), and counting every forty-ninth letter from right to left spells *rahshum* רשום, which means "make a record."

2. In Isaiah 52:7, starting with the mem (מ) in the Hebrew word *shalom* שלום, the eighth word, taking the fourth letter, and counting every forty-ninth letter from right

to left spells *me'chatimo* מחתימו, which means "His signature."

3. In Isaiah 52:7, starting with the first letter in the fifth word and counting every forty-ninth letter from left to right spells "the Lord God," "Yoel" יואל, which is also the name of the prophet Joel.

4. In Isaiah 53:2, starting with the third letter in the fifteenth word and counting every forty-ninth letter from right to left spells "mountain of grace, the prophets of God" חן הר נבאי-אל or, better stated, "the grace prophets (on the) mountain of God."

5. In Isaiah 53:9, starting with the second letter in the third word and counting every forty-ninth letter from right to left spells "the Lord Almighty" שדיהו. In Isaiah 53:3, starting with the second letter in the thirteenth word and counting every fifty-fifth letter from left to right also spells "the Lord Almighty" שדיהוה. Notice that the same yod is used in *Shaddai* and *Jehovah* in both of these insights.

6. In Isaiah 54:1, starting with the first letter in the sixteenth word and counting every forty-ninth letter from right to left spells "Lord God" *Eliyah* אליה.

7. In Isaiah 52:1, starting with the first letter in the fourth word and counting every forty-ninth letter from right to left spells "Obed" עובד, of the tribe of Judah. The ayin (ע) is taken from the word "for your strength" עזך.

8. In Isaiah 53:2, starting with the second letter in the tenth word and counting every forty-ninth letter from left to right spells "the Levites" לוים. The tribe of Levi will function as priests throughout the messianic kingdom.

Messiah, the One Who Rose Again

In these messianic chapters in the book of Isaiah, we have discovered many wonderful insights. These final paragraphs reveal the season of Messiah's crucifixion and resurrection. They also uncover the feeling that the disciples had at these events. Finally, they reveal what our attitudes should be in light of Messiah's sacrifice.

In Isaiah 52:4, starting with the first letter in the fourth word and counting every sixteenth letter from right to left spells *aviv* אביב, which is the head of the year on the sacred calendar and the month of the great Passover when our Jesus sealed our salvation on the cross. In the same verse we have additional insights concerning the above.

In Isaiah 52:4, starting with the first letter in the thirteenth word and counting every sixteenth letter from left to right spells "the covenant sealed" *brit chahtum* ברית חתום. The new covenant was ratified when Yeshua, the Lamb of God, sealed it with His death, burial, and resurrection, as described in Isaiah 53. The Hebrew word for "sealed" חתום is found in Isaiah 8:16: "Bind up the testimony, seal [חתום] the law among my disciples [*be'limmudai* בלמדי]." Starting with the yod (י) in "disciples" and counting every sixty-second letter from left to right spells *Yeshua* ישוע. Also, David is encoded in this area several times. Surely, Yeshua is the Son of David!

In Isaiah 52:1, starting with the third letter in the eighth word and counting every twenty-seventh letter from right to left spells *aviv ve'moriah* אביב ומריה, which means "Aviv of Mount Moriah" — this is the time and the place of the sacrifice. The adjacent letters spell *rosh* ראש, which means "the first or the head of the year." The other adjacent letters spell "from the shade of the skirt (train)" מהשול בצל. The word for "in the shade (shadow)" בצל is found in Psalm 91:1: "He that dwelleth in the secret place of the most High shall abide under the shadow (בצל) of the Almighty."

In Isaiah 53:12, starting with the third letter of the second word and counting every fifty-fifth letter from left to right spells *limmudim ahnan* למדים אנן, which means "the disciples mourn." In this same count of fifty-five, but adjacent to "disciples" the word "priest" is spelled. In Isaiah

53:5, starting with the second letter in the first word and counting every fifty-fifth letter from left to right spells *ha'kohain* הכהן. The word for "disciples" is the same word that is used in Isaiah 8:16. Mark 16:9–10 says, "Now when Jesus was risen early the first day of the week, he appeared first to Mary Magdalene, out of whom he had cast seven devils. And she went and told them [the disciples] that had been with him, as they mourned and wept." All who have been washed in the blood of the Lamb of God are called to be kings and priests for our Lord and Savior. In glory our weeping shall cease. There will only be praise and adoration throughout the ceaseless ages to come. We read in Revelation 19:5, "And a voice came out of the throne, saying, Praise our God, all ye his servants, and ye that fear him, both small and great."

A final thought with reference to Isaiah 53. The great price that Yeshua paid for our redemption is far beyond man's ability to comprehend. The finite minds of mankind cannot understand the love, power, design, and intelligence behind God's redemptive plan for fallen man. We can only praise Him for our eternal and perfect salvation. In Isaiah 53:10, starting with the third letter in the first word, which is "Adonai" יהוה, and counting every 196th letter from left to right spells *Halleluyah* הללויה, which means "Praise the Lord." The adjacent letters spell *ha'rahm shachah* הרם שחה, which means "the extolling (lifted up) worship." The Hebrew word *shachah* שחה, means "to worship royalty or God." The first letter in the above insight, where we found *Halleluyah*, begins in the word *Jehovah* "Adonai" יהוה, and the last letter ends in the word *Jehovah* "Adonai" יהוה. We should begin and end our day with a praise offering unto Him. "Let everything that hath breath praise the Lord, Praise ye the Lord [הללויה]." (Psalm 150:6)

A Challenge to the Yeshua Code Critics

When my book *YESHUA* was published in the fall of 1996, tens of thousands of readers rejoiced in this new discovery that the Bible Codes revealed the encoded name of Jesus in dozens of well-known messianic prophecies throughout the Old Testament. However, a number of Bible Code scholars, as well as orthodox Jewish rabbis, have disputed the significance of this discovery of Yeshua's name encoded in dozens of prophecies. They have pointed out that the name *Yeshua* יֵשׁוּעַ is a relatively small word with only four letters and two common vowels. Some of these critics have contemptuously challenged the significance of the Yeshua Codes discovery and declared that one could find the name *Yeshua* יֵשׁוּעַ in virtually any passage in Hebrew literature (from a novel to the Israeli phone book). However, these critics are ignoring the fact that the name *Yeshua* appears at very small ELS intervals (i.e., every 5th, 9th or 20th letter) inside dozens of familiar messianic prophecies. We have not found any other significant names of individuals appearing at small ELS intervals appearing repeatedly in dozens of messianic prophecies.

However, my recent discovery of over forty names of individuals and places associated with the crucifixion of Jesus of Nazareth in the Suffering Servant messianic passage in Isaiah is unprecedented. I would like to issue a challenge to the critics who reject the Yeshua Codes to find any passage in Hebrew literature, other than the Bible, that contains the names of Jesus, the Nazarene, Passover, Herod, Mary, and the names of Christ's disciples at minimal ELS intervals, such as is found in Isaiah's prophecy.

A partial list of my code discoveries in Isaiah's prophecy is provided at the end of this chapter to help the reader realize the breadth of information encoded in this remarkable prophecy. The critics claim that you can find these codes by random chance in any Hebrew literature, and they, therefore, reject the significance of this discovery. Let them produce an example of these codes in any other Hebrew literature of the same length as or shorter than this Isaiah passage that contains all of the names listed in the summary that follows. If they cannot, and I believe it will be impossible, we will have additional evidence that these codes are truly unprecedented.

Jesus and His Disciples Found Encoded in Isaiah 53
The Suffering Servant Prophecy of the Messiah

Name	Begins	Word	Letter	Interval
Yeshua	Isa. 53:10	11	4	(-20)
Nazarene	Isa. 53:6	11	3	(47)
Messiah	Isa. 53:11	1	1	(-42)
Shiloh	Isa. 53:12	21	4	(19)
Passover	Isa. 53:10	13	3	(-62)
Galilee	Isa. 53:7	1	2	(-32)
Herod	Isa. 53:6	4	1	(-29)
Caesar	Isa. 53:11	7	4	(-194)
The evil Roman city	Isa. 53:9	13	2	(-7)
Caiaphas, High Priest	Isa. 52:15	7	3	(41)
Annas, High Priest	Isa. 53:3	6	5	(-45)
Mary	Isa. 53:11	1	1	(-23)
Mary	Isa. 53:10	7	3	(6)
Mary	Isa. 53:9	13	3	(44)
The Disciples	Isa. 53:12	2	3	(-55)
Peter	Isa. 53:10	11	5	(-14)
Matthew	Isa. 53:8	12	1	(-295)
John	Isa. 53:10	11	4	(-28)
Andrew	Isa. 53:4	11	1	(-48)
Philip	Isa. 53:5	10	3	(-133)
Thomas	Isa. 53:2	8	1	(35)
James	Isa. 52:2	9	3	(-34)
James	Isa. 52:2	3	4	(-20)
Simon	Isa. 52:14	2	1	(47)

Thaddaeus	Isa. 53:12	9	1	(-50)
Matthias	Isa. 53:5	7	4	(-11)
Let Him be crucified	Isa.53:8	6	2	(15)
His Cross	Isa. 53:6	2	2	(-8)
Lamp of the Lord	Isa. 53:5	5	7	(20)
His signature	Isa. 52:7	8	4	(49)
Bread	Isa. 53:12	2	3	(26)
Wine	Isa. 53:5	11	2	(210)
From Zion	Isa. 52:14	6	1	(45)
Moriah	Isa. 52:7	4	5	(153)
Obed (servant)	Isa. 53:7	3	2	(-19)
Jesse	Isa. 52:9	3	1	(-19)
Seed	Isa. 52:15	2	2	(-19)
Water	Isa. 52:7	9	1	(-19)
Levites	Isa. 54:3	3	6	(19)
From the Atonement Lamb	Isa. 52:12	12	2	(-19)
Joseph	Isa. 53:2	1	2	(210)

2

Yeshua יֵשׁוּעַ:
The Aleph and the Tav אֵת

His Name Is Jesus reveals powerful new evidence about the life, death, and resurrection of the Lord Jesus the Messiah יהוה ישׁוע המשׁיח *Jehovah Yeshua HaMashiach*. As we examine these intriguing new insights embedded in the Hebrew text of the Old Testament Yeshua alone deserves our praise and adoration.

The System of Analysis

One method that I use to find the coded words is called *equidistant-letter sequence* (ELS). During the last few years, I have analyzed the Hebrew Scriptures using this method, examining particular Hebrew letters that are distributed at equal intervals (i.e., fifth, tenth, seventeenth) throughout the text.

The Hebrew word for equidistant sequence is *shalav* שׁלב. It has at least two meanings: (1) the rungs on a step ladder that are equally spaced; (2) three or more objects that are equally spaced one from the other (in our case — letters).

Our friend and publisher, Grant Jeffrey, and his wife, Kaye, invited my wife, Yaphah, and me to be their guests at a Bible conference for scholars in January 1997 at Tyndale Theological Seminary in Dallas, Texas. Grant presented the phenomenon of the Hebrew codes and illustrated it with numerous encoded messages from his best-selling book, *The Signature of God*, including a number of my discoveries of the name "Jesus" *Yeshua* encoded in virtually every messianic prophecy in the Bible. This information was fascinating to these very respectful, learned Hebrew scholars. After Grant gave his exposition on the insights from the Masoretic Hebrew text, he introduced me to these serious scholars of the Word of God. Many questions were asked about the method of analysis that we use in our books. One of the scholars asked if we had discovered any direct reference to the Hebrew Code phenomenon encoded in the Scriptures itself. Immediately, Grant Jeffrey and I entered the Hebrew word *shalav* שׁלב, which means "equidistant," into Grant's Powerbook 1400 computer to search the Scriptures. It was fascinating to report to this group that we had discovered the encoded word "equidistant" *shalav* שׁלב in every one of the five books of the Torah. The full phrase "equidistant-letter sequence" was found in Hebrew at equal intervals in Genesis through Deuteronomy. We shared the following insight found in Genesis 20:2 that reveals this significant Hebrew phrase called "equidistant-letter sequence." The Scripture below is the example that we presented to our fellow believers in Yeshua HaMashiach because it gives absolute credence to this methodology. The majority of those who were present received the information with awe and respect.

Genesis [*Beresheet* בראשׁית] 20:2 says, "And Abraham said of Sarah, his wife, She is my sister: and Abimelech king of Gerar sent, and took Sarah." Below is the Hebrew for this verse, according to the Masoretic text. I have removed the spaces between each word and enlarged every fifth letter for your convenience.

וי אמר א ברהמ א ל שׁ רהא שׁ תוא ח תׁ יהוא
וי שׁל ח א בי מל ך מל ד ג ר ר ויק ח א ת שׂ ר ה

Starting with the last heh (ה) on the second line to the far left and counting every fifth letter from left to right is the phrase *hacharak oht shalav* הַחֲרָךְ אוֹת שָׁלָב, which means "the latticework of the equidistant-letter sequence." The Hebrew definition of this phrase is found by the very method of its meaning.

From the shin (שׁ) that forms the word *shalav* and counting every fifty-fifth letter from right to left, we again find *shalav* שָׁלָב. The adjacent letters to the Hebrew word *shalav* spell "letter" *oht* אוֹת. Thus, we have another phrase forming the same words, only in multiples of five.

Starting with the last heh (ה) in verse four, using the same five-letter sequence and counting every 125th letter (five to the third power) from left to right spells the words *Jehovah* "Adonai" יְהוָה. This insight proves to us that the Lord is the foundation of His own Word. The fifth letter of the Hebrew aleph-bet is the heh (ה). This letter represents many beautiful things. Five of its magnificent meanings are "the Holy Spirit," "the latticework," "covenant," promise," and "His Word."

> The voice of my beloved! behold, he cometh leaping on the mountains, skipping upon the hills. My beloved is like a roe or a young hart: behold, he standeth behind our wall, he looketh forth at the windows, showing himself through the lattice. [*ha'charak*].   (Song of Songs [Solomon] 2:8–9)

The Hebrew word for "looking" is *mash'gi'ach* מַשְׁגִּיחַ. If you remove the gimmel (ג), you have "Messiah" *Mashiach* מָשִׁיחַ. The Lord, our beloved, came to us in the person of Yeshua, the Messiah. Here we see the Lord as our beloved, looking at us through the lattice with tenderness, desiring our fellowship. The latticework represents the Word of God, and He speaks to us through His Word, as we see in John 1:14 ("And the Word was made flesh and dwelt among us.") and in Revelation 19:13b ("And his name is called The Word of God.").

These few insights prove the validity of the inspired Word of God. The method by which I acquire these findings is both scientific and sound. I wish to establish the importance of each letter, word, and phrase, as well as the original written position of all His Word. The Jewish sages taught that to change the Word of God would be equivalent to changing the course of the universe. A rabbi once suggested to me that if one letter of God's Torah were retracted, the whole universe would disappear.

> God, who at sundry times and in divers manners
> spake in time past unto the fathers by the prophets,
> Hath in these last days spoken unto us by his Son,
> whom he hath appointed heir of all things, by whom
> also he made the worlds; Who being the brightness
> of his glory, and the express image of his person, and
> upholding all things by the word of his power, when
> he had by himself purged our sins, sat down on the
> right hand of the Majesty on high;
>
> (Hebrews 1:1–3)
>
> Through faith we understand that the worlds were
> framed by the word of God.   (Hebrews 11:3a)

The first and last letters of the Hebrew aleph-bet, respectively, are the aleph (א) and the tav (ת). These two letters represent all the Word of God from the beginning to the end and speak of Him as the First and the Last. Genesis [Beresheet בְּרֵאשִׁית] 1:1 begins, "in the beginning," beresheet בְּרֵאשִׁית. The root of its understanding is in John (Yochanan יוֹחנן) 1:1: "In the beginning was the Word, and the Word was with God, and the Word was God." Not only is God referred to as the beginning and the end in the Old Testament, He is also referred to the same way in the New Testament: "I am Alpha [Aleph א] and Omega [Tav ת], the beginning and the ending, saith the Lord, which is, and which was, and which is to come, the Almighty" (Revelation 1:8).

Genesis 1:1 is the first time that the aleph (א) and the tav (ת) appear in the Scripture, and there they are used together as one unit (אֵת). These two letters of the Hebrew aleph-bet are used jointly twelve times during the six days of Creation. The number twelve means "theocracy" — a government based on the precepts of His Holy Word and led by the priests of the Lord through divine revelation. There is no surface interpretation or translation for this combination, but the two letters combined represent the ineffable name of the God of all creation.

Let me give you an illustration from the insights (the Hebrew Codes) of how God shows up on any level that you may pursue. Below we will see the aleph (א) and the tav (ת) directly associated with Elohim אֱלֹהִים "God."

> For I the Lord thy God will hold thy right hand,
> saying unto thee, Fear not; I will help thee.
> (Isaiah, [Yeshai'yahu יְשַׁעְיָהוּ] 41:13)

כִּי אֲנִי יְהוָה אֱלֹהֶיךָ מַחֲזִיק יְמִינֶךָ

yemi'neka macha'zik Elohekah Jehovah ani ki

הָאֹמֵר לְךָ אַל תִּירָא אֲנִי עֲזַרְתִּיךָ:

azar'ti'ka Ani el tirah lekah ha'omair

Starting with the second-to-the last word, which is "I" *Ani* אֲנִי, and taking the first letter of each word spells מ י ר ה ל א ת א. If these letters are reversed, we have *et Elohim* אֵת אֱלֹהִים, which means "God," preceded by the aleph and the tav. In Genesis 1:1, בְּרֵאשִׁית בָּרָא אֱלֹהִים אֵת, the aleph and the tav follow the name of God, but here these two letters precede His name. He is the first of all things, and He is the last of all things — the First and the Last, the Beginning and the Ending. Isaiah confirms this in chapter 44, verse 6: "Thus saith the Lord the King of Israel, and his redeemer the Lord of hosts; I am the first, and I am the last; and beside me there is no God."

> I have declared, and have saved, and I have showed, when there was no strange god among you: therefore ye are My witnesses saith the Lord, that I am God.   (Isaiah 43:12)

In Isaiah 43:12, the relevant words are in the phrase "I declared and I saved and I showed" *Anoki higadeti vehoshati vehishmatai* אָנֹכִי הִגַּדְתִּי וְהוֹשַׁעְתִּי וְהִשְׁמַעְתִּי. Starting with the second yod (י) to the right and counting every fourth letter from right to left spells *Yeshua* יְשׁוּעַ. In Hebrew, the number "four" represents creation and the creative power behind it — God.

To give a more powerful description of the Creator from the insights, we need to look at Genesis 24:8. Starting with the first letter in the fourth word and counting every 1,010th letter from right to left spells *haborai Yeshua* הַבּוֹרֵא יְשׁוּעַ, or "Yeshua the Creator." Do we need any more evidence to give verification to the Word of God? In this same letter count of 1,010, we discover three additional finds relative to Yeshua the Creator: "Jonah" *Yonah* יוֹנָה, "the place" *makom* מָקוֹם, and "truth" *emmet* אֱמֶת.

Yeshua is directly associated with the phrase "I have declared and I saved and I showed." This Scripture reflects the thought that is found in Acts 4:12: "Neither is there salvation in any other: for there is none other name under heaven given among men, whereby we must be saved." The insight from Isaiah 43:12 is not by chance, nor was it engraved in His Word by men.

The Lord is revealing His Word at a rapid pace in these last days. Daniel says that in the last days many shall run to and fro and knowledge will increase. This is happening now in both the secular world and in the spiritual realm. Since the invention of high-tech computers, God's people are running through His Word at a speed never before experienced. The awesome revelation of His Word is on a scale that is unprecedented. Why? Because it is the end of time when all things will be fulfilled. For example, Daniel 12:4, 9 says, "But thou, O Daniel, shut up the words, and seal the book, even to the time of the end: many shall run to and fro, and knowledge shall be increased. . . . And he said, Go thy way, Daniel: for the words are closed up and sealed till the time of the end."

I want to establish the authenticity of the precious Word of God by giving you some additional insights before I proceed into the main purpose of this book. I believe that Yeshua created all things and that all things are kept by the power of His Word. There are many jewels hidden deep within the book of Genesis. For me, Genesis has proven to be a lifelong study. I have mined many gems from this book, God's treasure house. Take, for example, Genesis 36:24. Starting with the second letter in the tenth word and counting every twenty-sixth letter from right to left spells *tav Emmanuel Aleph* ת-עמנו-אל-א. Here we find the tav preceding the name *Emmanuel* and the aleph following His name. In this twenty-six-letter count, we encounter the word "Jonah" *Yonah* יונה at fifty-two-letter intervals (2 × 26). "Jonah," meaning "dove," is a name that alludes to the *mikveh* (baptism) of Yeshua, and *Emmanuel* is a name for

Messiah which means "God with us." There are other jewels, as illustrated in the following passages:

> Therefore the Lord himself shall give you a sign; Behold, a virgin shall conceive, and bear a son; and shall call his name Immanuel [עמנו-אל].
>
> (Isaiah 7:14)

Starting with the mem (מ) in the word for virgin עלמה and counting every seventeenth letter from right to left spells *Messiah* משיח. From the same mem and counting every fourteenth letter from left to right spells *haShalom* השלום, which means "the peace." Jesus is the Prince of Peace. This is fulfilled in Matthew 1:21–23:

> And she shall bring forth a son, and thou shalt call his name JESUS [Yeshua]: for he shall save his people from their sins. Now all this was done, that it might be fulfilled which was spoken of the Lord by the prophet, saying, Behold, a virgin shall be with child, and shall bring forth a son, and they shall call his name Emmanuel, which being interpreted is, God with us.

When the Lord spoke to the children of Israel out of the fire, they feared greatly because of the awesome holiness of our Lord. But Moses spoke to Him face-to-face as a man speaks to a friend. The Lord knows our weaknesses and had compassion on us. He sent His Son, Jesus, so we may approach God through Him. God chose a virgin named Mary *Miryam* מרים to bring forth the Messiah.

Next is a passage in Deuteronomy 5:4–5: "The Lord talked with you face to face in the mount out of the midst of the fire, (I stood between the LORD and you at that time, to show you the word of the Lord: for ye were afraid by reason of the fire, and went not up into the mount)." From the ayin (ע) in the Hebrew phrase "with you" *immahkem* עמכם and counting every 1,325th letter forward spells "the Virgin Mary" *Almah Miryam* עלמה מרים. Mary was the person whom God used to bring us our Lord and Savior, Yeshua the Messiah. The fire of Deuteronomy 5:4 shows up as light in the New Testament, as in 2 Corinthians 4:6: "For God, who commanded the light to shine out of darkness, hath shined in our hearts, to give the light of the knowledge of the glory of God in the face of Jesus Christ."

Additional references to Jesus are found in the Old Testament. In Exodus 32:25, starting with the second letter in the eighth word and counting every tenth letter from right to left spells *Yeshua* יֵשׁוּעַ. The letters that are adjacent to the ones that spell *Yeshua* spell *melek* מלך, which means "king." Another group of adjacent letters spell *ha'aitzar*, which means "the prison." In this same series of ten-letter counts is the Hebrew phrase *ohrah Eliyahu* אורה אליהו, which means "the light of the Lord God." *Eliyahu* also means "Elijah." In addition, in this same series of ten-letter counts but at fifty-letter intervals spells the word *Elijah* אליהו. The word "Moses" מֹשֶׁה shows up at a ten-letter count as well. Moses represents the Torah, and Elijah represents the prophets — the two great witnesses to God's truth in the Old Testament. In this same verse (Exodus 32:25), starting with the ayin (ע) in *Yeshua* and counting every eleventh letter from left to right, we find the word *Emmanuel* אל-עמנו, which means "God with us."

The seven combinations of *Yeshua, light, Emmanuel, Elijah, Moses, prison,* and *king* give us a picture of Yeshua's destiny: Yeshua was born of a virgin; He is the light of the world; God was with us; Moses and Elijah appeared with Yeshua on the mountain to discuss His execution; He went to prison; and the Roman soldiers wrote the inscription "Jesus, the King of the Jews" on His cross.

Genesis 1:14–18 contains the narrative of the fourth day of Creation. Starting in verse 17 with the yod (י) in the name

Elohim אלהים and counting every twenty-sixth letter from right to left spells the word *Yeshua* ישוע. The adjacent letters to the right of each letter of *Yeshua* spell *ha'Moriah* המריה, which is the mountain range in Israel where the Temple stood and where our Lord was crucified. In Genesis 1:2, the word for "the waters" is *ha'mayim* המים. This is the first time that this word is mentioned in the Bible. Starting with the last mem (מ) and counting every twenty-sixth letter from right to left spells the word *Mir'yam* מרים, which not only means "bitter waters" but also "Mary," the name of the earthly mother of Yeshua.

In these combinations we find not only *Yeshua* but also the place of His death and His mother's name. The name of Jehovah "Adonai" יהוה has a value of twenty-six. The odds that these various insights occur by chance are ridiculously high. These three words also have a value of twenty-six times thirty-six, or twenty-six times six to the second power. If these few insights do not convince the skeptic of the authenticity of His Word, allow me to expound more in this area of Scripture and thought.

In Genesis 1:6, starting with the first yod (י) and counting every twenty-sixth letter from right to left spells the words *Yah Elohim* יה אלהים, which means "the Lord God."

In Genesis 1:14, starting with the first tav (ת) and counting every twenty-sixth letter from left to right spells *tikveh* תקוה, which means "the hope." Every believer has a hope in the hereafter, but for us who look for the catching up (Rapture) this is called the blessed hope.

See also Genesis 1:1: "In the beginning, God created the heavens." The Hebrew for "the heavens" is *et ha'shamayim* את השמים. Notice that the words "the heavens" are preceded by the aleph and the tav. Starting with the shin (ש) and counting every twenty-sixth letter from right to left spells *shophar* שופר, which means "the ram's horn" (the voice of the Lord). Could this be the *shophar* (trump)? It follows the law of first mention that was repeated at the first *Shavuot* (Pentecost) after Moses brought the children of Israel out of Egypt up to Mount Sinai and announced the descent of the Lord of Glory.

When God created the heavens and the earth, He spoke and it happened. If we could have been there to hear Him speak, I am sure that His voice would have sounded like a shofar. Notice that the Hebrew word *shophar* shows up in the first verse in all the Bible.

Exodus 19:19–20 says, "And when the voice of the trumpet sounded long, and waxed louder and louder, Moses spake, and God answered him by a voice. And the Lord came down upon mount Sinai, on the top of the mount: and the Lord called Moses up to the top of the mount; and Moses went up." God's voice sounded like a shofar, which announced His coming at the first Shavuot (Pentecost). The first shofar sounded from heaven, and the last shofar will also sound from heaven to announce the coming of the Lord.

For the Lord himself shall descend from heaven with a shout, with the voice of the archangel, and with the trump [*shophar*] of God: and the dead in Christ [Messiah] shall rise first: Then we which are alive and remain shall be caught up [raptured *natzal* נָצַל] together with them in the clouds, to meet the Lord in the air: and so shall we ever be with the Lord" (1 Thessalonians 4:16–17).

In addition to the Second Coming, we find in 1 Thessalonians 4:17 the biblical Hebrew root word for *natzal* נָצַל, which means "catch up, rescue, and deliver."

An encoded *natzal* appears in Genesis 2:12: "And the gold of that land is good; there is bdellium [gum resin] and the onyx stone." Starting with the third heh (ה) and counting every twenty-sixth letter from right to left spells *ha'natzal* הנצל, which means "the rapture, snatched up, saved, rescued." I wonder if the land of gold has something to do with this insight? Perhaps, the heavenly streets of gold? The word *natzal* is encoded at least three times in this area (Genesis 2:12; 2:14; 2:15).

Starting with the very first tav (ת) of Genesis 1:1 and counting every twenty-sixth letter from right to left spells *terumah* תרומה, which means "a gift, sacrifice, present, free-will offering." Yeshua is the gift to this world that was in the heart of God from the very beginning. Any gift must be received before one can benefit from it, and so it is with Yeshua: You must receive God's gift to obtain the gift of eternal life.

Starting with the first heh (ה) of Genesis 1:12 and counting every twenty-sixth letter from left to right spells *hai Shiloh* הא שילה, which means "behold, Shiloh." "Shiloh" is another name for the Messiah. The adjacent letters to the right of the letters that form *Shiloh*, spell *shevet* שבט, which means "scepter." The letters to the left of the letters that form *Shiloh* spell *yakum* יקום, which means "He rises, shall rise up."

> The scepter [*shevet* שבט] shall not depart from Judah, nor a lawgiver from between his feet, until Shiloh שילה [Messiah] come, and unto him shall the gathering of the people be. (Genesis 49:10)

Thus far, we have explored eleven words that are found at an interval of every twenty-sixth letter in the first two chapters of Genesis:

1. *Yeshua* ישוע — Jesus.
2. *Ha'Moriah* המריה — the mountain where the name of the Lord is written, where the temple stood, and where Yeshua was crucified. Also, this is the location of the holy city Jerusalem.
3. *Mir'yam* מרים — Mary, the name of Jesus' earthly mother.

4. *Yah Elohim* יה אלהים — the Lord God.

5. *Tikveh* תקוה — the hope.

6. *Shophar* שופר — the shofar (ram's horn).

7. *Ha'Natzal* הנצל — the Rapture (snatching up).

8. *Terumah* תרומה — the gift.

9. *Hai Shiloh* הא שילה — behold, Shiloh.

10. *Shaivet* שבט — scepter.

11. *Yakum* יקום — He rises; shall rise up.

Each of the above words are conspicuously related to one another. The Lord has divinely placed each of these precious gems in His Word for us to explore in these last days.

Every book of the Bible is unique and overlaps from one book to the other in sequence. While the whole Word of God is one composite unit, it has been divided into segments that we call books. It begins in the book of Genesis with the fountain of living waters that bring forth salvation (Yeshua) from God's throne room of plenty. The Word of God ends in the book of Revelation with the promise of eternal redemption for the believers and rejection for the ungodly. We can tap this reservoir of abundance through the Living Word (Yeshua) and receive salvation and the eternal sustenance of life today.

The first book of the Torah begins with Adam and ends with Joseph. The many events between these two patriarchs and those who portrayed the various types of the coming Messiah tell us of the planning and character of our God. The books of Exodus through Deuteronomy elaborate on the character-building experiences of the nation of Israel, the leaders, and the judgment on the rebellious. Moses, Aaron, and Joshua were types of Yeshua the Messiah — but only up to a point. None of those portraying His character could perfect their roles because they were just men, ordained of God, yes, but with the weaknesses that all of humanity has.

The first book of the Torah, Genesis, ends with the word

Egypt. The second book, Exodus, ends with the word *journeys.* The third book, Leviticus, ends with the word *Sinai.* The fourth book, Numbers, ends with the word *Jericho.* The fifth and last book of the Torah, Deuteronomy, ends with the word *Israel.* We can see the progressive travels of Israel in each book. They started in Egypt but were delivered by Moses and went on a journey through the desert to Mount Sinai. After forty years, they crossed over the Jordan River and went to Jericho. Then they entered the Promised Land (Israel). The believers' walk is a parallel journey. We began our earthly trek in the world (Egypt); we will one day arrive in the Promised Land (heaven) of glory. These words of the Torah were not put there by chance but by divine design.

Yeshua, The Aleph and the Tav

With permission, I quote from J. R. Church's and Gary Stearman's book, *The Mystery of the Menorah* (pp. 163, 173), published in 1993 by Prophecy Publications:

Genesis (Aleph א)

Genesis, the book of beginnings, is the ultimate statement of God's power and sovereignty. Here, He is expounded as Creator, Sovereign, Sustainer and Redeemer, who creates a perfect environment for man and woman — the primary purpose of His creation. He is the one and only constant throughout the events of their fall and the promise of mankind's redemption.

Through their sin and the sins of their progeny, He develops a redemptive plan that stretches out across the ages. Genesis is the setting for this immense journey. Without the simple understanding of man's creation and fall, the rest of the Bible becomes an inexplicable chronicle of man's repeated failure. The contrast between man's sinful nature and God's sinless perfection forms the foundation of divinely-inspired Scripture.

Revelation, Chapter 22 (Tahv ת)

The ת tahv symbolizes the Hebrew word *emet* "truth." In Hebrew, this word is said to be an acrostic that stands for "God is the Eternal King, in the infinite past, present and future."

The aleph (א) and the tav (ת) equal 401, but when spelled out together in Hebrew they equal 517; aleph (אלף) equals 111 and tav (ית) equals 406, respectively. Yeshua is not only known by the names Aleph and Tav; He is also known by many other names, as we see from the following Scripture snapshots.

In Genesis 36:35, starting with the third yod (י) and counting every 214th letter from right to left spells *Aleph Yeshua* אלף ישוע, which means "Yeshua the Aleph" or "Yeshua the First." *Aleph Yeshua* has a total mathematical value of 497. This value is the result of adding the numerical value of the aleph (אלף 111) and Yeshua (ישוע 386) together. The adjacent letters spell *tummim* תמים, which means "perfection or truth." A tummin was one of the items of clothing worn by the high priest.

In Genesis 42:24, starting with the third to last yod (י) and counting every thirty-first letter from left to right spells *Yeshua Aleph* ישוע אלף. In this combination, aleph follows Yeshua.

In Numbers 1:1, starting with the last mem (ם) and counting every ninth letter from right to left spells *Mashiach Tav* משיח תו, which means "Messiah, the Tav."

In Deuteronomy 31:27, starting with the second to last tav (ת) and counting every ninth letter from left to right spells *Tav Yeshua* תו ישוע.

In Numbers 6:5, starting with the first mem (מ) and counting every thirty-fifth letter from right to left spells *Mashiach oht* משיח אות, which means "Messiah, the sign (token or letter)."

Numbers 9:5 reads, "And they kept the Passover on the fourteenth day of the first month at even in the wilderness of Sinai [סיני]: according to all that the Lord commanded Moses, so did the children of Israel."

In Numbers 9:5, from the second letter, the yod (י) in the twelfth word "Sinai" (סיני) and counting every fifty-fourth letter from left to right spells *Yeshua ha'ait* ישוע האת, which means "Yeshua the Aleph and the Tav."

In Leviticus 27:29, starting with the last yod (י) and counting every thirty-eighth letter from left to right spells *Yeshua hadegel* ישוע הרגל, which means "Yeshua, the banner." The adjacent letters spell *Arayih* אריה, which means "the lion (of the Lord)."

In 1 Chronicles 4:13, starting with the fourth letter, the yod (י), of the third word "Othniel" עתניאל and counting every fourth letter from right to left spells *Yeshua ait* ישוע את. The Hebrew name "Othniel" means "the force of God." Remember that the name *Yeshua* is also encoded in Isaiah 43:12 at four-letter intervals within the statement "I declare, and I save, and I show." When Yeshua created the universe, He did it by the power (force) of God, which is His Word.

In 1 Chronicles 4:10, starting with the first letter in the thirteenth word and counting every tenth word from right to left, taking only the first letter of each word, spells *Yeshua* ישוע. This system of analysis is called "equidistant-word sequence" (EWS). In reality, it is called *Rosh Tov* ראש תוב, which means "to take the first letter or the head letter of a word." Thus, not only do we find *Yeshua* through ELS but also through EWS. (See the Foreword and the first part of this chapter for a fuller explanation of these terms.)

In 2 Chronicles 7:22, starting with the first letter, the aleph (א), in the fourteenth word *ait* אֵת and counting every eleventh letter from right to left spells *ait Yeshua* אֵת יֵשׁוּעַ, which means "Yeshua the aleph and the tav."

Also in 2 Chronicles 7:22, starting with the second to last aleph (א) and counting every eleventh letter from right to left spells *ait Yeshua* אֵת יֵשׁוּעַ.

In 2 Kings 18:4, starting with the eighth tav (ת) and counting every fiftieth letter from right to left spells *tav Yeshua o'ded* תּו יֵשׁוּעַ עֹדֵד, which means "Yeshua continually the Tav (last)."

In Ezra 2:9, starting with the first aleph (א) and counting every twenty-third letter from left to right spells *Ait Mashiach* אֵת מָשִׁיחַ. In other words, not only is Yeshua the Aleph and the Tav, but also Messiah is the Aleph and the Tav.

Jesus is known as the Aleph and the Tav in the New Testament as well as in the Old Testament. John the Baptist had received a revelation that Jesus was the preexisting Holy One of Israel. Considering John's background for holiness and detail, he would not have made such an assumption if it was not true. John equated Jesus, the almighty God of creation with Jesus the Lamb of God who would take away the sins of the world. He knew that Jesus was a man, born of a virgin, yet He was also God in the flesh. We see this in John 1:15: "John bare witness of him, and cried, saying, This was he of whom I spake, He that cometh after me is preferred before me: for he was before me."

John the apostle also saw Him as the Beginning and the End, the Aleph (א) and Tav (ת), the First and the Last. John writes in Revelation 1:8, "I am Alpha (א) and Omega (ת), the beginning and the ending, saith the Lord, which is, and which was, and which is to come, the Almighty." The phrase "which is, and which was, and which is to come" is the meaning of the ineffable name *Jehovah* יהוה. In this text, Jesus, the man, is claiming to be the Lord Jehovah, God.

Revelation 5:5 says, "And one of the elders saith unto me, Weep not: behold, the Lion of the tribe of Judah, the Root of David, hath prevailed to open the book, and to loose the seven seals thereof." In the final book of the Bible, Yeshua is a lion. Finally, Revelation 1:11 reveals that Jesus said, "I Am Alpha [aleph א] and Omega [tav ת] the first and the last."

Yeshua was a Jew by birth; His natural mother was from the royal tribe of Judah; His Father was God. God has placed encoded messages within the text of Genesis 2:7–8, which speaks of the creation of Adam. Starting with the fourth letter in the third word of Genesis 2:8 and counting every thirty-third letter in reverse spells *Yeshua* ישוע. We will find different words and phrases with the thirty-three-letter count in the same area of Scripture (Gen. 2:13; 2:6). The various words are (1) *Yeshua* ישוע; (2) "the Jew" יהודי; (3) *Moreh* מורה, which means "the teacher of righteousness, and, the early rain;" (4) *Shabbat* שבת; (5) *Hinnai Yah* הנה יה, which translates "behold the Lord." Within this text, Yeshua's name is encoded twice.

When God breathed the breath of life into Adam, he became a living soul without sin. His blood was pure — free from any defilement whatsoever. When Adam sinned, something happened to his pure blood — it became contaminated with his sin. Because life is in the blood, which God has given to sustain us, the sin contamination led to physical death. Jesus was born of the royal house of Judah. He was a Jew by birth, but His Father was God. His blood was therefore pure and remained so because He was without sin. This is evident in Genesis 5:3. Starting with the third letter in the eleventh word and counting every 124th letter from right to left spells "the blood of Messiah" משיח דם. Also, in the adjacent letters in the same count of

124 spells "to bury" קבר , "to humble" שׁוח, and "sin offering" אשׁם. In this one verse, we have *the blood, Messiah, sin offering, to humble*, and *burial*.

Genesis 5:3 is not the only verse that links the words "Messiah" and "blood." In Leviticus 23:34, starting with the third letter in the sixth word and counting every 159th letter from right to left spells "blood and Messiah" משׁיח דם. Also in this same verse but with a count of 124 spells "psalm of praise" תהלה and "faith" אמנה. The blood that Jesus had in His veins did not come from His earthly mother, Miryam; it came from His Father and was pure from all defilement. Many times, I will see insights from the Hebrew Codes where blood is directly associated with the name "Jesus" or "Messiah." There are reasons for encoded messages such as these. One reason is to prove that Jesus was a man, and as a man, He had to give His blood and His life a ransom for the sins of the world. One of the truths that we can glean from the meaning of the Aleph and Tav is that Jesus died for the first as well as the last man in this world. He ransomed all humankind from the death penalty, and He patiently waits for your earnest response to Him so that He may give to you eternal life with Him. Romans 5:8–11 reflects this thought:

> But God commendeth his love toward us, in that, while we were yet sinners, Christ [Messiah] died for us. Much more then, being now justified by his blood, we shall be saved from wrath through Him. For if, when we were enemies, we were reconciled to God by the death of his Son, much more, being reconciled, we shall be saved by his life. And not only so, but we also joy in God through our Lord Jesus Christ, by whom we have now received the atonement.

3

The Abounding Grace of God

The people of this world who decline the offer of salvation through Jesus the Messiah give many different excuses that are not sensible nor legitimate. The most frequent response is based on conjecture or hearsay. Some say they just cannot believe that all the stories of the Bible are true; they claim there is no real proof. This response is quite absurd. There are volumes of facts that provide verification of the source and authenticity of the Bible. This argument reminds me of a college professor who tried to justify his atheism by discrediting the infallible Word of God based solely on his mistaken belief that the Bible claimed that the children of Israel carried Noah's ark around the wilderness for forty years. These types of misconceptions are easily corrected by simply reading the Bible. The professor needed only to compare the measurements of the Ark of the Covenant with those of Noah's ark. This type of excuse is not reasonable; it is an insult to intelligent, thinking people.

The criticism that comes from the unsaved should never set the standard by which we who have the heavenly vision are influenced in making decisions for our spiritual walk with the Lord. Should an unbeliever plan your sermon for the next service, or should a person who takes counsel from the ungodly tell you what you should believe or not believe concerning eternal things? This is what the worldly, being full of opinions, try to do in controversial matters concerning the Bible. We can gain much from philosophical and scientific knowledge, but the thoughts of the natural mind are not in tune with the realm of the Spirit of God.

> For they that are after the flesh do mind the things of the flesh; but they that are after the Spirit the things of the Spirit. For to be carnally minded is death; but to be spiritually minded is life and peace. Because the carnal mind is emnity against God: for it is not subject to the law of God, neither indeed can be.
>
> (Romans 8:5–7)

There is an attack against the proper Hebrew spelling of the name *Yeshua* ישׁוע by some anti-messianics. Some unbelievers claim that Jesus is a pagan Gentile demi-god and that, therefore, it is blasphemous to accept Him as the true Messiah. By dropping the last letter of Jesus' name — the ayin (ע) — from the Biblical spelling *Yeshua* ישׁוע, they claim His name is spelled *Yeshu* ישׁו, which is a derogatory term. They solidify their arguments that He is a false messiah by claiming that His name appears in certain Scriptures associated with evil or sin. This is one of the methods they use to deprogram Jewish believers in *Yeshua HaMashiach*. Deuteronomy 28:36 is one Scripture frequently used to prove their confusing point: "The Lord shall bring thee, and thy king which thou shalt set over thee, unto a nation which neither thou nor thy fathers have known; and there shalt thou serve other gods, wood and stone."

In this Scripture, they have found the word *yeshu* יְשׁוּ at five-letter intervals in the part of the verse speaking of other gods of wood and stone. This does not make sense, nor does it prove anything. Since the name *Yeshua* and several other key words like *Torah* appear frequently, it is inevitable that you will find various words encoded in passages dealing with both good and evil. For example, we also find encoded within this same area of the Scripture the name "Moses" מֹשֶׁה, "Exodus" שְׁמוֹת, and "salvation" יֵשַׁע. In Deuteronomy 28:34, starting with the first letter in the seventh word, counting every 20th letter in both directions, spells *Nathani Yeshua* נְתַנִי יֵשׁוּעַ, which means "My gift, Yeshua." Also, in this same twenty-letter count, we will find, "Shiloh" שִׁילֹה and "Adonai" יְהֹוָה. If we continue counting, this time at 100-letter intervals, we will find "Adonai" יְהֹוָה. Little do they know that wherever sin is, Jesus will be there, full of love and grace, ready to forgive all manner of sins, even those who oppose Him. Did He not forgive those who crucified Him at Jerusalem almost 2,000 years ago? Remember, He died for all sinners of all nations for all time.

There are several computer programs available on the market that can be used to calculate ELS, but some have been proven faulty. Be very careful when you purchase programs with the Hebrew text. The mistakes may not be intentional, but the effect is the same. In one example, Isaiah 53:5, the Hebrew phrase "for our transgressions" מִפְּשָׁעֵינוּ is the correct Hebrew spelling according to the Masoretic text, but one of the Torah programs lacks the yod (י) in this word. The *Interlinear Bible*, by Hendrickson Publishers, also adds a letter in Isaiah 53:5. The fifth word, which is "for our iniquities" מֵעֲוֹנֹתֵינוּ, has no vav (ו) between the nun (נ) and tav (ת). An extra letter is also added by the *Interlinear* in Daniel 9:27. The 14th word is "a desolator" מְשֹׁמֵם in the Masoretic text, but in the *Interlinear* the vav (ו) is omitted.

In Psalms 22:28 the sixth word means "the ends of" אפסי. This is the correct spelling, according to the Masoretic text. However, one of the computer programs omits the peh (פ) and samech (ס) in this word. They spell it אי. Here again, we need to be very careful when using such imperfect programs. These errors upset the original pattern of words and letters. This should not be! These examples may help you to better appreciate the methods used by the ancient rabbis in their analyses, which are done manually. This is why I use this same method; there is less room for mistakes.

The Lord prophesied through Moses in Deuteronomy 28 about a king that would desecrate His people and His house. This certainly is not *Yeshua HaMashiach*.

> Manasseh was twelve years old when he began to reign, and he reigned fifty and five years in Jerusalem: But did that which was evil in the sight of the Lord, like unto the abominations of the heathen, whom the Lord had cast out before the children of Israel. For he built again the high places which Hezekiah his father had broken down, and he reared up altars for Baalim, and made groves, and worshipped all the host of heaven, and served them. Also he built altars in the house of the Lord, whereof the Lord had said, In Jerusalem shall My name be for ever. And He built altars for all the host of heaven in the two courts of the house of the lord. And he caused his children to pass through the fire in the valley of the son of Hinnom: also he observed times, and used enchantments, and used witchcraft, and dealt with a familiar spirit, and with wizards: he wrought much evil in the sight of the Lord, to provoke Him to anger. And he set a carved image, the idol which he had made, in the house of God, of

which God had said to David and to Solomon his son, In this house, and in Jerusalem, which I have chosen before all the tribes of Israel, will I put My name forever: (2 Chronicles 33:1–7)

Not only did Jewish kings desecrate God's people, the Jews, but so did Gentile kings. Nebuchadnezzar was a Gentile king who besieged Jerusalem in 606 B.C. and took the Jews captive to Babylon. He was yet another tyrant who persecuted Israel because of their sinful rebellion. In the midst of their captivity, the God of grace was ready to forgive and save anyone who would call upon Him.

There are many places throughout the Scriptures where we will find Yeshua encoded within a text that speaks of the sins and transgressions of His people. Why is this? God loves the sinner but not his sins. He will always be present where sin abounds, ready to forgive and bring restitution to the offenders.

Another area of Scripture that is used to discredit the name of Jesus (*Yeshua*) is found in the book of Deuteronomy.

Thou shalt have none other gods before Me. Thou shalt not make thee any graven image, or any likeness of any thing that is in heaven above, or that is in the earth beneath, or that is in the waters beneath the earth. Thou shalt not bow down thyself unto them, nor serve them: for I, the Lord [*Jehovah*] your God am a jealous God, visiting the iniquity of the fathers upon the children unto the third and fourth generation of them that hate Me.

(Deuteronomy 5:7–9)

Yeshu ישׁו is also encoded within these Scriptures. However, this does not indicate in any way that Jesus (*Yeshua*) is a pagan messiah. If we look closer at the original

Hebrew text of the last portion of verse nine, we will see a beautiful message of salvation to the rebellious and the name of the city where His Name is written: "For I, the Lord [*Jehovah*] your God am a jealous God, visiting the iniquity of the fathers upon the children unto the third and fourth generation of them that hate Me."

כי אנכי יהוה אלהיך אל קנא פקד עון
אבות על — בנים ועל-שלשים ועל-רבעים לשנאי:
(Deuteronomy 5:9b)

Encoded at five-letter intervals in the Hebrew passage above is the name *Yeshua* ישוע, which means "salvation," and, at three-letter intervals, "Jerusalem (the city of peace) exists" יש ירושלם. Why would His name and the city of Jerusalem appear here? The city was not founded until 400 years later by King David. This is the place where He demonstrated the full grace of God to a rebellious nation and world. This event took place almost 1,500 years after Moses wrote this text.

And doing kindness to thousands of those who love Me and keep My commandment.
(Deuteronomy 5:10)

Moreover the Law [*Torah*] entered, that the offence might abound. But where sin abounded, grace did much more abound: That as sin hath reigned unto death, even so might grace reign through righteousness unto eternal life by Jesus Christ [*Yeshua HaMashiach*] our Lord.   (Romans 5:20–21)

For the wages of sin is death; but the gift of God is eternal life through Jesus Christ [*Yeshua HaMashiach*] our Lord.   (Romans 6:23)

For the Son of man [*Yeshua*] is come to seek and to save that which was lost.   (Luke 19:10)

And I thank Christ Jesus [*Yeshua HaMashiach*] our Lord, who hath enabled me, for that he counted me faithful, putting me into the ministry; Who was before a blasphemer, and a persecutor, and injurious: but I obtained mercy, because I did it ignorantly in unbelief. And the grace of our Lord was exceeding abundant with faith and love which is in Christ Jesus [*Yeshua HaMashiach*]. This is a faithful saying, and worthy of all acceptation, that Christ Jesus [*Yeshua HaMashiach*] came into the world to save sinners; of whom I am chief.

(1 Timothy 1:12–15)

Recently, I received some disturbing information from the Internet. Someone was trying to associate Yeshua with the false messiah by using the system of analysis called ELS. The Scripture to which they were referring for this blasphemous accusation is found in Isaiah 11, which is a messianic prophecy concerning Yeshua the Messiah and the messianic kingdom. As usual, when I examine these anti-Yeshua insights, I prove them to be faulty.

And there shall come forth a rod out of the stem of Jesse, and a Branch shall grow out of his roots: And the spirit of the Lord shall rest upon him, the spirit of wisdom and understanding, the spirit of counsel and might, the spirit of knowledge and of the fear of the Lord: And shall make him of quick understanding in the fear of the Lord: and he shall not judge after the sight of his eyes, neither reprove after the hearing of his ears: But with righteousness shall he judge the poor, and reprove with equity for the meek of the earth: and he shall smite the earth with the rod of his mouth, and with the breath of his lips shall he slay the wicked. And righteousness shall be the girdle of his loins, and faithfulness the girdle of his reins. The wolf also shall dwell with the lamb, and the leopard shall lie down with the kid: and the calf and the young lion and the fatling together; and a little child shall lead them.   (Isaiah 11:1–6)

In Isaiah 11:3, starting with the second letter in the sixth word, which is "His eyes" עיניו, and counting every 88th letter from right to left spells *Yeshua* ישוע. The anti-Yeshua discreditors claim that the Hebrew word "false" *sheker* שקר overlaps this insight of Yeshua at 82-letter increments, thereby suggesting that He (*Yeshua*) is a false-messiah. When I made my analysis to prove or disprove this ludicrous statement, I discovered the Hebrew word *ha'chashak* החשק, which means "to cling to; to love; to desire." The location of this insight is found in Isaiah 11:3, starting with the third letter of the ninth word and counting in both directions.

Another combination that is unique is found in Isaiah 11:6. Starting with the first letter of the eighth word and counting from right to left, taking the first letter of every forty-ninth word from right to left spells *Yeshua* ישוע. *Yeshua* ישוע shows up at a thirty-four word count with the adjacent letters spelling "the Fire of the Lord" יראש. Also, in this chapter we will find Yeshua at least four additional times and "Messiah" at least once.

There is archeological evidence from the first century that the Hebrew name of Jesus, *Yeshua* ישוע, is spelled in this manner. With Grant Jeffrey's permission, I wish to quote from pages 318 and 319 in his book *Final Warning*, released May 1995. I might add that this book is a must-read for everyone.

In the spring of 1873, Effendi Abu Saud, while constructing his house on the eastern slopes of the Mount of Olives near the road to ancient Bethany, accidently discovered a cave that proved to be an ancient burial catacomb. Inside, he found thirty ancient stone coffins. Professor Charles Claremont-Gannueau examined the ossuaries in this ancient family sepulchral cave carved out of limestone rock. The Jews in the first century buried their dead either in the ground or in atomb. Several years later they would clean the bones of the skeleton and re-bury these bones in a small limestone ossuary, often forty-five inches long, twenty inches wide and twenty-five inches high. The lids of these ossuaries are triangular, semi-circular, or rectangular. Inscriptions containing the name and identification of the deceased were painted or engraved on the sides or on the lids of the ossuaries in Hebrew or Greek. Claremont-Gannueau was excited to note that several ossuaries were inscribed with crosses or the name "Jesus" יְשׁוּעַ, proving that these Jewish deceased were Christians.

Engraved on the sides of three of these ossuaries from this cave were the names of "Eleazar אֶלְעָזָר" (the Hebrew form of the Greek name "Lazarus"), "Martha," and "Mary." Those names were followed by the sign of the cross, proving they were Christian. In the Gospel of John we read the touching story of Christ raising His friend Lazarus from the dead. "Now a certain man was sick, Lazarus of Bethany, the town of Mary and her sister Martha" (John 11:1). Claremont-Gannueau noted that this was one of the most important archeological discoveries ever made concerning the origins of the early New Testament Church. He wrote, "This catacomb on the Mount of Olives belonged apparently to one of the earliest families which joined the new religion of Christianity. In this group of sarcophagi some of which have the Christian symbol and some have not, we are, so to speak, (witnessing the) actual unfolding of Christianity. Personally, I think that many of the Hebrew-speaking people whose remains are contained in these ossuaries were among the first followers of Christ. . . . The appearance of Christianity at the very gates of Jerusalem is, in my opinion, extraordinary and unprecedented. Somehow the new [Christian] doctrine must have made its way into the Jewish system. . . . The association of the sign of the cross with (the name of Jesus ישוע)) written in Hebrew alone constitutes a valuable fact."

There are additional Scriptures about sin or evil where Yeshua is encoded. Each one of these has a prophetic overtone. The fourth chapter of Leviticus gives us an unusual, but firm, message. The last four words in verse two will be used at the beginning of the Hebrew below.

> If the priest that is anointed do sin according to the sin of the people; then let him bring for his sin, which he hath sinned, a young bullock without blemish unto the Lord for a sin offering.

תעשׂינה ועשׂה מאחת מהנה: אם הכהן המשׁיח יחטא לאשׁמת העם
והקריב על חטאתו אשׁר חטא פר בן בקר תמים ליהוה לחטאת:
(Leviticus 4:3)

Starting with the sixth letter to the far right and counting every sixth letter from right to left spells "Behold, Behold Yeshua" הא הן ישוע. Notice, the word before the yod (י) in Yeshua's name is *HaMashiach* המשׁיח. Now we have "Behold, Behold Yeshua the Messiah (*Yeshua HaMashiach*)."

One may ask the question: Why does Yeshua show up where the priest has sinned? Is not Yeshua the High Priest?

Here again, we look to the phrase "Where sin abounds, grace does much more abound." Jesus was the perfect one for the sacrifice of the sins, not only for the priest, but of the whole world: "For He hath made Him to be sin for us, Who knew no sin; that we might be made the righteousness of God in Him" (2 Corinthians 5:21). Now we understand why the name of Jesus appears in Leviticus 4:3, revealing insights about the sins of the priest, whose sins He took, as well as yours, when He became our sin-offering.

> And it came to pass, that, as Jesus sat at meat in His house, many publicans and sinners sat also together with Jesus and His disciples: for there were many, and they followed Him. And when the scribes and Pharisees saw Him eat with publicans and sinners, they said unto His disciples, How is it that He eateth and drinketh with publicans and sinners? When Jesus heard it, He said unto them, "They that are whole have no need of the physician, but they that are sick: I came not to call the righteous, but sinners to repentance. (Mark 2:15–17)

These Scriptures explain why the names *Yeshua, Mashiach,* and *Lord* are encoded in areas of the Word where sin and related subjects are recorded.

The book of Proverbs was written by Solomon, who was inspired by God to receive great wisdom. He wrote many hidden messages throughout this book. Truly, this is a book of direction and godly character. In the book of Proverbs all the feasts of the Lord and many insights concerning Yeshua are encoded. Solomon built the first Temple, which was the most magnificent structure in all the earth. He also was considered the wisest man in the world. However, Yeshua, when speaking of Himself in Luke 11:31, declared, "Behold, a greater than Solomon is here."

We have established the fact that where sin abounds, the

grace of God abounds much more. In other words, the grace and love of God overcomes sin and degradation through Yeshua the Messiah. Proverbs 21:24 declares, "Proud and haughty scorner is his name, who dealeth in proud wrath."

זד יהי ר ל ץ שׁמו ע ל שׁה ב ע ברת זדון.

The enlarged letters above, spelling *Yeshua* יֵשׁוּעַ, are spaced at four-letter intervals. Here again, we see Yeshua encoded in the verses dealing with man's sin, showing He is ready to deliver — yes — even the proud and arrogant. Also, encoded in this same area, starting with the first heh (ה) in verse 24 and counting every 21st letter from left to right spells the ineffable name "Adonai" *Jehovah* יהוה. Those critics who would impune the name of Yeshua because it happens to appear near a mention of sin must logically and consistently impune the holy name of Jehovah which is also encoded in this scriptural passage.

The last word in Proverbs 21:31 is "deliverance" (salvation by the Lord through a man) *Hat'teshuah* התשׁועה. Counting every 16th letter from left to right from the shin (שׁ) spells *Shiloh Yeshua* שׁילו ישׁוע. Genesis 49:10 states, "The sceptre shall not depart from Judah, nor a lawgiver from between his feet, until Shiloh come; and unto Him shall the gathering of the people be." The Hebrew word *Shiloh* שׁילה can be spelled four different ways. It is a prophetic term for the Messiah that means "tranquil" or "calm" (as the calming of the waters).

In Genesis 49:9, starting with the first letter in the eleventh word, counting every forty-fourth letter from right to left spells *Mashiach* משׁיח. Also, from the same mem (מ) in Mashiach, taking the first letter of every sixth word, from right to left, spells *Moshi'ah* מושׁע, which means "Savior." These wonderful insights substantiate the divine arrangement of the Bible and the fact that God's Word is one אחד.

They demonstrate, also, the absolute holiness and expression of God. While many have tried to discredit these insights from the Masoretic Hebrew text, this new discovery of over forty names associated with the historical event of the crucifixion eliminates any possibility that these patterns are simply random appearances by chance. The Psalmist David declared thousands of years ago, "All that hate Me whisper together against Me; against Me do they devise My hurt" (Psalm 41:7).

יחד עלי יתלחשו כל-שׂנאי עלי יחשבו רעה לי:

Every second letter in the Hebrew phrase "they plot evil" *yachshvu ra'ah* יחשבו רעה spells *Yeshua* ישׁוע. Also, the remaining letters spell *chavrah* חברה, which means "the association" or "the group." It was some of Yeshua's own people — the very ones He came to save — that plotted evil against Him by every possible means. However, the Lord laid upon Him the iniquity of us all. In the final analysis, it was neither the Romans nor the Jews, but the sins of the whole world that caused His death.

> Hast thou commanded the morning since thy days; and caused the dayspring to know his place; That it might take hold of the ends of the earth, that the wicked might be shaken out of it?   (Job 38:12–13)

וינערו רשׁעים ממנה
that the wicked might be shaken out of it

Every second letter starting with the yod (י) in "the wicked" רשׁעים spells *Yeshua* ישׁוע in reverse. Remember, Yeshua reversed the curse that was on us. Also, He will judge the wicked nations on the day He returns to earth.

> And I saw heaven opened, and behold a white horse; and He that sat upon him was called Faithful and

> True, and in righteousness He doth judge and make
> war. His eyes were as a flame of fire, and on His
> head were many crowns; and He had a name
> written, that no man knew, but He Himself. And He
> was clothed with a vesture dipped in blood: and His
> name is called the Word of God. And the armies
> which were in heaven followed Him upon white
> horses, clothed in fine linen, white and clean. And
> out of His mouth goeth a sharp sword, that with it
> He should smite the nations: and He shall rule them
> with a rod of iron: and He treadeth the winepress of
> the fierceness and wrath of Almighty God. And He
> hath on His vesture and on His thigh a name written,
> KING OF KINGS, AND LORD OF LORDS.
>
> (Revelation 19:11–16)

The messianic kingdom will be set up at this time, ushering in a time of tranquility and peace such as the world has never known. This kingdom age has been prophesied from the beginning. As we draw closer to the time of the Kingdom, conditions in the world, both from a personal and international point of view, will grow more perplexing and chaotic at an exponential rate, a condition never before witnessed since the beginning of human history.

I personally praise God for 1 Thessalonians 4. For the believer, this is called the blessed hope, but for the unbeliever, it is called the day of gloom and trouble.

> But I would not have you to be ignorant brethren,
> concerning them which are asleep, that ye sorrow
> not, even as others which have no hope. For if we
> believe that Jesus died and rose again, even so them
> also which sleep in Jesus will God bring with Him.
> For this we say unto you by the word of the Lord,
> that we which are alive and remain unto the coming
> of the Lord shall not prevent [go before] them which

are asleep. For the Lord Himself shall descend from heaven with a shout, with the voice of the archangel, and with the trump of God: and the dead in Christ shall rise first: Then we which are alive and remain shall be caught up together with them in the clouds, to meet the Lord in the air: and so shall we ever be with the Lord. Wherefore comfort one another with these words.   (1 Thessalonians 4:13–18)

Nothing could be any clearer; those who have placed their faith in Jesus Christ as their Lord God shall be raptured up into the air and rescued from all the terrible times that are coming upon this earth. We shall meet our Lord Jesus face to face. What a blessed hope!

The Word of God says that offenses must come. Until the day that Jesus calls us home, those who follow Jesus Christ will suffer contradiction and ridicule for their faith in Him. Paul said, in Romans 8:18, "For I reckon that the sufferings of this present time are not worthy to be compared to the glory that shall be revealed in us."

Such contradictions and ridicule from men, are normal reactions from those who do not have the same hope. They see things from an earthly perspective, but we have glimpsed the eternal and have seen our destiny. What an awesome thought! We shall behold Him, who created all things for His good pleasure. He is none other than the Lord Yeshua HaMashiach!

In every situation during the centuries when Israel was persecuted by their enemies, the Lord always stretched forth His hand to save them. Even though they were in error, God shed forth His grace and love to a rebellious people.

And it shall come to pass in that day, that the Lord shall set His hand again the second time to recover the remnant of His people, which shall be left, from

Assyria, and from Egypt, and from Pathros, and from Cush [Ethiopia], and from Elam [Persia], and from Shinar, and from Hamath, and from the islands of the sea. And He shall set up an ensign for the nations, and shall assemble the outcasts of Israel, and gather together the dispersed of Judah from the four corners of the earth.

(Isaiah 11:11–12)

Notice the Hebrew phrase "the remnant of His people, which shall be left."

אֶת-שְׁאָר עַמּוֹ אֲשֶׁר-יִשָּׁאֵר

Starting with the yod (י) and counting every other letter from left to right spells *Yeshua* יֵשׁוּעַ. This combination shows up twice in the same area of Scripture. The phrase "His hand is still stretched out" refers to the Messiah, as the arm of the Lord. It is Yeshua (Jesus) who will retrieve the lost sheep of Israel when He returns the second time. We are seeing a partial fulfillment of the regathering of Israel, but the full recovery will not be complete until His return. Notice, at the worst time in the history of the nation of Israel, the Lord will come to their rescue and destroy their enemies. It is no wonder then that the name of Yeshua would show up at the most sinful time and when most needed.

There is no other name under heaven whereby we must be saved than by the name of Jesus. When Philip asked Jesus to show him the Father, Philip knew He was the Son of God, or this question would not have been asked.

Philip saith unto Him, "Lord, shew us the Father, and it sufficeth us." Jesus saith unto him, "Have I been so long time with you, and yet hast thou not known Me, Philip? He that hath seen Me hath seen the Father; and how sayest thou (then), Shew us the

Father? Believest thou not that I am in the Father, and the Father in Me? The words that I speak unto you I speak not of Myself: but the Father that dwelleth in Me, He doeth the works. Believe Me that I am in the Father, and the Father in Me: or else believe Me for the very works' sake.   (John 14:8–11)

This is an awesome response by Jesus. He told Philip that if you have seen Me, you have seen the Father. Colossians 2:8–10 declares, "Beware lest any man spoil you through philosophy and vain deceit, after the tradition of men, after the rudiments of the world, and not after Christ [Messiah]. For in Him dwelleth all the fullness of the Godhead bodily. And ye are complete in Him, which is the head of all principality and power." The Scriptures declare that to reject Jesus as the true Messiah is to reject God the Father. This truth is evident also from Colossians 2:8–10, 1 John, and Psalm 20.

Behold, what manner of love the Father hath bestowed upon us, that we should be called the sons of God: therefore the world knoweth us not, because it knew Him not.   (1 John 3:1)

Who is a liar but he that denieth that Jesus is the Christ [Messiah]? He is antichrist, that denieth the Father and the Son. Whosoever denieth the Son, the same hath not the Father: but he that acknowledgeth the Son hath the Father also.   (1 John 2:22–23)

The Lord hear thee in the day of trouble; the name of the God of Jacob defend thee; Send thee help from the sanctuary, and strengthen thee out of Zion; Remember all thy offerings, and accept thy burnt sacrifice; Selah. Grant thee according to thine own heart, and fulfill all thy counsel.   (Psalm 20:1–4)

Starting with the third letter in the third word in verse five in Psalm 20:5 and counting every forty-fourth letter from right to left spells "In Jesus and the Father" *be'Yeshua ve'ha'av* ביׁשוע והאב. Can anything be clearer? If we are in Jesus, we are also in the Father. This insight is the answer to Philip's question.

As believers in Yeshua HaMashiach, Colossians 3:1–4 becomes our hope:

> If ye then be risen with Christ [Messiah], seek those things which are above, where Christ [Messiah] sitteth on the right hand of God. Set your affection on things above, not on things on the earth. For ye are dead, and your life is hid with Christ [Messiah] in God. When Christ [Messiah], who is our life, shall appear, then shall ye also appear with Him in glory.
>
> (Colossians 3:1–4)

In every generation since the beginning, there have been groups of people who attempt to pervert the Word of God. There will be those who claim they are in God's camp but who try to change the meaning of the Word of God and the insights (codes that God has placed throughout His Word). One person told me that he did not need the insights to prove to him that Jesus was the Messiah. My response was instant! What about those who do not believe? Shall we not try any legitimate means within the boundaries of God's Word to convince them of His grace and love?

4

The Building of God and the Number of His Name

God has numbered our days and has counted the hairs on our heads. God deals with mathematical values much more than many of us have been led to believe. I reject the occult study of numerology that suggests that there is a message in the Bible that can be revealed by the study of numbers in the codes or the Scriptures in general. God forbids fortune-telling, regardless of the method used. However, the evidence that God has constructed the Hebrew text of the Bible using a mathematical design is obvious to anyone who will examine the Scriptures closely. This phenomenon of mathematical design, or Bible numerics, in the Holy Scriptures can be demonstrated to anyone who will actually examine the evidence for themselves. Since the ancient Hebrews did not possess any Arabic numbers (5, 6, 7, etc.) they used the twenty-two Hebrew letters to indicate numbers (a = א = 1, etc.).

For example, there are 144,000 set-apart people in the book of Revelation — 12,000 out of each tribe of the twelve tribes of Israel. The New Jerusalem is 12,000 furlongs high, 12,000 furlongs long, and 12,000 furlongs wide, with a volume of approximately 1,500 cubic miles. This means that the heavenly city is 12,000 furlongs (1500 miles) in every direction. To understand the awesome size of the New Jerusalem, multiply the height times the length times the width. This equals one trillion, seven-hundred twenty-eight billion (1,728,000,000,000) cubic furlongs. A furlong is about 220 feet long. Take a moment to reflect on this magnificent, heavenly structure. Imagine your living room being 220 feet long, wide, and high — one cubic furlong. Now imagine an area the size of the New Jerusalem. How many people could comfortably live in a city of that size? Heaven, which contains the New Jerusalem, is a real place as Jesus indicated in the gospel of John.

> Let not your heart be troubled: ye believe in God, believe also in Me. In My Father's house are many mansions [*chuppahs*]: if it were not so, I would have told you. I go to prepare a place for you. And if I go and prepare a place for you, I will come again, and receive you unto Myself; that where I am, there ye may be also. (John 14:1–3)

The Bible reaffirms the existence of heaven in Revelation 21:9b–10: "Come hither, I will shew thee the bride, the Lamb's wife. And he carried me away in the spirit to a great and high mountain, and shewed me that great city, the Holy Jerusalem, descending out of heaven for God."

The Tabernacle in the Wilderness and both Temples were mathematically designed, including specified dimensions for the furniture. God has given us, in advance, the dimensions of the New Jerusalem, the Holy City, of which Jesus is the Master Designer.

God arranged each season to be four months long, each day to be a specific number of hours. God gave us seven days for a week; the seventh day, called the Sabbath, is a day of rest. God created Adam on the sixth day, and the next day was Adam's first Shabbat. On the seventh day God ceased from His labors of creation. When the first six days were finished, God had completed His work. Did God or Adam need to rest on the seventh day? Of course not, but God set a standard for all people in all generations to observe.

When the Lord spoke the universe into existance, He also brought forth a language so that humankind could converse with Him and with one another. The Bible records that God spoke to Adam on different occasions. What language did He speak if it was not the Hebrew of the Bible? After all, that was the only language spoken at that time. The Lord set the standard for this wonderful language to later be used to bring forth His written Word, which was originally written in Hebrew. When Moses went to Mount Sinai, God brought forth the Ten Commandments, written with His finger in Hebrew on two stone tablets. From that time forward, all that God had to say to this world was written by holy men as they were moved by the Spirit of God to inscribe for all generations God's plan of redemption and the penalty for refusing His commands.

God, however, will speak by His Spirit to any of us in the language we understand. There are twenty-two letters in the Hebrew aleph-bet, and each letter has a mathematical value. The name of every person in the Bible has a numerical value based on the Hebrew aleph-bet, but that does not imply that we should engage in any type of numerology, other than biblical mathematics. The enemy has taken God's mathematics and used it to discredit the original use of the biblical structure of the divinely arranged system called the inerrant Word of God.

God determined the amount of rain during the forty-day deluge when the heavens opened and the deep burst forth. Had it rained too much, it would have been against God's timetable for restoration; therefore, the cleansing of the earth would not have been according to heavenly specifications. Noah's ark was mathematically designed to comfortably accommodate all the occupants. It was 300 cubits long, 50 cubits wide, and 30 cubits high — 450,000 cubic cubits. Had Noah designed it with specifications other than those God had given him, the ark would have been incomplete. God caused the flood to top the highest mountain by 15 cubits, or about 22 feet. All living creatures, including humankind, were destroyed. Only those within the ark were saved. There are two Hebrew words for "ark." One is *tevah* תבה, which means "a box." The other is *aron* ארון, which is the Ark of the Tabernacle that was in the Holy of Holies. The ark that Noah built is called *tevah*, and the Ark of the Covenant is called *aron*. We find the account of Noah in Genesis. His salvation is recorded in Genesis 7:5-7: "And Noah did according unto all that the Lord commanded him. And Noah was six hundred years old when the flood of waters was upon the earth. And Noah went in, and his sons, and his wife, and his sons' wives with him, into the ark, because of the waters of the flood."

ויעש נח ככל אשר-צוהו יהוה: ונח בן-שש
מאות שנה והמבול היה מים על-הארץ: ויבא נח
ובניו ואשתו ונשי-בניו אתו אל-התבה מפני מי המבול:

There are some very interesting insights in this area of Scripture. Starting with the first letter, the yod (י), in the name *Jehovah* יהוה, counting every third word, and taking the first letter of each word from right to left spells *Yeshuanu* ישׁענו, which means "our Jesus." This method of analysis is called *Rosh Tov* ראשׁ טוב. Also, the Holy names "Elohim" אלהים, which means "God," and *Tzion* ציון, which means "Zion," are found at four-letter intervals in the same area where we found *Yeshua*. The name *Yoel* יואל, which means "Lord God" or "God is willing" is found at eight-letter intervals. The word *Torah* תורה is also encoded at eight-letter intervals.

In Genesis 7:11, the phrase "the fountains of the great deep" מעינות תהום רבה has the encoded word *Torah* at two-letter intervals. The seven common laws of the Torah were the standard in the days of Noah.

Noah and his family had heavenly support and security during the judgment of God on the earth as long as they were in the ark. They entered the ark before the waters came and evacuated the ark after the floodwaters subsided. That not one drop of water touched them is a picture of all believers who are secure in Jesus. Not one ounce of the Lord's wrath will fall on God's people during the coming judgment of the earth and the nations. Thank God, there is a rapture coming to take us to the heavenly ark of safety.

You might say that God has a heavenly calculator that surpasses all the super-computers on earth. He has placed in His wonderful Word a certain number of letters and words. To add or subtract from His Word would change the prearranged, mathematical structure, thereby causing, if it were possible, an imbalance in His plan of redemption. It has been said by many Hebrew sages that the name of every person in this world is recorded on the surface reading or encoded in hidden form somewhere in the original Scriptures. The Hebrew Scripture has been called a book of life, but it is not the Lamb's Book of Life, which is in heaven. Every letter and word in the Bible is equivalent to the structure of a magnificent building; taking away one item or adding something that does not belong would cause the building to be incomplete. Summed up, the Holy Bible reveals a complex architecture of codes and information, both on the surface and in the hidden levels.

God knows the name of every star in the heavens. Psalm 147:4–5 says, "He telleth the number of the stars; He calleth them all by their names. Great is our Lord, and of great power: His understanding is infinite."

> For there is hope of a tree, if it be cut down, that it will sprout again, and that the tender branch thereof will not cease. Though the root thereof wax old in the earth, and the stock thereof die in the ground; Yet through the scent of water it will bud, and bring forth boughs like a plant. (Job 14:7–9)

כי יש לעץ תקוה אם־יכרת ועוד יחליף וינקתו לא תחדל: אם־יזקין
בארץ שרשו ובעפר ימות גזעו: מריח מים יפרח ועשה קציר כמו־נטע

Starting with the second letter, the mem (מ), of the sixth word in verse eight and counting every eighth letter in reverse, we find "Messiah, the fire of the Lord" משיח יואש. God is an all-consuming fire and is expressed as such in the Messiah. In Revelation 1, John saw Jesus the Messiah, whose eyes were as flames of fire.

Job, in chapter 14, likens himself to a tree that will wither one day, but he knew that water would bring life again. The Psalmist likens us to trees that are planted by the rivers and to stars that shine in the heavens. The water represents the powerful Word of the Lord when He speaks; even those in their graves will hear His voice. The trees represent our roots in a sure foundation, and the stars speak of the glory of God by which we will shine throughout the ages to come.

Job 14:14–16 says, "If a man die, shall he live again? all the days of my appointed time will I wait, till my change come. Thou shalt call, and I will answer Thee: Thou wilt have a desire to the work of Thine hands. For now Thou numberest my steps: dost Thou not watch over my sin?" Job asked a question about his death; then in the same breath, he answered the question. He spoke of a time after he fulfilled his days on earth when God would call for him and he would answer from the grave. This speaks of the

Resurrection. Encoded in these verses are insights referring to our Lord and Savior.

In Job 14:8, starting with the fourth letter of the second word, which is the chet (ח), and counting every seventy-fifth letter from right to left spells *chaiker Yeshua* חקר ישוע, which means "enquire about Yeshua." Here, the word is instructing us to ask Jesus; He will answer every question. Jesus answers Job's question, "If a man die, shall he live again?" In John 11:25 Jesus said to Martha, "I am the resurrection, and the life: he that believeth in me, though he were dead, yet shall he live."

Job speaks of our days being numbered by God. God also knew the number of Israelites who would come out of Egypt. In preparation for the building of the Tabernacle, when the sons of Israel came out of Egypt, they took with them some of the wealth of the Egyptians. Exodus 12:35 says, "And the children of Israel did according to the word of Moses; and they borrowed of the Egyptians jewels of silver, and jewels of gold, and raiment."

It was time for the Lord to require something of reasonable value from the sons of Israel. God had a purpose behind every request or commandment that He administered. Silver speaks of redemption and gold of perfection.

> And the Lord spake unto Moses, saying, When thou takest the sum of the children of Israel after their number, then shall they give every man a ransom for his soul unto the Lord, when thou numberest them; that there be no plague among them, when thou numberest them. This they shall give, every one that passeth among them that are numbered, half a shekel after the shekel of the sanctuary: (a shekel is twenty gerahs:) an half shekel shall be the offering of the Lord. Every one that passeth among them that are numbered, from twenty years old and above,

shall give an offering unto the Lord. The rich shall not give more, and the poor shall not give less than half a shekel, when they give an offering unto the Lord, to make an atonement for your souls.

(Exodus 30:11–15)

The half-shekel, or ten gerahs, is equivalent to thirty-three cents. God wanted all the sons of Israel, twenty years of age and over, to have a part in His redemptive plan. At that time, they did not have complete knowledge of the details of that plan, nor the purpose of that plan.

There are, however, encoded messages within these Scriptures that give us an answer. In Exodus 30:12, starting with the second letter in the fourth word and counting every forty-eighth letter from right to left spells "My tabernacle" אהלי. Israel was having a part in the building of God's dwelling place, *haMishkon* המשכן.

In Exodus 30:13, starting from the mem (מ) in the Hebrew phrase "half a shekel" and counting every tenth letter from right to left, we again find "Messiah" משיח. Though thirty shekels of the sanctuary were paid for the betrayal of Yeshua, the fact that His name is associated with *shekels*, *Tabernacle*, and *ransom for the soul* reflects a greater plan yet to unfold.

God counted the sons of Israel who were twenty years old and up while they were in bondage to the Egyptians. Had Israel left Egypt before or after God's perfect timing, the plan would have been disrupted. The Scriptures below reflect this thought.

All the gold that was occupied for the work in all the work of the Holy Place, even the gold of the offering, was twenty and nine talents, and seven hundred and thirty shekels, after the shekel of the sanctuary. And the silver of them that were numbered of the congregation was an hundred talents, and a thousand seven hundred and threescore and fifteen shekels, after the shekel of the sanctuary: A bekah for every man, that is, half a shekel, after the shekel of the sanctuary, for every one that went to be numbered, from twenty years old and upward, for six hundred thousand and three thousand and five hundred and fifty men. (Exodus 38:24–26)

This tells us how many men over twenty years of age came out of Egypt. Also, they used 600,000 half-shekels for the making of the talents of silver to be used as a foundation, which left 3,550 half-shekels for the hooks and the other needs. Every ounce of gold and silver was used. Not one half-shekel was left over, nor were they short a half-shekel. This took divine planning by the Master Builder. Each person among the children of Israel had some part, small though it may have seemed, in the building and finishing of the Tabernacle of the Wilderness.

There were 600,000 men, twenty years and older, who came out of Egypt. The Bible reveals how many men had their twentieth birthday from the time they left Egypt to the time they reached the place in the wilderness for the building of the Tabernacle. God knew each Israelite to the finest detail. The way you can figure this fact is by counting the total number of half-shekels used in the Tabernacle that surpassed the 600,000 men who were twenty years or older at the time of their departure. This is the same number of the sons of Israel who had birthdays from the first Passover until the call went out for the half-shekel of silver, the price of redemption.

All the gold that was occupied for the work in all the work of the holy place, even the gold of the offering, was twenty and nine talents, and seven hundred and thirty shekels, after the shekel of the sanctuary.
(Exodus 38:24)

כל הזהב העשוי למלאכה בכל מלאכת הקדש ויהי זהב התנופה
תשע ועשרים ככר ושבע מאות ושלשים שקל בשקל הקדש:

In Exodus 38:24, the Hebrew phrase "and thirty shekels" *veshloshim shekel* וֹשְׁלֹשִׁים שֶׁקֶל gives us an awesome insight into Christ's betrayal. Starting with the yod (י) in "thirty shekels," which is the last yod of the above verse, and counting every third letter from left to right, we find the words "Yeshua cut off" יֹשׁוּעַ וכרות. It was thirty pieces of silver from the sanctuary that the high priest paid for the betrayal of our Lord Jesus, as we find in Matthew 27:3, 5: "Then Judas, which had betrayed him, when he saw that he was condemned, he repented himself, and brought again the thirty pieces of silver to the chief priests and elders . . . And he cast down the pieces of silver in the temple, and departed, and went and hanged himself."

Also, from the first mem (מ) in the far upper right and counting every sixty-sixth letter from right to left spells "Messiah" מֹשִׁיט. The adjacent letters to the right of each letter that forms the name "Messiah" in both directions every sixty-sixth letter spell "Prince, Son (of the) commandment" *sar, yeled, tzevah* שׂר ילד צוה. We can find Yeshua in many significant places in the Scripture. The reason for this is because He is the Creator and the center of God's plan to redeem mankind.

Zechariah 11:12 says, "And I said unto them, If ye think good, give Me My price; and if not, forbear. So they weighed for My price thirty pieces of silver." In this passage, the name *Yeshua* יֹשׁוּעַ is found at twenty-four-letter intervals. He gave His soul a ransom for all, but Israel only needed to give half a shekel. Why the great difference in price? Because Israel's sins were only temporarily atoned for by the free-will offering, but Yeshua atoned for all sins forever. Incidentally, the word "Passover" פסח is also encoded within these Scriptures.

In Daniel 9:26 we read, "And after sixty-two weeks,

Messiah shall be cut off, . . ." *ayikrit* יכרת. This Hebrew word means "to be cut off in death." In verse 26, beginning with the fourth letter in the ninth word and counting in increments of twenty-six letters from left to right, we find *Yeshua* ישוע. The prophet Daniel wrote by the unction of the Holy Spirit, naming the Messiah and the fact that He would be cut off in death but not in death for Himself.

We see this "cutting off" in Psalm 22:13. Starting with the second letter of the sixth word and counting every twenty-sixth letter from right to left spells *tok Yeshua* תך ישוע, which means "Yeshua cut in pieces."

The Hebrew word for "thorns" *kotzim* קצים is found at least three times throughout Psalm 22. After Adam and Eve sinned, the ground was cursed and many plants grew thorns and briars. This was part of the curse that Jesus took with Him on the cross by receiving a crown of thorns.

In Psalm 22:3, starting with the second letter in the second word and counting every ninety-second letter from right to left, we find "thorn" *kutz* קוץ. Starting with the same letter and counting every 126th letter from right to left, we also find "thorn." In Psalm 22:12, starting with the first letter in the sixth word and counting every third letter from left to right, we find *kutzim* קוצים, which means "thorns." Thus, we have *Yeshua, Messiah, cut in pieces* (put to death), and *thorns*. This is verified in the New Testament in John 19:1–3: "Then Pilate therefore took Jesus, and scourged Him. And the soldiers plaited a crown of thorns, and put it on his head, and they put on him a purple robe, And said, Hail, King of the Jews! and they smote him with their hands." This was the price that Jesus paid for our redemption, so we could have the privilege of citizenship in the heavenly city, the New Jerusalem.

Now we come to the heavenly picture that was portrayed by Moses and the whole house of Israel when they built the Tabernacle in the Wilderness. The Tabernacle and the two Temples were pictures of a greater building of God, one of which you are a part if you have been washed in His blood. This great salvation cost us nothing except our dedication and love of God. What a small price to pay for such a valuable possession! The prophetic messianic Scriptures in Isaiah 55 reflect this thought.

> Ho, every one that thirsteth, come ye to the waters, and he that hath no money; come ye, buy, and eat; yea, come buy wine and milk without money and without price. Wherefore do ye spend money for that which is not bread? and your labour for that which satisfieth not? hearken diligently unto Me, and eat ye that which is good, and let your soul delight itself in fatness. Incline your ear, and come unto Me: hear, and your soul shall live; and I will make an everlasting covenant with you, even the sure mercies of David. Behold, I have given Him for a witness to the people, a leader and commander to the people. ... Behold, thou shalt call a nation that thou knowest not, and nations that knew not thee shall run unto thee because of the Lord thy God, and for the Holy One of Israel; for He hath glorified thee. Seek ye the Lord while He may be found, call ye upon Him while He is near.   (Isaiah 55:1–3, 5–6)

In Isaiah 55:5, starting with the third letter in the eleventh word and counting every 116th letter from left to right spells "Jesus" יֵשׁוּעַ. Also, in verse 11, starting with the second letter in the second word and counting every thirty-second letter from right to left, we find *HaMashiach huben* הַמָּשִׁיחַ הוּבַן, which means "the Messiah to be understood." In that day, we shall know Him as we are known. This is echoed in 1 Corinthians 13:12: "For now we see through a glass, darkly; but then face to face: now I know in part; but then shall I know even as also I am known."

> Wherefore, holy brethren, partakers of the heavenly calling, consider the Apostle and High Priest of our profession, Christ Jesus [Yeshua ha'Mashiach]; Who was faithful to Him that appointed Him, as also Moses was faithful in all his house. For this Man was counted worthy of more glory than Moses, inasmuch as he who hath builded the house hath more honour than the house. For every house is builded by some man; but He that built all things is God. And Moses verily was faithful in all his house, as a servant, for a testimony of those things which were to be spoken after; But Christ [Messiah] as a Son over His own house; Whose house are we, if we hold fast the confidence and the rejoicing of the hope firm unto the end.   (Hebrews 3:1–6)

We, as believers, are God's house, and He is the Master Builder. Everyone who is a member of His household is very important to the eternal structure of His divine plan. In His infinite wisdom, He chose you to be part of the everlasting temple in which he will dwell. Without you His body would be incomplete. The children of Israel offered up to God sacrifices in numbers that go beyond one's imagination, but you and I need only to offer our hearts and our lives to become a living sacrifice unto Him. We are lively stones appointed unto glory for His good pleasure, as Peter says in 1 Peter 2:5, 9: "Ye also, as lively stones, are built up a spiritual house, an holy priesthood, to offer up spiritual sacrifices, acceptable to God by Yeshua the Messiah. . . . But ye are a chosen generation, a royal priesthood, an holy nation, a peculiar people; that ye should shew forth the praises of Him who hath called you out of darkness into His marvellous light."

Every building that is solid and strong is built by stones of some sort. The foundation should be the strongest part of any structure. We see a magnificent description of God's eternal city in the closing chapters of Revelation. This great house that God is building is founded upon the Rock of Ages, Yeshua HaMashiach. The only part that is not yet finished are the lively stones — the believers, you and I.

> And I John saw the holy city, new Jerusalem, coming down from God out of heaven, prepared as a bride adorned for her husband. And I heard a great voice out of heaven saying, Behold, the tabernacle of God is with men, and He will dwell with them, and they shall be His people, and God Himself shall be with them, and be their God.   (Revelation 21:2–3)

> And had a wall great and high, and had twelve gates, and at the gates twelve angels, and names written thereon, which are the names of the twelve tribes of the children of Israel. . . . And the wall of the city had twelve foundations, and in them the names of the twelve apostles of the Lamb [Yeshua].
>
>   (Revelation 21:12, 14)

Someone once asked me when the heavenly city was built. My reply was simple: "Since eternity past, but the add-ons for you and me are taking place now." Then I was asked, "When were the names of the tribes of Israel and the apostles inscribed on the gates and the foundations?" My reply was, "Since God knows all things past, present, and future, He wrote their names before the foundation of this world and the universe. God knows you from ages past, but you were not born until this generation. However, in the Lord's infinite wisdom, He knew you were coming to Him, so He created a position for you in His household before the stars sang together. What God has settled in heaven is irreversible and irrevocable on earth."

Throughout the Holy Scriptures there are many things that we will never understand in this life. When we are clothed with His magnificent divine nature, then we will comprehend the mysteries that cloud us today. God has engraved His signature on His Word in a variety of ways; His Word is scientific, mathematical, prophetic, historic, and spiritual — all are divinely administered by the handwriting of God.

The biblical mathematics to which I alluded in the opening pages of this chapter go beyond human comprehension and ability. There is a magnificently splendid insight that gives absolute proof that Jesus (*Yeshua* ישׁוע) is none other than the Lord (*Jehovah* יהוה) and Creator. We need not look too far nor go beyond the boundaries of the Word of God to receive His awesome truth. Truly, He has put His signature throughout His divinely inspired written Word.

Looking very closely at the Scripture below will give us an exhilarating experience that goes beyond natural abilities to describe. In Exodus 15:27 we read, "And they came to Elim, And there were twelve springs of water and seventy palm trees. And they camped by the waters." Notice that there were twelve springs with seventy palm trees nearby. Water always cleanses and gives life if properly administered. The Israelites camped by the waters and received much comfort by the shade of the palm trees. What a delight to come upon a place of such beauty and sustenance after treking through the unknown wilderness. God knew what they needed and supplied it at a time when most appreciated. There are twelve tribes of Israel, twelve apostles, twelve gates, and twelve foundations in the New Jerusalem. Also, there were seventy elders in Israel. According to the book of Numbers, God instructed Moses to gather seventy elders from the different tribes of Israel to assist him in judging the people. The Lord Jesus sent the twelve disciples and the seventy elders as trees of righteousness to minister to the people. They healed the sick, and the Good News was brought forth as rivers of living waters.

As God had instructed Moses to bring forth twelve tribal leaders and seventy elders, so Yeshua chose His twelve disciples and gave authority to the seventy elders and sent them forth. The seventy elders and twelve tribal leaders were to help Moses judge the children of Israel. But we see a greater fulfillment when Yeshua chose His twelve and seventy to heal the sick, cast out devils, and preach the Good News. They were not sent to judge but to deliver.

In Exodus 15:27, starting with the third letter in the thirteenth word, which is the yod (י) in the Hebrew word for "water" הַמַּיִם, and counting every 235th letter from right to left spells "Lord Jesus" *Jehovah Yeshua* יְשׁוּעַ יהוה. This encoded message proves beyond a shadow of a doubt who Jesus is.

This next Scripture stands out from all the surrounding verses in Genesis 49. It seems that the Lord placed the three Hebrew words that form this awesome verse in a most unusual area. They are sandwiched between Dan, as a serpent "by the way," and Gad, who shall "overcome him." I believe that the reason for this rare location is because wherever trouble abounds, the Lord abounds much more.

Genesis 49:18 says, "I have waited for Your Salvation [*Yeshua*] O Jehovah," לִישׁוּעָתְךָ קִוִּיתִי יהוה. Notice the names *Jehovah* יהוה and *Yeshua* יְשׁוּעַ in the same very short verse. Some may say that the name of Yeshua in Hebrew simply means "salvation." This is correct. But take the name "Joel." In Hebrew his name means "the Lord God." This does not change the fact that God gave a man a name that reflects His glory. Was Joel the Messiah? No. But he played an integral part in bringing forth the message of salvation (*Yeshua*). We know for a fact that the name of the Messiah is Lord Yeshua (Jesus). The Genesis 49:18 passage gives credence to this fact.

Starting with the yod (י) in *Jehovah* "Adonai" יהוה and counting every 180th letter in reverse, we find *Yeshua Jehovah* ישוע יהוה. Now we have His ineffable name twice in the Torah. Can we ever doubt that Jesus really is Jehovah, our Lord God? It is no wonder why the world hates His name so much. It brings us to a place of ultimate decision — to accept Him or reject Him on the basis of the scientific information available. In Yeshua we have a sure foundation.

The mathematical value of the name *Yeshua* ישוע equals 386: (1) yod (י) equals 10; (2) shin (ש) equals 300; (3) vav (ו) equals 6; and (4) ayin (ע) equals 70. Adding together the numerical value of all the letters in His name gives us a total of 386. This method has been used for thousands of years by our ancient Jewish sages and is scientific and credible. According to the ancient rabbis, if a word is found at intervals that are the same as its numerical value, it is very significant. Significantly, in the book of Revelation, the apostle John used this same technique to identify the name of the future Antichrist to the Tribulation saints when he declared, "Here is wisdom. Let him that hath understanding count the number of the beast: for it is the number of a man; and his number is Six hundred threescore and six" (Revelation 13:18). The inspired prophet of God wrote out this numerical value of the Antichrist's name using three Greek letters (χξς) that stood for the number 666 in the Greek language. Both biblical languages, Hebrew and Greek, used the letters of their alphabet to indicate numbers because they did not have the Arabic numbers (1, 2, 3, etc.) that we use today.

The twelve gates and foundations of the heavenly Jerusalem were created by Yeshua, the Lord of Glory. He has put His signature on the city and adorned it with His beauty and eternal magnificence. Throughout the Torah, the five books of Moses, are encoded messages that radiate this truth and wisdom.

We find in Exodus 3:15 that starting with the fourth letter of the twelfth word and counting every 386th letter from left to right spells *Yitron Yeshua* יתרן ישוע, which translates "Jesus the Excellency" — a title of honor and glory.

In Leviticus 22:14, starting with the fourth letter in the first word and counting every 386th letter from left to right spells *Yeshua* ישוע. At the same interval of 386 letters and adjacent to the name of Yeshua are two words that add more information concerning Him. One word is "truth" אמת, the other is "wisdom" החכמה. Yeshua is all truth and all wisdom.

The name of Yeshua is found twelve times at 386-letter intervals throughout the whole Torah. Remember, there are twelve tribes of Israel, twelve disciples of Yeshua, twelve gates in the heavenly Jerusalem, and twelve foundations that give it solidness and sureness. In other words, the heavenly city is four-square. You became a citizen of the eternal city of God when Yeshua saved you and made you to be a lively stone for His building.

A brief comment about the numbering of the name of Yeshua is in order. The apostle John spoke about the numerical value of the letters composing the future Antichrist's name in Revelation 13. If the numbering of a person's name was not biblical, the Lord Jesus would not have given John the revelation of the numerical value of the letters in the name of the anti-messiah (Antichrist). To my amazement, many are foolishly trying to find out who the Antichrist is by adding up the letter values of different likely suspects whom they believe may fit the description of the false messiah. However, the Bible teaches us that we shall not know who he is until he is revealed, when the Holy Spirit no longer restrains him from appearing. The time of the revelation of that ominous person will come when the believers are translated out of this world and into heaven. We do not need to know his name; it shall be manifested at the proper time, as we see from the book of Revelation.

> And he causeth all, both small and great, rich and poor, free and bond, to receive a mark in their right hand, or in their foreheads: And that no man might buy or sell, save he that had the mark, or the name of the beast, or the number of his name. Here is wisdom. Let him that hath understanding count the number of the beast: for it is the number of a man; and his number is Six hundred three score and six (666).   (Revelation 13:16–18)

Looking through the corridors of time that were illuminated by the prophetic eyes of the Holy Spirit (*Ruach haKodesh*), John caught a glimpse into the future of the overcomers — the tribulation saints — who had been taken to heaven. "And I saw as it were a sea of glass mingled with fire: and them that had gotten the victory over the beast, and over his image, and over his mark, and over the number of his name, stand on the sea of glass, having the harps of God" (Revelation 15:2).

Nothing could be clearer than the above verses as to the method of identifying the Antichrist. Each Hebrew letter has a mathematical value. The numbering system of ancient Israel was done, in many cases, by the letters of the aleph-bet. For instance, Psalms 50 was identified, and still is, by the Hebrew letter with that numerical value, which is the nun (נ). Now we need not be in the dark about how to prove who the Antichrist is; but whomever he is, he must fulfill all the other requirements as well.

We who are saved are not looking for the Antichrist

(false messiah), though we are to observe the signs of the end, for we have a sure foundation in God and cannot be moved. We are sealed by God until the day of redemption with the Spirit of promise. 2 Timothy 2:19 says, "Nevertheless the foundation of God standeth sure, having this seal, The Lord knoweth them that are his. And, Let every one that nameth the name of Christ depart from iniquity."

5

Equidistant Letter and Word Sequences
Shalav Oht Ve'debar,
שלב אות ודבר

The purpose of this chapter is to open up our understanding concerning the prearranged divine Word of God. God knew from before the beginning exactly which letters, words, or phrases would be incorporated within His final Word to us. The Bible is a reflection of God's holiness and redemption that demonstrates an order far beyond our greatest imaginations or concepts. We have yet to tap this reservoir of knowledge and wisdom; we can only glean small particles from the fringes of His truth and magnificence. One day, in the not-too-distant future, we shall see Him as He is. Until then, we fervently search the Scriptures that we may know in part, until we know as we are known.

I gave an illustration of the system of equidistant-letter sequence in chapter one of this book, so there will be no need to reiterate that example. However, I will bring forth additional information about the logic of the letter-spacing science. What is the purpose of equidistant-letter spacing? Consider, for a moment, that you are an accomplished pianist, and someone — unknown to you — changes one of the keys on the piano. The moment you sat down to play, you would know it had been tampered with. For instance, the C cord is called a triad because it is composed of three notes — C, E, and G. Starting with the first note, which is middle C, and skipping one note would bring you to the E, and skipping another note would give you the G. Hitting all three of these notes simultaneously would give you the C cord in perfect harmony. If a key had been removed or another put in its place, the perfect balance of this wonderful instrument would be thrown off and the result would be a very unpleasant sound. Suppose all the instruments in an orchestra had been tampered with. Could they play the concerto as written? It is the same with His precious Word. If the enemy would change one letter, word, or phrase of the divine Scriptures, this would cause a complete change in the meaning and mathematical structure of the whole Bible.

Allow me to elaborate further on this thought from the book of Leviticus. Leviticus 4:24 is a prophecy of the perfect sin offering that was fulfilled by Yeshua the Messiah: "And he shall lay his hand upon the head of the goat, and kill it in the place where they kill the burnt offering before the Lord: it is a sin offering."

במקום אשר-ישחט את-העלה

Bi'mekom asher yishchat et ha'olah

If we count every second letter from right to left, starting with the second mem (מ) from the right, this spells "Messiah, Tabernacle" *Mashiach Ohail* משיח אהל. We know that the sacrifice of our Messiah was our sin offering and that it happened on Mount Moriah in Jerusalem.

Leviticus 9:3 gives us background into sacrifices: "And unto the children of Israel thou shalt speak, saying, Take ye a kid of the goats for a sin offering; and a calf and a lamb, both of the first year, without blemish, for a burnt offering."

ואל-בני ישראל תדבר לאמר קחו שעיר-
עזים לחטאת ועגל וכבש בני-שנה תמימם לעלה

Speaking of the most perfect sacrificial animal — the one without blemish — consider this very rare combination. Starting with the third letter, the yod (י), in the fourteenth word and counting every third letter in reverse spells *Yah Yeshua El* אל ישרע יה, which means "Lord Jesus" and "God." Then in Leviticus 4:22, starting with the third letter in the sixth word and counting every ninth letter forward spells *Yeho Yeshua* ישוע יהו, which means "Lord Jesus." Here again, we see Him as the perfect one of the flock, the sacrificial sin offering. If someone had removed or added a single letter in the above Hebrew Scripture, it would completely change the harmony and prearranged structure of His Word and would eliminate the name of the person who was to be sacrificed as our sin offering.

There are warnings in both Deuteronomy and Revelation about adding or subtracting one iota from the Word of God. Some translators have tried to change His Word by introducing their own concepts. However, we need to understand why God has forever settled His Word in heaven. In Deuteronomy 4:2 we read, "Ye shall not add unto the Word which I command you, neither shall ye diminish aught from it, that ye may keep the commandments of the Lord your God which I command you."

> For I testify unto every man that heareth the words of the Prophecy of this Book, If any man shall add unto these things, God shall add unto him the plagues that are written in this Book: And if any man shall take away from the words of the Book of this

Prophecy, God shall take away his part out of the book of life, and out of the Holy City, and from the things which are written in this Book.

(Revelation 22:18–19)

There is a foolproof, mathematical design throughout the Bible that will let us know if His Word has been tampered with. If one letter had been added or subtracted from Genesis 22:13, it would have eliminated His precious name in this area of Scripture: "And Abraham lifted up his eyes, and looked, and behold behind him a ram caught in a thicket by his horns: and Abraham went and took the ram, and offered him up for a burnt offering in the stead of his son."

The ram that was caught in the thicket is a picture of Yeshua the Messiah, caught in the thicket of our sins and sacrificed in our place. God has encoded, by equidistant-letter spacing, the name of the person who would be sacrificed for us. Starting with the second letter in the fifth word in Genesis 22:13 and counting every seven thousandth letter in reverse spells "Jesus" *Yeshua* יֵשׁוּעַ. If someone had changed His Word in this area, His name would not show up at this equal spacing of letter-distances, as originally placed there by God.

Genesis 22:17 says, "That in blessing I will bless thee, and in multiplying I will multiply thy seed as the stars of the heaven, and as the sand which is upon the sea shore; and thy seed shall possess the gate of his enemies." What a wonderful Scripture! It is very close to Genesis 22:13. Not only has God put the name of our substitute in verse 13; He has also included the name of our blesser in verse 17. Notice that the Lord is speaking in the first person: "I will Bless thee." Starting with the second letter in the first word in verse 17, and counting in reverse every seven thousandth letter, we also find "Jesus" *Yeshua* יֵשׁוּעַ. Not once, but twice in the same area, the name "Jesus" shows up at seven thousand-letter increments. The name "Jesus" ישוע is recorded at least twelve times at seven-thousand-letter increments throughout the five books of the Torah תורה. How awesome, phenomenal, stupendous, magnificent, and divine is the Word of God! I would know if anyone had tampered with His Word because the above count would not be the same. Thank God that we can prove His Word to be true. All of the above insights are taken from the Masoretic text.

The text itself tells us about equidistant-letter sequences. In Genesis 41:50, starting with the last shin (ש) and counting every sixth letter from right to left spells *shalav* שלב, with the adjacent letters spelling *Torah* תורה. Regardless of the system of analysis, if that system is orderly and sets a continuous pattern, then it should be considered scientific.

In addition to the equidistant-letter sequence, there is another divine arrangement of His Word. This arrangement will enable us to uncover additional information for His glory. This method is normally called *Rosh Tav* ראש טוב, but the name that I give this system is "equidistant-word sequence" (EWS) or *shalav debar* שלב דבר. This arrangement takes the first or last letter of each word that is equally distributed throughout the Scripture, but not each word as a whole.

When Jesus healed the ten lepers, He instructed them to go show themselves to the priests in accordance with the Torah. In Luke 17:14 Jesus said, "And when he saw them, he said unto them, Go shew yourselves unto the priests. And it came to pass, that, as they went, they were cleansed." In Leviticus 13:10–11a God commanded, "And the priest shall see him: and, behold, if the rising be white in the skin, and it have turned the hair white. . . . "

וראה הכהן והנה שאת-לבנה בעור והיא
הפכה שער לבן ומחית בשר חי בשאת

Starting with the first letter of the fourth word from the right and taking the first letter of each word spells the phrase "the interlaced of the equidistant sequence" *shalav veha'shaluv* שלב והשלוב. All Scripture is interwoven together, thereby making one complete unit. In Leviticus 13:10, starting with the fourth letter in the eleventh word, and counting every eighth letter from right to left spells *Yeshua* ישוע. Also, from the same yod (י) and counting every twenty-eighth letter forward spells *Yeshua* ישוע. The name of Yeshua appears twice in the same area and from the same yod.

In Leviticus 13:12, starting from the fourth letter in the seventh word, which is the ayin (ע) from the name of Yeshua in the above insight, and counting every eighty-second letter forward spells "Yeshua to be ashamed" *Yeshua bosh* ישוע בוש. The adjacent letters spell *ha'chattat* החטאת, which means "punishment for sin" (or sinners). It is quite phenomenal to find interwoven insights centered around both Jesus and the sin offering. Hebrews 12:2–3 says, "Looking unto Jesus (Yeshua) the author and finisher of our faith; who for the joy that was set before him endured the cross, despising the shame, and is set down at the right hand of the throne of God."

> O house of David, thus saith the Lord; Execute judgment in the morning, and deliver him that is spoiled out of the hand of the oppressor, lest my fury go out like fire, and burn that none can quench it, because of the evil of your doings.
>
> (Jeremiah 21:12)

בית דוד כה אמר יהוה דינו לבקר משפט והצילו גזול מיד
עושק פן תצא כאש חמתי ובערה ואין מכבה מפני רע מעלליהם:

Starting with the second letter in the sixth word from the far right, which is *dayeinu* דינו, and counting every eighth

letter from right to left spells "Jesus my power" *Yeshua oni*
ישוע אורי. This is the only place in the Holy Scriptures
where the word *dayeinu* דינו appears, a word which means
"it would have been enough," "to do justice," or, "justice
was done." This is the word we use at Passover when we
sing, "It Would Have Been Enough." It is quite amazing that
this word should appear with the insight of "Jesus my
power." These combinations directly radiate the power,
beauty, and splendor of our Lord Jesus. Revelation 4:11
says, "Thou art worthy, O Lord, to receive glory and honor
and power: for Thou has created all things, and for Thy
pleasure they are and were created."

In Genesis 41:36, starting with the second letter in the
fifth word, counting every 234th letter from right to left
spells *shalav dabar* שלב דבר, which means "equidistant-
word sequence" or EWS. In Numbers 21:20, starting with
the third letter in the eighth word, and counting every thirty-
second letter from right to left spells *dabar shalav* שלב דבר.
In Numbers 21:17, starting with the first letter in the third
word, and counting every tenth word — taking only the first
letter of each word — spells *Yeshua* ישוע. By finding the
name of Yeshua encoded in the same area, we can better
understand why EWS is a legitimate system of analysis. I
have found many examples of equidistant-word sequence.
The examples that follow are but a few combinations,
compared to the massive array of intertwined codes
throughout the whole Bible. Occasionally, it will be
necessary to jump from one book to another to show various
combinations that are relevant.

In Genesis 4:1, starting with the last word, which is
יהוה, and counting from left to right every 144th word,
taking the first letter of each word, spells *Jehovah* יהוה. Does
this allude to the 144,000 in the book of Revelation?

In Malachi 3:23 in the Hebrew Tanakh, start with the first
letter of the eleventh word "Israel" and count the first letter

of every thirty-fifth word. The last two letters, the yod and the heh, begin the word *Jehovah* יהוה. If we overlap back into Genesis, we find that the first two letters in Genesis 1:1, the vav and the heh, complete the word *Jehovah*. This insight shows us how there is both overlapping from book to book and equidistant word sequence at the same time.

In Genesis 1:9, starting with the first letter of the eighth word "the place" מקום, and counting evey ninetieth word from right to left, taking the first letter of each word, spells משיח. The Hebrew word *maqom* מקום is another word that alludes to the Messiah, as we saw in Leviticus 4. In Genesis 3:4, starting with the first letter in the sixth word, counting every seventy-ninth word from right to left, and taking only the first letter of each word, uncovers nine letters (א א ל א ה ח י ש מ). The first four letters from the right spell "Messiah" משיח at seventy-nine-word increments, and every other letter from the left spells "God" אלהים at 158-word increments. This is yet another proof of the divine arrangement of His word.

In Genesis 4:3, starting with the first letter of the third word, counting every seventh word, and taking the last letter only from left to right spells יהוה. In Genesis 5:23, starting with the last letter of the first word, counting every seventh word, and taking the last letter of each word spells *Yeshua* ישוע. This area of Scripture is about Enoch (the seventh generation from Adam), his godly walk and his translation. Genesis 5:23–24 says, "And all the days of Enoch were three hundred sixty and five years: And Enoch walked with God; and he was not; for God took him."

In Deuteronomy 12:11, the first letter of each word starting with the thirteenth word and counting from left to right gives us *et shaish shalav* את שש שלב, which means "six equidistant sequence." Thus, it seems that the Word is instructing us to count the equidistant-word or -letter sequence at intervals of six. We see this in Deuteronomy

12:10, starting with the fifth word and counting every sixth word from left to right spells "Elul" אלול, which is the sixth month on the sacred calendar. Counting at thirty-word increments (the six-word sequence times five), you will have *Jehovah* "Adonai" יהוה, the first letter of every thirtieth word. In the same sequence (six times six), counting left to right every thirty-sixth letter from the chet (ח) in the place where "Messiah" משיח is found at two-letter intervals in verse 11, from left to right, spells *chakmah* חכמה, which means "wisdom." Also, in this series you will find *aron* ארון, which means "the ark."

In Genesis 7:5, starting with the first letter of the last word, counting from right to left, and taking the first letter of each third word spells *Yeshuanu* ישועינו, which means "our Jesus." God had just commanded Noah and his family to enter the ark before the flood of judgment came. Noah was six hundred years of age at that time. Could this allude to the six thousand years when the Lord will judge the world through Yeshua? In Genesis 7:9, starting with the second bet, and counting every sixtieth letter from left to right spells *b'natzal lunb*, which means "in the rapture." In Genesis 37:9, starting with the fifth letter in the tenth word and counting in reverse every six thousandth letter spells *Yeshuayehu* ישועיהו, which means "Jesus Lord." Genesis 7:5–6 says, "And Noah did according unto all that the Lord commanded him. And Noah was six hundred years old when the flood of waters was upon the earth."

In Genesis 22:8, starting with the second to the last word, taking the first letter, the shin (ש), and counting every nineteenth word in both directions, reading only the first letter of each word, spells *Yeshua* ישוע. Doing this again from the same shin and counting every fifty-first word in both directions, uncovers *Yeshua* ישוע. This is a phenomenal insight. Both combinations emanate from the same shin. Also, the first letter of every fifth word in verse eight spells *Jehovah* יהוה. The adjacent words (first letters only) spell *hallu* הללו, which means "praise." In verse seven, starting with the first letter of the second word and taking only the first letter of every fifth word from left to right spells *Jehovah* יהוה.

In Genesis 22:9 God tells us, "And they came to the place which God had told him of; and Abraham built an altar there, and laid the wood in order, and bound Isaac his son, and laid him on the altar upon the wood." Starting with the first letter of the twelfth word, and counting every sixth word, taking only the first letter from left to right spells *halilah* הלילה, which means "the night." Find the adjacent letters to the previous word *halilah*. Take the last letter of each word and count every sixth word, and it spells *terumah* תרמה, which means "a free-will offering." Jesus was sacrificed as a free-will offering for the sins of all the world. From the sixth to the ninth hour, there was gross darkness, as He hung in agony upon the tree. In Genesis 22:7, starting with the last yod (י), and counting every fourth letter from right to left spells *Yah ha'mar lilah* יה המר לילה, which means "the bitter night of the Lord." This was the time when God had commanded Abraham to sacrifice his son Isaac. Again, this reminds us of when Yeshua was bitterly sacrificed, and day became as night.

In Genesis 22:8, starting with the last letter of the fourth word, counting every tenth word, and reading the first letter of each word spells *Jehovah* "Adonai" יהוה. The adjacent letters of every tenth word to the right spell *malach* מלח, which means "salt." The first letter of each tenth word to the left spells *chak'mah* חכמה, which means "wisdom." In this same series of ten-letter counts, but counting every thirtieth word, and reading the last letter of each word spells "Mary" *Miryam* מרים. We see many words and names that are prophetic in nature that are encoded within this messianic portion of Scripture about Isaac and Abraham.

In Genesis 37:30, starting with the first letter of the last word and taking only the first letter of the next eleven words spells *bo kiyoshiah ve'ahav* בוא כירשע ואהב, which means "come for salvation and love." John 13:1 says, "Now before the Feast of the Passover, when Jesus knew that His hour was come that He should depart out of this world unto the Father, having loved His own which were in the world, He loved them unto the end."

In Genesis 28:13, starting with the first letter in the seventh word and counting every sixteenth word from right to left spells *Yeshua* ישוע. The adjacent letters spell "Hamman the Syrian" המן רמי. Could this insight allude to Yeshua when He confronts the Antichrist — of whom Hamman was a type — at the last battle?

Genesis 35:22 says, "And it came to pass, when Israel dwelt in that land, that Reuben went and lay with Bilhah his father's concubine: and Israel heard it." Reuben's great sin caused him to forfeit his birthright as the firstborn or firstfruit of Israel. The firstborn took the place of authority in the family or nation when the father passed away. God, however, had a plan in spite Reuben's sins. We must remember that God controls the beginning from the end. Reuben's promise as a son of vigor, dignity, power, and might was inherited by Yeshua as the Kinsman-Redeemer. In Genesis 35:22, starting with the first letter in the third word, which is *Yisrael* ישראל, and taking the first letter of every thirty-third word from right to left spells *Yeshua* ישוע. Here, we see Yeshua within the same Scripture where Reuben sinned. We must look a little deeper to find the reason for this. We find that reason in Genesis 49:3: "Reuben, thou are my firstborn, my might, and the beginning of my strength, the excellency of dignity, and the excellency of power."

עז   יתר שאת ויתר

might highest and dignity highest the

Notice that the first letter of each word spells Yeshua יֵשׁוּעַ. In this world or the world to come, no other person but Yeshua the Messiah could qualify for this position, as we see in Matthew and Revelation.

> And Jesus [Yeshua] came and spake unto them, saying, All power is given unto Me in Heaven and in earth. (Matthew 28:18)

> And they sung a new song, saying, Thou art worthy to take the book, and to open the seals thereof: for Thou wast slain, and hast redeemed us to God by Thy blood out of every kindred, and tongue, and people, and nation; And hast made us unto our God kings and priests: and we shall reign on the earth. And I beheld, and I heard the voice of many angels [messengers] round about the throne and the beasts and the elders: and the number of them was ten thousand times ten thousand, and thousands of thousands; Saying with a loud voice, Worthy is the Lamb that was slain to receive power, and riches, and wisdom, and strength, and honor, and glory, and blessing. (Revelation 5:9–12)

The most magnificant Scripture of the firstborn in the Old Testament is found in Zechariah, where Yeshua returns to take the leadership of Israel and the nations at the beginning of the messianic kingdom. Zechariah 12:10 says, "And I will pour upon the house of David, and upon the inhabitants of Jerusalem, the spirit of grace and of supplications: and they shall look upon Me whom they have pierced, and they shall mourn for Him, as one mourneth for his only Son, and shall be in bitterness for Him, as one that is in bitterness for His firstborn." The Hebrew word here for firstborn is *hayahchid* הַיָּחִיד, which translates "an only son." Counting every thirty-eighth letter from the chet (ח), in reverse, spells *Mashiach* מׁשׁיח. Also, every seventh letter in this verse spells "Savior" מׁשׁיע. At the beginning of the messianic kingdom, Yeshua will be recognized and exalted by Israel and the world. John 3:16 says, "For God so loved the world, that He gave His only begotten Son, that whosoever believeth in Him should not perish, but have everlasting life." Yeshua the Messiah is the firstborn and only begotten Son of God and the One for whom they shall weep in that day.

In Genesis 47:29, starting with the first letter of each fifteenth word spells *Yeshua* יׁשׁוע. Joseph, who was a type of our Savior, was exalted to the throne while in Egypt. This area of Scripture reflects the closeness that Joseph had with Israel, his father. This scenario will be fulfilled when Yeshua comes back to Israel and when He is recognized as the Messiah.

In Genesis 48:12, starting with the first letter of the fourth word, and counting every fifty-seventh word in reverse — the first letter only — spells *mahla Yeshua nahkar* מלא יׁשׁוע נכר, which means "consecrated (confirmed), Yeshua, acknowledge (recognize fully)." This combination also contains the same shin (ׁש) where we found *Yeshua* at fifteen-word intervals.

In Exodus 1:10, starting with the last letter of the seventh word, and counting the last letter of every other word spells יהוה. Exodus 1:12, starting with the first letter of the last word, reading the first letter of each word from right to left spells *beyom aviv* ביום אביב, which means "in the day of Aviv." Also, in Exodus 1:10, starting with the first peh and counting every ninety-eighth letter from right to left spells *Pesach* פסח. In this series of the ninety-eight-letter count, we will find *mo'aid* מוער, which means "the feast (appointment)." Also we find אמך, and *gili* גילי, which means "joy."

In Exodus 1:4, starting with the fourth yod, counting

every 116th letter from right to left spells *Yeshua shabar li* ישוע שבר לי, which means "wait patiently (with hope) for Me Yeshua (Jesus)." The adjacent letters spell *chan'not ram* חנות רם, which means "an exalted (lifted up) prayer."

In Exodus 19:13, starting with the first letter of the sixteenth word, counting every third word, and reading only the first letter spells *Jehovah* יהוה. In Exodus 19:15, starting with the seventh word, and reading the first letter of every third word spells *Jehovah* יהוה. In Exodus 19:16, starting with the first letter and reading only the first letter spells *Oshiah* הושע, which means "He will save." Note that in Exodus 19:23 when we combine in sequence the second, third, and fourth words, it spells "Moses and Elijah" *Moshe Eliyahu* משה אליהו. Moses and Elijah were together on the Mount of Transfiguration with Jesus many years later.

In Exodus 19:18, starting with the ninth word and counting the first letter of every sixteenth word from left to right spells יהוה. In Exodus 19:15, starting with the seventh word, the first letter of every fourth word from left to right uncovers יהוה. In Exodus 19:11, starting with the first letter of the fourth to last word, counting every third word, and reading only the first letter spells "the jubilee" היבל. In Exodus 19:10, starting with the first letter of the second word and counting every sixteenth word spells *yabail* יבל. In Exodus 19:19, starting with the first letter of the eighth word and counting every sixteenth word from left to right spells יבל. Also, from the same yod, and counting every sixty-first letter from right to left spells ישוע. The adjacent letters spell האבה, which means "the Father." In Deuteronomy 32:11, starting with the first letter in the ninth word, the yod (י), counting every seventeenth word from right to left, and reading only the first letter of each of the words spells *Yeshua* ישוע.

God appointed Aaron as the high priest to bring praise unto the Lord, to minister to, and intercede for Israel. We can see a picture of our High Priest and Lord in the functions of Aaron and the garments he wore.

> And thou shalt make holy garments for Aaron thy brother for glory and for beauty. And thou shalt speak unto all that are wise hearted, whom I have filled with the spirit of wisdom, that they may make Aaron's garments to consecrate him, that he may minister unto Me in the priest's office. And these are the garments which they shall make; a breastplate, and an ephod, and a robe, and a broidered coat, a mitre, and a girdle: and they shall make holy garments for Aaron thy brother, and his sons, that he may minister unto Me in the priest's office. And they shall take gold, and blue, and purple, and scarlet, and fine linen. And they shall make the ephod of gold, of blue, and of purple, of scarlet, and fine twined linen, with cunning work. It shall have the two shoulder-pieces thereof joined at the two edges thereof; and so it shall be joined together. And the curious girdle of the ephod, which is upon it, shall be of the same, according to the work thereof; even of gold, of blue, and purple, and scarlet, and fine twined linen. And thou shalt take two onyx stones, and grave on them the names of the children of Israel. (Exodus 28:2–9)

The following is the Hebrew text of verse three and the first two words in verse four:

ואתה תדבר אל-כל-חכמי-לב אשר מלאתיו רוח חכמה
ועשׂו את-בגדי אהרן לקדשׁו לכהנו-לי: ואלה הבגדים

In Exodus 28:4, starting with the second word, taking the first letter of every second word from left to right spells *hallah Boray* הלל בורא, which means "praise the Creator." In Exodus 28:7, starting with the first letter of the third word and reading the first letter of every third word from right to left spells Yeshua יֵשׁוּעַ. In Exodus 28:10, starting with the last letter of the last word, reading the first letter of every second word spells *Mashiach* מָשִׁיחַ, which means "the Messiah."

> And thou shalt put the two stones upon the shoulders of the ephod for stones of memorial unto the children of Israel: and Aaron shall bear their names before the Lord upon his two shoulders for a memorial. And thou shalt make ouches of gold.
>
> (Exodus 28:12–13)

ושמת את-שתי האבנים על כתפת האפר אבני זכרן לבני ישראל
ונשא אהרן את-שמותם לפני יהוה על-שתי כתפיו לזכרן:
ועשית משבצת זהב:

Starting with the third letter in the eleventh word of Exodus 28:12 and counting every seventh letter forward spells ראם ישוע, which means "Yeshua lifts up." Aaron was portraying the position of Yeshua the High Priest.

In Exodus 28:20, starting with the second to last word, reading the first letter of every sixth word from left to right spells *Jehovah* יהוה.

In Exodus 40:36, starting with the first letter of the fourth word, and counting every seventieth word, reading the first letter of each word from left to right spells *Yeshua* ישוע. Continue counting every seventieth word and you will come to a tav, which is the last letter of the seventieth word. This time, read only the last letter of each 280th word (4 × 70), which spells *Torah* תורה.

> Gather the people, sanctify the congregation, assemble the elders, gather the children, and those that suck the breasts: let the Bridegroom [Yeshua] go forth of His chamber, and the bride [body of believers in Heaven] out of her closet. (Joel 2:16)

The first letter of each word spells *Yeshua az* יׁשוע אז, which means "Yeshua at that time." In verse 17, the last letter of each word spells *Jehovah* יהוה. Also, this is true of the last letter of every fifth word. We can see by these insights that a great event is going to take place relative to the feast of Yom Kippur on some future date.

In Amos 1:3, starting with the third word and reading the first letter of every sixth word spells *Yeshua* יׁשוע. Also, in Amos 1:1, starting with the first ayin, counting every sixth letter, and overlapping into the book of Joel spells *Yeshua* יׁשוע.

In Malchi 3:23, Hebrew Tanakh . . . but in the King James Version it is Malachi 4:3; starting with the first letter in the sixth word, counting every other word, and reading only the first letter spells "Elijah" *Eliyahu* אליהו. This is his full name, but in this Scripture the vav (ו) is omitted. The first letter of every second word uncovers the following:

Malachi 1:14; *Iyob* איוב Job
Malachi 1:14; *Benim* בנים Sons
Malachi 2: 8; *Sa'rah* שרה Sarah
Malachi 2:15; *Moshe* מׁשה Moses
Malachi 3: 5; *Miryam, shalom, Levi* לוי, שלום, מרים Mary, peace, Levi
Malachi 3:24; *Eliyahu* אליהו Elijah
Malachi 3:24; *Yoel* יואל Joel
The first letter of every seventh word uncovers:
Malachi 1:7; *Manorah* מנרה Lampstand
Malachi 1:14; *Yehudah har* יהורה הר Judah the Mountain
Malachi 2:1; *Elohim* אלהים God
Malachi 3:19; *Yarah Adonai* ירה יהוה Adonai, to teach, flow as water.

In Malachi 1:1, starting with the last resh, and counting every fifteenth letter from right to left spells *Rachel* רחל. In Malachi 1:14, starting with the third resh, counting every fifteenth letter spells *Rachel* רחל. In Malachi 2:14, starting with the third-to-the-last resh, counting every fifteenth letter spells *Rachel* רחל. *Rachel* is a name for the suffering Messiah Who took all the sins of the world on His shoulders. He was as a Lamb, *Rachel* רחל, being led to the slaughter. We see a clearer picture of this event in Isaiah 53 (see chapter 1).

In Psalm 23:4, starting with the last letter of the ninth word and counting the last letter of every twenty-sixth word spells *Jehovah* יהוה. In Psalm 150:5, starting with the last letter of the second word, and counting every twenty-sixth letter from left to right spells *Jehovah* יהוה. The name *Jehovah* in the Hebrew has a mathematical value of twenty-six.

In Psalm 23:4, starting with the first letter of the last word and reading the first letter of each word from left to right spells *Joshuah* יהושע. Also, in Psalm 23:2, starting with the fourth letter in the third word, and counting every twenty-fourth letter from right to left spells *Yeshua* ישוע. Psalm 23:1–2, a psalm of David says, "The Lord is my Shepherd; I shall not want. He maketh me to lie down in green pastures." The Hebrew for "He maketh me to lie down" ירביצני gives us the name of the person who will give us green pastures and supply our daily food. Starting with the second yod (י) and counting every twenty-fourth letter from right to left spells *Yeshua* ישוע. Also, in Psalm 23:4, starting with the second letter in the third word and counting every twenty-fourth letter from left to right spells *lachem* לחם, which means "bread." If we stop now, we would not get a complete picture of all that this Psalm holds for us. In Psalm 23:5, starting with the third letter in the eighth word and counting every twenty-fourth letter from left to right spells *salamo* סלמו, which means "His ladder." This is the same word used in Genesis 28:12, where Jacob saw the Lord at the top of the ladder with angels ascending and descending.

Psalm 41 is also a powerful prophecy concerning the

Messiah and the enemies of God who seek His life by plotting evil against Him. Within this Psalm is encoded the name of the Messiah. In Psalm 41:3, starting with the first letter in the first word, counting every thirty-eighth word from right to left, and taking only the first letter of each word spells *Yeshua* ישוע. The last letter of each word in this combination spells *ha'ohail* האהל, which means "the tabernacle." Yeshua tabernacled with us to give us life in spite of the evil done to Him.

In Psalm 96:2, starting with the first letter of the last word, counting every thirteenth word, reading the first letter of each spells *Jehovah* יהוה. Psalm 95:11 says, "Unto whom I sware in my wrath that they should not enter into My rest." Starting with the first letter of the fifth word, and counting every fourteenth word from right to left spells *Yeshua* ישוע. This extends into Psalm 96. In Deuteronomy 5:26, starting with the first letter in the seventh word, counting every fifty-second word from right to left, and reading only the first letter of each word spells *Eliyahu* אליהו, which means "the Lord is my God." This is also the name of Elijah. Then in Deuteronomy 5:30, starting with the first letter in the fourteenth word, counting every twelfth word, and reading only the first letter of each word spells *Jehovah* יהוה. Finally, in Deuteronomy 6:21, starting with the first letter in the eighth word, counting every thirty-fourth word, and reading only the first letter from left to right spells *Jehovah* יהוה.

The second time Moses went up to Mount Sinai, he requested of the Lord to see His glory.

And he said, I beseech thee, shew me Thy glory. And He said, I will make all My goodness pass before thee; and I will proclaim the name of the Lord before thee; and will be gracious to whom I will be gracious, and will shew mercy on whom I will shew mercy. And He said, Thou canst not see My face: for there shall no man see Me, and live. And the Lord said, Behold, there is a place by Me, and thou shalt stand upon a rock: And it shall come to pass, while My glory passeth by, that I will put thee in a clift of the rock, and will cover thee with My hand while I pass by: And I will take away Mine hand, and thou shalt see My back parts: but My face shall not be seen. (Exodus 33:18–23)

In verse 20, starting with the third letter in the sixth word, which is yod (י) in the Hebrew phrase "My face" *et pahni* את-פני and counting every 139th letter from left to right spells *Yeshua El* ישוע אל, which translates "Jesus God." The Scriptures below will explain why the name, Jesus God, is encoded within these wonderful verses:

For now we see through a glass, darkly, but then face to face: now I know in part; but then shall I know even as also I am known.

(1 Corinthians 13:12)

For God, who commanded the light to shine out of darkness, hath shined in our hearts, to give the light of the knowledge of the glory of God in the face of Jesus Christ. (2 Corinthians 4:6)

And there shall be no more curse: but the throne of God and of the Lamb shall be in it; and his servants shall serve Him: And they shall see his face; and his name shall be in their foreheads.

(Revelation 22:3–4)

Notice the singular use of the pronouns "His" and "Him." Whom shall we see? None other than Jesus.

Moses was commanded by God to make the Tabernacle according to the pattern seen on the mountain. This pattern was to be followed to the utmost, without any deviation whatsoever. We understand by the Word of God that the Tabernacle was a picture of Yeshua the Messiah. All the things that Moses saw on the mountain can only be speculated on, but one thing is certain. Moses saw a pattern for an earthly dwelling of our Lord that would be fulfilled in Yeshua the Messiah. Throughout the Scriptures where Moses is repeating the Lord's command concerning the building of the Tabernacle *mishkan* מִשְׁכָּן, you will find many wonderful insights about Yeshua our Lord.

The true Hebrew rendering of Exodus 36:22 reads, "By two board pins, the one was connected (*meshullavot* מְשֻׁלָּבֹת), one to another, so he did to all the boards of the tabernacle."

שְׁתֵּי יָדֹת לַקֶּרֶשׁ הָאֶחָד מְשֻׁלָּבֹת אַחַת
אֶל-אַחַת כֵּן עָשָׂה לְכֹל קַרְשֵׁי הַמִּשְׁכָּן

The Hebrew word *meshullavot* מְשֻׁלָּבֹת, means "to connect at equidistant spacing." An amazing insight is seen in this verse. Starting with the first letter of the first word and reading only the first letter of each word from right to left spells *Shiloh* שִׁילֹה, which is a term for the Messiah.

Exodus 36:26–27 says, "And their forty sockets of silver; two sockets under one board, and two sockets under another board. And for the sides of the tabernacle westward he made six boards."

וְאַרְבָּעִים אַדְנֵיהֶם כָּסֶף שְׁנֵי אֲדָנִים תַּחַת הַקֶּרֶשׁ הָאֶחָד
וּשְׁנֵי אֲדָנִים תַּחַת הַקֶּרֶשׁ הָאֶחָד: וּלְיַרְכְּתֵי הַמִּשְׁכָּן יָמָּה עָשָׂה
שִׁשָּׁה קְרָשִׁים וּשְׁנֵי קְרָשִׁים עָשָׂה לִמְקֻצְעֹת הַמִּשְׁכָּן בַּיַּרְכָתָיִם:

In the same area of Scripture, speaking of the Tabernacle in verse 27, starting with the first letter of the third word and reading the first letter of each word from left to right spells *Jehovah* יהוה. Continuing with the first letter of the third word and counting every other word from right to left, reading only the first letter, spells *Yeshua* ישוע. Now we have *Shiloh, Jehovah,* and *Yeshua* in the same area concerning the structure of the Tabernacle. What did Moses see when he looked into the heavens? Could it have been the Lord Yeshua Himself? In Exodus 36:24, starting with the third letter of the eighth word and counting every twenty-seventh letter from right to left spells *Yeshua* ישוע.

In Daniel 9:23, starting with the first letter in the twelfth word, counting every tenth word in both directions, and reading only the first letter of each word spells *torah b'qodesh* תורה בקודש, which means "the Torah in the sanctuary."

In Isaiah 66:20, taking the first letter of every seventieth word, beginning with the first letter of the twenty-third word, and counting every seventieth word from left to right spells *Yoshiah* יושיע, which means "He will save."

In Isaiah 63:11, reading the first letter of every 169th word and counting from right to left, beginning with the *Ruach Kodsho* רוח קדשו (His Holy Spirit) spells *rebo Yeshua* רבו ישוע, which means "Yeshua to increase in dignity and power." The ayin (ע) in Yeshua's name overlaps into the book of Jeremiah. Oddly enough, this phrase equals 596, which is the same number as *Yerushalayim* ירושלים, when it is spelled with the extra yod. In this same series of 169-word counts — but this time, 2 × 169th word, or every 338th word — we will find the word *hashachim* השחים, which means "to be very humble." This is a picture, leading up to His own sacrifice, of our Messiah when He was on earth.

In Leviticus 9:9, starting with the first letter of the thirteenth word, counting every seventh word, and reading the first letter of each seventh word from right to left spells *havah Yeshua* הוה ישוע, which means "Yeshua exists." Notice that from the yod in Yeshua's name and counting from left to right spells "Adonai" *Jehovah* יהוה. "And the sons of Aaron brought the blood unto him: and he dipped his finger in the blood, and put it upon the horns of the altar, and poured out the blood at the bottom of the altar." It is quite interesting that *Yeshua* and *Jehovah* would show up in the insight where it is speaking of the blood sacrifice. When Yeshua ascended into heaven after Mary had approached Him, He sprinkled the altar in heaven for our redemption. This act represents one complete work for all time.

Finally, in Revelation 6:9 we read, "And when He had opened the fifth seal, I saw under the altar the souls of them that were slain for the Word of God, and for the testimony which they held." Why were the souls of them that were slain for His name under the altar? Because that is where the blood of Jesus was applied. In other words, they were under the blood of the Lamb. In type, we who are washed in the blood of the Lamb are under the altar. There is saving power and keeping power in the blood of Jesus Christ.

6

The Overlapping Sequences to the Infinite

To grasp the full height and depth of the Word of God would take an eternity of study in the Holy Scriptures. In this carnal body and mind, it would be impossible, however, to understand the full meaning of all that God has for us. From time to time, God's people receive glimpses of His infinite glory as the Lord lifts our limitations and opens our spiritual minds to receive a small portion of His beauty. On the day when we stand in His presence, we shall see Him in all His glory and shall comprehend not only His purposes but also the reason He saved us. Then we shall have the clear vision and perfect love that abundantly transcends our natural abilities and faculties. Many people of faith do not understand that new revelation takes us beyond our comfort zones. We are similar to babies who do not want to be taken from the womb because the new surroundings are so unfamiliar; or we are similar to a person who does not want to be in a contest because he or she fears failure. God does not lead us into dangerous circumstances past the place of retrieving us because He is our Good Shepherd who will never leave us nor forsake us. There is great new revelation coming forth in these last days — new to us, but not new to God. Knowledge about the Bible and about Jesus is being revealed today at an awesome rate that surpasses the rate of revelation of all previous generations. This is mind-boggling; nevertheless, this is the time for His Word to be manifested by His Spirit to His people before the end of time.

> But we speak the wisdom of God in a mystery, even the hidden wisdom, which God ordained before the world unto our glory: Which none of the princes of this world knew: for had they known it, they would not have crucified the Lord of glory. But as it is written, Eye hath not seen, nor ear heard, neither have entered into the heart of man, the things which God hath prepared for them that love Him. But God hath revealed them unto us by His Spirit: for the Spirit searcheth all things, yea, the deep things of God. (1 Corinthians 2:7–9)

We can know the things of God, but we must walk in the light as He is in the light. In His light, we shall see more light. There is a secret place in God for every believer, but He will not reveal His great mysteries to babes or disobedient children. If, however, we have childlike faith, and if we love Him, He will give us the desires of our hearts.

> And there was a voice from the firmament that was over their heads, when they stood, and had let down their wings. And above the firmament that was over their heads was the likeness of a throne, as the appearance of a sapphire stone: and upon the likeness of the throne was the likeness as the appearance of a Man above upon it. And I saw as the color of

amber, as the appearance of fire round about within it, from the appearance of His loins even upward, and from the appearance of His loins even downward, I saw as it were, the appearance of fire, and it had brightness round about. As the appearance of the bow that is in the cloud in the day of rain, so was the appearance of the brightness round about. This was the appearance of the likeness of the Glory of the Lord. And when I saw it, I fell upon my face, and I heard a voice of One that spake.

(Ezekiel 1:25–28)

His head and His hairs were white like wool, as white as snow; and His eyes were as a flame of fire; and His feet like unto fine brass, as if they burned in a furnace; and His voice as the sound of many waters. (Revelation 1:14–15)

And immediately I was in the spirit: and, behold, a throne was set in heaven, and One sat on the throne. And He that sat was to look upon like a jasper and a sardine stone: and there was a rainbow round about the throne, in sight like unto an emerald.

(Revelation 4:2–3)

The person whom Ezekiel saw was the same person whom John saw. Ezekiel 1:27 gives us an insight to this fact. Starting with the yod (י) in the Hebrew phrase "His loins" מתניו and counting forward every thirty-sixth letter (1/10 of a full circle) spells *Yeshua* ישוע. Also, from the fourth letter in the fourth word and counting every twenty-first letter in reverse spells "Messiah the truth" אמת המשיח. There is no question about the identity of the Lord of Glory. His name is Yeshua HaMashiach.

When God destroyed the earth and its inhabitants during the time of Noah, He promised Noah and all His generations to follow that He would not judge the earth nor destroy it again in this manner. God put the signature of His covenant in the heavens as a reminder for all people of all generations. Every time there is a rainbow, which is the pattern of the heavenly rainbow in His throne room, we are reminded of the promises that God has made to humankind.

> And I, behold, I establish My covenant with you, and with your seed after you; . . . And I will establish My covenant with you; neither shall all flesh be cut off any more by the waters of a flood; neither shall there any more be a flood to destroy the earth. And God said, This is the token of the covenant which I make between Me and you and every living creature that is with you, for perpetual generations: I do set My Bow in the cloud, and it shall be for a token of a covenant between Me and the earth. And it shall come to pass, when I bring a cloud over the earth, that the bow shall be seen in the cloud.
>
> (Genesis 9:9, 11–14)

I am reminded of an article I read that stated that the rainbow makes a complete circle that can be detected when viewed from above. This speaks of infinity because when God makes a covenant, He will never break His part of that promise. It is as though God is the wheel-within-the-wheel of the rainbow, from which all light radiates. The spectrum of the rainbow is a prophetic announcement of the Good News (Gospel). Sir Isaac Newton, who is considered to be one of the greatest geniuses of all time, used a spectrum in some of his scientific research. He found that from a source of white light, the spectrum gives wavelengths of seven shades of color. This is exactly what the rainbow does. God is the source of all light that radiates from His covenant through the spectrum of His heavenly rainbow. The colors are violet, indigo, blue, green, yellow, orange, and red.

These shades of color give us a wonderful, prophetic picture of the Good News and the love of God for all His creation that is proclaimed throughout the world. In Genesis 9:9, starting with the first letter in the third word and counting every 144th letter from right to left spells *me'basair tov* מבשר טוב. This same statement is also found in Isaiah 52:7 and means "bringing good tidings" or "bringing the good news."

God demonstrated his love for Noah and all humankind by the sign of the rainbow. Jesus demonstrated his love for the whole world by the sign of the cross. It has been said by many doctors and scholars that the punishment Jesus received before He was nailed to the cross was so horrible that He was disfigured beyond recognition. His face was swollen. His flesh was ripped from His body to the point that His organs showed openly from His back. His beard was ripped from His face. He was beaten on the head with reeds, thus mutilating His appearance. He was ridiculed, mocked, spat upon, and rejected by His friends as He carried the sins of the whole world to His grave. This is what the Good News is all about: Jesus paid the ultimate price for the ratification of the covenant that God made with all humanity. God made a covenant with Noah, Abraham, Isaac, Jacob, and Moses, as well as a new covenant with believers in Yeshua HaMashiach. All these covenants were like stepping stones from glory to glory, culminating in Yeshua and the finished work of His death, burial, and resurrection.

Each color of the rainbow has an eternal meaning:

1. *Blue* depicts heaven, infinity, Son of God. Hebrews 1:1–2 says, "God, Who at sundry times and in divers manners spake in time past unto the fathers by the prophets, Hath in these last days spoken unto us by His Son, Whom He has appointed heir of all things, by Whom also He made the worlds."

2. *Red* is for scarlet, blood, redemption. Ephesians 1:6–7 says, "To the praise of the glory of His grace, wherein He hath made us accepted in the beloved. In Whom we have redemption through His blood, the forgiveness of sins, according to the riches of His grace."

3. *Orange* means fruit, fruit of atonement, fruits of the Spirit, trees of righteousness. Psalms 1:3 says, "And he shall be like a tree planted by the rivers of water, that bringeth forth his fruit in his season; his leaf also shall not wither; and whatsoever he does shall prosper."

4. *Indigo* stands for the dark blue dye from plants; it was one of the dyes used for the skins for the Tabernacle covering. This is yet another picture of the humanity of Jesus; the dyed rams' skin was the outer visable covering of the dwelling place of God. First Timothy 3:16 states, "And without controversy great is the mystery of godliness: God was manifest in the flesh, justified in the Spirit, seen of angels, preached unto the Gentiles, believed on in the world, received up into glory."

5. *Green*: depicts resurrection, newness of life, growth. The storm that brings the rain also brings with it newness of life for the soil and plants. Each storm is accompanied by lightning, thunder, and a rainbow — yet another signature of God in the heavens. Revelation 21:5 says, "And he that sat upon the throne said, Behold, I make all things new. And he said unto me, Write: for these words are true and faithful."

6. *Gold* is for deity, purity, perfection. Gold speaks of the perfect Son of God from heaven. Second Corinthians 5:21 states, "For He hath made Him [Messiah] to be sin for us, Who knew no sin; that we might be made the righteousness of God in Him."

7. *Violet*, or bluish purple, is royalty, kingship, love. John 3:16 states, "For God so loved the world, that He gave His only begotten Son, that whosoever believeth in Him should not perish, but have everlasting life."

The Torah is also likened to the wheel-within-the-wheel that reaches from Genesis through Deuteronomy and returns from Deuteronomy to Genesis. The Torah is infinity disguised behind the surface writing of the Word of God and contains hidden messages for all of us to heed. The mysteries of God are revealed to us through His Divine word by His Spirit, and all that we need to know about life, death, past, present, future, eternal life, or eternal damnation is written within the Torah. All things are written by God through His Holy Spirit, as seen in Ezekiel 1:19. Starting with the seventh letter in the eleventh word "the wheels" האופנים and counting every tenth letter from right to left spells *Mashiach* מ׳שׁ׳ח. Also, from the shin (שׁ) in *Mashiach* and counting every seventh letter in reverse spells "the fire of the Lord" or "the Lord is strong" יוראשׁ. In verse 20, we will find *Yeshua* ישׁוע at two-letter intervals woven within the Hebrew phrase "and the wheels were lifted along with them" והאופנים ינשׂאו לעמתם. Also within this text at two-letter intervals, we find the phrase "wealth from the (Kinsman) Redeemer" *hone me'go'el* הון מגאל.

> And when the living creatures went, the wheels went by them: and when the living creatures were lifted up from the earth, the wheels were lifted up. Withersoever the spirit was to go, they went, thither was their spirit to go; and the wheels were lifted up over against them: for the spirit of the living creature was in the wheels. (Ezekiel 1:19–20)

ובלכת החיות ילכו האופנים אצלם
ובהנשׂא החיות מעל הארץ ינשׂאו האופנים:
על אשׁר יהיה-שׁם הרוח ללכת ילכו שׁמה הרוח
ללכת והאופנים ינשׂאו לעמתם כי רוח החיה באופנים:

In Ezekiel 1, we see the wheel-within-the-wheel from a new perspective of infinity *netsech* נצח. Every tenth letter from the kaph (כ) in the phrase "to go" ללכת in Ezekiel 1:20 spells "for infinity" כי נצח. The hidden secrets of the Lord can only be revealed by the Lord. We should never speculate on whether or not the Word of God is for us. His Word is not a subject for debate outside the godly, spiritual realm. Since God is revealing His secrets at a prodigious rate in these last days, we should take heed of the generation in which we have been born.

Another beautiful insight is found in Ezekiel 1:16. Starting with the third letter in the tenth word and counting every seventieth letter from right to left spells "hidden secret" עלום. Without question, the wheel-within-the-wheel represents Yeshua HaMashiach in the power, and of the power, of God. All the mysteries — past, present, and future — are hidden in Jesus, for He knows all things.

I have always believed that infinity is like a complete circle, without beginning or end. Lately, I believe that the Torah is the reflection of the wheel-within-the-wheel, and that the remaining books of the first covenant are the outer wheel. The books of the Bible, other than the Torah, are an expression and confirmation of all of the Torah, and the new covenant is the fulfillment of the first. To give credence to this thought, let us examine some wonderful encoded messages that the Lord has for us.

In Ezekiel 1:1, starting with the second letter in the second word and counting every 360th letter from right to left spells *Shalom* שלום. The letters adjacent to *Shalom* spell, *Ki Tahmid* כי תמיד, which translates "for eternity, for always, continually, perpetual." We can readily understand the importance of this find; it gives us hope of eternal peace. All that was, is, and will be, including the universe, revolves around our Lord and Savior, Yeshua HaMashiach.

One additional group of combinations that deserves our attention at this time is found in Ezekiel 1:3. Starting with the fourth letter in the fourth word, which is the ineffable name

Jehovah יהוה, and counting every 235th letter from right to left spells "knowledge, understanding" בינה. In this same count of 235, we find "truth" אמת.

In Ezekiel 1:1, starting with the first letter in the ninth word and counting every 235th letter from right to left spells "the light" האור. In Ezekiel 1:5, starting with the first letter in the sixth word and counting every 235th letter from right to left spells "who is like the Lord" מיכה. This name is asking a question: "Is there anyone like the Lord?" We get an answer for this question from His Word. The 235-letter count is the same count found in Exodus 15:27 where we found *Yeshua Jehovah* ישוע יהוה.

> I, even I, Am the Lord; and beside Me there is no saviour. I have declared, and have saved, and I have shewed, when there was no strange god among you: therefore ye are my witnesses, saith the Lord, that I Am God. (Isaiah 43:11–12)

אנכי אנכי יהוה ואין מבלעדי מושיע: אנכי הגדתי והושעתי
והשמעתי ואין בכם זר ואתם עדי נאם-יהוה ואני-אל:

Every fourth letter from right to left spells *Yeshua* ישוע, which is none other than Jesus. Jesus said that all power was given unto Him and that no man could come to the Father but by Him. Is Jesus another God? No. Are He and the Lord God one and the same? Yes. Since the Tanakh is a reflection of the Torah, we should be able to find some magnificent insights that are relative to the above.

Exodus 15:27 says, "And they came to Elim, And there were twelve springs of water and seventy palm trees. And they camped by the waters." What a wonderful place to be after treking through the wilderness! There is a greater, hidden message for us within this text than what appears on the surface. I have elaborated on this insight in chapter three, where the Scripture reveals the name *Jehovah*

"Adonai" *Yeshua* יהוה ישוע emanating from the waters of
Elim. He is the Living Waters and the Tree of Life, without
which we all would perish.

John 14:9b says, "He that hath seen Me [Jesus] hath seen
the Father." As Jacob in Genesis 28:12 was viewing the
ladder extending from the earth into heaven, He saw the
Lord at the top of the ladder with His angels ascending and
descending. The person whom he saw was the Lord Yeshua
in His glory and splendor, radiating His magnificence and
beauty. The Lord told Jacob of his destiny and that he would
inherit the land that was promised to Abraham and Isaac. In
Genesis 28:15, starting with the fifth letter in the seventeenth
word for "I have spoken" דברתי and counting every 140th
letter from right to left spells *Yeshua eh'heyeh* ישוע אהיה,
which means "Jesus will be what He will be" or "I Am
Jesus." This is same phrase that Jehovah used when he
spoke to Moses in the third chapter of Exodus. This term is
only used when referring to the ineffable God of Abraham,
Isaac, and Jacob, as seen in Exodus 3:14: "And God, said
unto Moses, I AM THAT I AM: and He said, Thus shalt thou
say unto the children of Israel, I AM (*eh'heyeh* אהיה), hath
sent me unto you."

Throughout the third chapter of Exodus, there are many
insights that reveal the name of Jesus the Messiah in various
combinations. One of the encoded sequences that is most
remarkable begins in Exodus 3:7, in the second letter of the
first word: "And the Lord said, I have surely seen the
affliction of My people which are in Egypt, and have heard
their cry by reason of their taskmasters; for I know their
sorrows." Starting with the second letter in the first word
and counting every 120th letter from left to right spells
Yeshua ישוע both forward and backward by starting with
the same yod (י) ישועושי.

Another awesome insight did not come into existence
until Israel entered the Promised Land many years later. In

Genesis 28:13, starting with the first letter in the ninth word and counting every twenty-sixth letter from left to right spells the "Tabernacle of Zion" *Ohail Tziyon* אהל ציון. The Lord spoke many things to Jacob from the top of the ladder that gave Jacob not only faith but also courage to carry him through his trek in the wilderness. The Lord will also strengthen us as we go through this life of difficulties and disappointments; then one day we shall enter our promised land in glory. In Genesis 1:1, starting with the first yod and counting every thirtieth letter in reverse, extending into the last book of the Torah (Deuteronomy) spells Yehovah יהוה. Starting with the second shin in Genesis 1:1 and counting every twenty-seventh letter in both directions spells *Yeshua* ישוע. This combination also overlaps into the book of Deuteronomy.

In Genesis 1:4, starting with the yod (י) and counting every 102nd letter from left to right (extending into the last chapter of Deuteronomy) spells *kayam Yeshua* קים ישוע, which means "permanent Yeshua" or "Yeshua is permanent." In Deuteronomy 34:11, starting with the first yod (י) and counting every eighty-second letter from right to left spells *Yischak* ישחק, which is the name of Isaac. This spelling of Isaac occurs at least five times throughout the Bible. This insight goes into the book of Genesis where you will find *Yoshiah* יושע, which means "He (Yeshua) will save," and "Jesse" ישי.

In Deuteronomy 34:10, starting with the last yod, counting every seventy-second letter in both directions, and extending into the book of Genesis spells *Moreh, chai, Yeshua,* מורה חי ישוע, which means "the teacher of righteousness of life, Yeshua." Then, starting with the second-to-the-last yod and counting every 120th letter from right to left spells *Yeshua* ישוע. This extends into the book of Genesis. The adjacent letters spell *Abi* אבי, which means "my Father."

In the next verse, Deuteronomy 34:11, starting with the second shin and counting every ninetieth letter from right to left spells "Solomon" *Shlomoh* שלמה. In this same series of the ninety-letter count, we will find *Miryam, Moshe,* and *Sarah*. These combinations overlap into the book of Genesis. Also in verse 11, starting with the second-to-the-last yod and counting every 117th letter from right to left spells *Yeshua* ישוע. The adjacent letters spell *chaii* חיי.

In Genesis 50:24, starting with the last yod and counting every thirty-sixth (six to the second power [6 × 6]) letter from right to left spells *Jehovah* יהוה, which overlaps into the book of Exodus. The adjacent letters to the right of each letter that spell His name is *hallal* הלל, which translates "praise." The adjacent letters to the left spell *Yoshiah* ירשע, which means "He will save us." Also, this is another name for Yeshua.

In Exodus 40:30, starting with the second-to-the-last yod and counting every 134th letter from right to left, extending into the book of Leviticus spells *Yeshua* ישוע. The adjacent letters spell *Oved* עבד, which means "servant." *Oved* is also the name of David's grandfather.

In Leviticus 27:34, starting with the third-to-the-last yod and counting every sixth letter from right to left spells *Jehovah* יהוה, which overlaps into the book of Numbers. The overlapping from Genesis to Exodus was six to the second power, but here His name shows up at six-letter intervals.

Numbers 36:8, starting with the fourth-to-the-last yod and counting every 160th letter from right to left spells *Yeshua* ישוע. This combination extends into the book of Deuteronomy. Starting with the third-to-the-last yod in Deuteronomy 34:12 and counting every twenty-second letter from right to left spells *Yeshua* ישוע. This combination extends into Joshua.

Ruth 1:1, starting with the first mem and counting every twenty-first letter from left to right spells *Mashiach* משיח.

This combination extends into the book of Judges. Starting with the third letter in the fifth word of Ruth 4:19, which is "Rahm," counting every fifty-first letter from right to left, and extending into the book of 1 Samuel spells "Messiah" מ̇שׂיח. The Messiah is a direct descendant of Rahm. In 2 Samuel 1:1, starting with the first yod and counting every fifty-fifth letter from left to right spells *Yeshua* ישׂוע. This overlaps into 1 Samuel. In 2 Samuel 1:4, starting with the first mem and counting every seventy-sixth letter from left to right spells *Mashiach* מ̇שׂיח. This insight extends into the book of 1 Samuel also.

In Kings 1:8, starting with the last heh and counting every eighty-fifth letter from left to right spells *ha'shai Yeshua* השׂי ישׂוע, which means "the gift, Yeshua." This overlaps into 2 Samuel. In 2 Kings 1:2, starting with the third heh and counting every twelfth letter from left to right spells *hai Yoshiah* הא̇ ירשׂיע, which means "Behold, He will save us." Starting with the last yod of 2 Kings 1:2 and counting every seventy-sixth letter from left to right spells *Yeshua* ישׂוע. Both of these insights overlap into 1 Kings.

In 1 Chronicles 1:2, starting with the last mem and counting every 101st letter from right to left spells *Mashiach* מ̇שׂיח. The adjacent letter to the right of the mem is the chet (ח). From this chet, counting every 101st letter from left to right spells *Mashiach* מ̇שׂיח the second time. This combination extends (overlaps) into 2 Kings 25. What are the odds of these two combinations occurring by chance with the same letter count and being adjacent one to the other?

In Nehemiah 1:1, starting with the fifth yod and counting every fourth letter from right to left spells *Yeshua* ישׂוע. Continually counting every fourth letter from the yod in *Yeshua* gives you the word *ha'cha'yim* החיים, which means "the life." The adjacent letters spell *kohain* כהן, which means "priest." This phrase extends into Ezra. Starting with the sixth letter of the fifth word in Ezra 10:43 and counting every 150th letter from right to left spells *Torah* תורה, which extends into the book of Nehemiah. Starting with the third letter of the fifth word in Nehemiah 13:28 and counting every fifty-second letter from right to left spells *ha'hallal shophar* ההלל שופר, which means "the shofar of praise." The praise is in Nehemiah, but the shofar is in Esther.

Starting with the last mem of Esther 1:17 and counting every 486th letter from left to right spells *Mashiach* משיח. The adjacent letters to the right spell *tehudah* תהודה, which means "resonance." The root word is *hud* הוד, which means "glory, majesty, magnificent." The adjacent letters to the left spell *hillel* הלל, which means "praising" (namely, God). The chet (ח) that is in Mashiach's name overlaps into Nehemiah.

In Job 1:2, starting with the first mem and counting every thirty-second letter from left to right spells *Mashiach* משיח. The adjacent letters spell *Torah yelamed* תורה ילמד, which means "to teach the Torah." Messiah will teach the Torah. The combination extends into the book of Esther.

In Psalm 5:6, starting with the last kaph (כ) and counting every 273rd letter from left to right spells *ki Yeshua v'erepha'aik* כי ישוע וארפאך, which means "for Yeshua will heal you" or "for Yeshua is your healing." The adjacent letters spell, *natzal ha'b'pri* נצל הבכרי, which means "the fruit in the rapture (snatching up)." The ayin (ע) in *Yeshua* overlaps into the book of Job. Also, in Job 42:17, starting with the second letter in the second word and counting every twenty-seventh letter from right to left, overlapping into Psalms spells *Jehovah* יהוה forward and backward. In Proverbs 1:14, starting with the second-to-the-last heh and counting every 139th letter from left to right spells *HaMashiach* המשיח. The adjacent letters spell *halal* הלל. This insight overlaps into Psalm 149.

In Ecclesiastes 1:2, starting with the fourth heh and counting every twenty-seventh letter from left to right spells *Jehovah* יהוה, in reverse. This extends into the book of

Proverbs. This is the same count as in Proverbs 1:14. In Ecclesiastes 1:3, starting with the second-to-the-last mem and counting every seventy-sixth letter from left to right spells *Mashiach*. This combination extends into the book of Proverbs.

In Song of Songs (Song of Solomon) 1:1, starting with the third shin and counting every twenty-eighth letter from left to right spells *Shlomoh* שלמה. This extends into the book of Ecclesiastes. Solomon is the writer of both books. In Song of Songs 1:1, starting with the third mem and counting every eighteenth letter from left to right spells *mishnah* משנה, which means "a copy, the second, the copy of the original Torah." Each king of Israel was supposed to make a personal copy of the Torah for his own record. In the same verse, starting with the third heh and counting every sixth letter from right to left spells *ha'bikurim* הבכרים, which means "the Feast of Firstfruits."

In Song of Songs 8:13, starting with the last yod and counting every seventy-third letter from right to left spells *Yeshua* ישוע, which extends into the book of Isaiah. "Wisdom" *chakmah* חכמה also has the value of seventy-three. The phrase "cause me to hear it" *hashmi'ini* השמיעני is where the yod in *Yeshua* begins. Starting with the nun in this word and counting every sixteenth letter from right to left spells *natzal* נצל, which means "rescue, rapture, snatch up."

A very interesting set of combinations in the first chapter of Isaiah overlaps back into the Song of Solomon. Starting with the very last yod (י) of Song of Solomon 8:14, counting every twenty-third letter from right to left, and extending into the book of Isaiah spells *Jehovah* יהוה. Compare that to Isaiah 1:1. Starting with the last letter in the sixth word, the heh (ה), and taking the last letter of every fifth word spells *Jehovah* יהוה. What is so interesting about this combination is that three of the letters in His name are used in the twenty-three-letter count of the above. Then in Isaiah 65:20, starting with the first letter of the twelfth word, counting every 169th word from left to right, and reading only the first letter of each word spells *Yeshua* יְשׁוּעַ. The ayin in Yeshua's name overlaps into the book of Jeremiah. This is called, equidistant-word sequence, the same system of analysis as the above.

Isaiah 66:24, starting with the third tav and counting every seventeenth letter from right to left, leads you into the book of Jeremiah and spells *Torah*. There are at least ten combinations in the seventeen-letter series: *ahabah* אַהֲבָא *love*; *gili* גִּילִי *joy*, *oved* עֶבֶד *servant*, *rav cha'kam* רַב חָכָם *great wisdom*, *michah* מִיכָה *who is like God*; *Torot* תֹּורֹת *the laws*, *Adon* אָדֹון *Lord*, *a'uriyah* אוּרִיָה *light of the Lord*, *sari my* שָׂרִי *prince*, and *Shaddai* שַׁדִּי *The Almighty*.

In Lamentations 1:3, starting with the first aleph and counting every thirty-first letter spells *El* אֵל, which means "God"; it has a mathematical value of thirty-one. Continue counting every thirty-first letter, and we will have אֵלִי יְהֹוָהִי, which means "My God, Adonai." Notice that "Adonai" *Jehovah* is spelled in both directions. This also overlaps into the book of Jeremiah. In Ezekiel 1:1, starting with the second yod and counting every eightieth letter from left to right spells *Yeshua* יְשׁוּעַ, which also overlaps into the book of Lamentations.

In Daniel 1:15, starting with the last yod and counting every 239th letter from left to right spells *da'yee toshiah da'yee* דִי תֹושִיעַ דִי, which means "sufficiently, He will save sufficiently." This overlaps into the book of Ezekiel. The last yod is also used in the combination of a 321-letter count that forms the name Mashiach. In Ezekiel 46:20, starting with the second shin and counting every 478th letter (2 × 239) from right to left spells *shamayim galah dor* שָׁמַיִם גָּלָה דֹור, which means "the heavens reveal the generation (age)." This phrase extends into Daniel 1:7, to the last resh. Deleting the first three letters will give you *magillah dor* מגלה דור, which means "scroll of the generation (age)."

In Hosea 1:1, starting with the first chet and counting every fortieth letter from left to right spells *Mashiach* משיח. The adjacent letters spell *emmet* אמת, which means "truth." This also extends into the book of Daniel. In Joel 1:2, starting with the second-to-the-last yod and counting every fifty-one letters from right to left spells *Yeshua ki ki shmitah* ישוע כי כי שמטה, which means "Yeshua, for the remission of a debt (labor)." The adjacent letters spell *natzar gamal* נצר גמל, which means "conceal, (guard), treat a person well (benefit)." The other adjacent letters spell *amatz* אמץ, which means "to confirm, courageous, steadfast." An interesting word shows up in the fifty-one-letter count of this series. This is *hatzureh* הזורה, which means "crushed, trodden down."

In Amos 1:1, starting with the first ayin and counting every sixth letter from left to right spells *Yeshua* ישוע. In verse 4, starting with the second yod and counting every seventy-eighth letter from left to right spells *Jehovah* יהוה. Both of these insights extend into the book of Joel. In Obadiah 1:1, starting with the third yod and counting every eighth letter spells *Jehovah* יהוה. This overlaps into the book of Amos. Starting with the second chet in the same verse and counting every eighty-sixth letter from left to right spells *chad'shi* חדשי, which means "a new thing." *Elohim* has a mathematical value of eighty-six. This insight overlaps into the book of Amos.

In Obadiah 1:21, starting with the first ayin and counting every thirty-third letter from right to left spells *almah harah* עלמה הרה, which means "virgin to become pregnant." The adjacent letters spell *ki tav Mashiach* כי תו משיח, which means "Messiah for a sign." Note also Isaiah 7:14. This insight tells us that a virgin will conceive and that the Messiah will be the sign and the fruit of her womb. This insight overlaps into the book of Jonah. From the mem in Messiah and counting every forty-two letters from right to left spells *shalom* שלום. This overlaps into the book of Jonah. Also counting every forty-ninth letter from left to right from the same mem spells *shalom*. From the shin in Messiah and counting every thirty-third letter from right to left spells *shemot* שמות, which means "the book of Exodus (the names)." This overlaps into the book of Jonah. This is also verified from the Jerusalem Hebrew Tanahk, the Masoretic text, and the Rock of Israel Tanahk. In Obadiah 1:19, starting with the third aleph and counting every seventieth letter from right to left spells *elul* אלול, which is the sixth month on the Hebrew sacred calendar. This insight overlaps into the book of Jonah 1:2. Starting with the first heh and counting every fourteenth letter from left to right spells *haohail sahrag* האהל שרג, which means "the tabernacle intertwined (wrapped together; wreathed)." This insight overlaps into the book of Obadiah.

Micah 7:19, starting with the second tav and counting every sixty-third letter from right to left spells *Teshuah* תשועה, which means "salvation by God through a man." The adjacent letters spell *levim* לוים, which means "the Levites (the priestly tribe)." Salvation would come through a man who would be a priest, and that man is Yeshua. The tav is in Micah 7:19, but the rest of the insight shows up in the next book, Nahum, and continues through Habakkuk. There are many names and phrases that show up in the sixty-three-letter count: *tevel* תבל, which means "the world"; *shamayim* שמים, which means "the heavens"; *halal* הלל, which means "praise"; *Jehovah* יהוה, which means "the Lord"; *Micah* מיכה, which means "who is like God"; *Noach* נח, which means "favor (Noah)"; *Dinah* דינה, which means "the Lord is judge" (also the name of Jacob's daughter); *Yonah* יונה, which means "dove" (also the name of a prophet); *berahm kehillah* ברם קהלה, which means "in the great assembly"; *Moshe* מֹשֶׁה, which means "Moses"; *ishah* אִשָּׁה, which means "woman (wife)"; and *eshet* אֵשֶׁת, which means "the woman." There are many more such combinations in multiples of the sixty-three-letter count.

In Nahum 3:18, starting with the last yod and counting every sixty-seventh letter from right to left spells *Yeshua* יֵשׁוּעַ. The adjacent letters spell *Jehovah* יהוה. This spells *Jehovah* in both directions. There are other insights that go with this combination: *rimon* רִמֹן, which means "pomegranate"; *metzev* מֹזֵר, which means "gather in (granary)"; and *shamahsh* שַׁמַּשׁ, which means "servant lamp, caretaker, the sun." These insights overlap from Nahum to Habakkuk. In Zephaniah 1:3, starting with the fifth mem and counting every 101st letter from left to right spells *Mashiach* מָשִׁיחַ. The adjacent letters spell *Jehovah* יהוהי in both directions. The name of Adonai is found every 202nd letter in this series. Also, every 101st letter spells *lerimonim ruv* לִרְמֹנִים רוּב, which means "the abundance of the pomegranates." The pomegranates were worn on the fringe of the high priest's garments. These insights overlap into the book of Habakkuk.

In Zephaniah 3:20, starting with the yod in the phrase "when I return" *be'shuvi* בְּשׁוּבִי and counting every ninety-first letter from right to left spells *Yeshua* יֵשׁוּעַ. His name overlaps into the book of Haggai. In the ninety-one-letter series, we encounter several insights relative to Yeshua. In Haggai 2:13, starting with the second-to-the-last aleph and counting every 364th letter spells *Adonai* אֲדֹנָי. Starting with the second tav of Haggai 1:9, every 273rd letter from right to left spells *Torati* "My Laws" תּוֹרָתִי. In Zechariah 1:9, starting with the fourth-to-the-last heh and counting every ninety-first letter spells *hod emmet'yahu* אֱמִתִּיהוּ, which means "the truth of the Lord;" *shalav* שָׁלָב, which means "equidistant sequence"; *hod aviv* הוֹד אָבִיב, which means "the first month on the sacred calendar, spendor, majesty."

In Zephaniah 3:20, starting with the second-to-the-last shin (שׁ) and counting every seventh letter from right to left spells *shaveh* שׁבע, which means "seven." Continue counting every seventh letter and you will overlap into the book of Haggai. This process forms four different words: "seven," "from fulless," "the Messiah," "Lord God" *shevah, me'shalom, HaMashiach, El'Yah* שׁבע, משׁלם, המשׁיח, אליה.

In Haggai 2:22, starting with the first mem and counting every twentieth letter from left to right spells *Mashiach'yahu ve'shmo* משׁיחיהו ושׁמו, which means "the Lord Messiah is His name." In this series of the twenty-letter count, we will find at every 120th-letter intervals the word *Shalom* שׁלום, which extends into the book of Zechariah. Shalom shows up twice in this series. In the next verse, starting with the second-to-the-last chet and counting every 181st letter from right to left spells *Mashiach* משׁיח. This extends into the book of Zechariah, as found in chapter 14, verse 20. Starting with the first yod and counting every seventy-seventh letter from right to left spells *Yeshua ve'dav'a* ישׁרע ורבע. The word *dav'a* in reverse means "the servant." This extends into the book of Malachi. The adjacent letters spell *abo* אבוא, which means "I come." In Zechariah 14:21, starting with the third letter in the seventh word, counting every twenty-eighth letter from right to left, and extending into the book of Malachi spells *Jehovah*, "Adonai" יהוה. From the book of Zechariah extending into the last book, Malachi, there are astonishing insights that never cease to amaze me. To any unbiased seeker after the truth, these discoveries should prove the validity of the Word of God.

> In that day shall there be upon the bells of the horses, HOLINESS UNTO THE LORD; and the pots in the Lord's house shall be like the bowls before the altar. Yea, every pot in Jerusalem and in Judah shall be holiness unto the Lord of hosts: and all they that

sacrifice shall come and take of them, and seethe
therein: and in that day there shall be no more the
Canaanite in the house of the Lord of hosts.

(Zechariah 14:20–21)

In Zechariah 14:18, starting with the first letter of the
fourteenth word, which is *Jehovah* יהוה, taking the first
letter of every sixty-second word from right to left, and
overlapping into the book of Malachi spells *Jehovah*
"Adonai" יהוהי forward and backward. Also, the first and
last words used in this insight are *Jehovah* יהוה. The
adjacent letters spell "the truth" האמת.

These are awesome combinations that give us a clearer
understanding of how the Word of God was written and
encoded beneath the surface, giving absolute credence to
the divine authorship of all the Bible. The insights that link
together His Word and those that overlap the books of the
Bible have opened to us a clearer revelation of our Lord and
Savior, Yeshua HaMashiach. It would take volumes upon
volumes to bring forth all the overlapping combinations that
God has placed in His Word. We may have to wait until we
stand in His presence before we can rehearse the remainder
of this thought.

7

The Witness of the Torah: The Five Books of Moses

Each book of the Bible, beginning with Genesis, gives us a stunning array of portraits in type and prophecy of Jesus the Messiah. By dipping into God's reservoir of wisdom, we see Him portrayed by events and people throughout the Scriptures. A brief study of His magnificent Word will reflect some of these facts. When we treat the complete Bible as one seamless unit with various books, chapters, verses, and letters, we will have an understanding of why God wrote His Word in this manner. For example, Genesis 1:1 says, "In the beginning God created the heavens and the earth." Insights from separate books throughout the Bible reveal that Jesus is the Creator.

> Then He [Yeshua] said unto them, O fools, and slow of heart to believe all that the prophets have spoken: Ought not Christ [Messiah] to have suffered these things, and to enter into His glory? And beginning at Moses and all the prophets, He expounded unto

them in all the Scriptures the things concerning
Himself . . . And He said unto them, These are the
words which I spake unto you, while I was yet with
you, that all things must be fulfilled, which were
written in the law of Moses, and in the prophets, and
in the psalms, concerning Me. Then opened He their
understanding, that they might understand the
Scriptures.   (Luke 24:25–27, 44–45)

In the first book of the Torah, Genesis, we see Yeshua as
the Creator, the beginning, the seed of the woman, and the
promised Redeemer.

Genesis בראשית, The Creator and the Beginning

God, who at sundry times and in divers manners
spake in time past unto the fathers by the prophets,
Hath in these last days spoken unto us by His Son,
whom He hath appointed heir of all things, by whom
also He made the worlds.   (Hebrews 1:1–2)

He was in the world, and the world was made by
Him, and the world knew Him not.   (John 1:10)

In Whom we have redemption through His [Jesus']
blood, even the forgiveness of sins: Who is the image
of the invisible God, the firstborn of every creature:
For by Him [Jesus] were all things created, that are in
heaven, and that are in earth, visible and invisible,
whether they be thrones, or dominions, or principalities, or powers: all things were created by Him, and
for Him: And He is before all things, and by Him all
things consist. And He is the head of the body, the
church: Who is the beginning, the firstborn from the
dead; that in all things He might have the preemi-
nence. For it pleased the Father that in Him should
all fullness dwell.   (Colossians 1:14–19)

We can readily understand from the above Scriptures that Jesus (Yeshua) is the Creator. But there are many insights in the Torah and Tanakh that *prove* that Jesus is the Creator. We should never doubt God's Word under any circumstances.

> My words shall be of the uprightness of my heart: and my lips shall utter knowledge clearly. The Spirit of God hath made me, and the breath of the Almighty hath given me life. (Job 33:3–4)

רוח-אל עשתני ונשמת שדי תחיני
The Spirit of God hath made me, and the
breath of the Almighty hath given me life.

Every fifth letter from left to right gives us the name of the Maker, who is *Yeshua* ישוע. Also, every second letter spells "Messiah" משיח. The Word of God confirms that Yeshua the Messiah is the Maker and Creator. To give more proof that Jesus is the Maker, we need to go to the Torah. In Deuteronomy 22:27, starting with the second letter in the fourth word and counting every 270th letter from left to right spells *ohsai Yeshua* עשי ישוע, which means "Jesus my Maker." The Hebrew word for "my maker" עשי, when read in reverse, spells *Yeshua* ישע, which means "salvation" and is another way to spell the name of Jesus. Thus, we can see by this insight that not only is He our maker but He is also our salvation.

In Numbers 23:9, starting with the fourth letter in the fifth word and counting every 612th letter from right to left spells *Yeshua bara* ברא ישוע, which means "Jesus created." In Genesis 43:18, starting with the second letter in the twenty-second word and counting every 1084th letter from left to right spells "Jesus my Maker" עשי ישוע.

> I, even I, Am the Lord; and beside Me there is no saviour. I have declared, and have saved, and I have

showed, when there was no strange god among you: therefore ye are My witnesses, saith the Lord, that I Am God.   (Isaiah 43:11–12)

אנכי אנכי יהוה ואין מבלעדי ממשי: אנכי הגדתי והושעתי
והשמעתי ואין בכם זר ואתם עדי נאם יהוה יהוה ואני אל:

Every fourth letter gives us the name of the Creator, who is Jesus (*Yeshua* ישׁוע). In Deuteronomy 31:9, starting with the third letter in the fourteenth word, which is the yod (י) in the Hebrew word "covenant" ברית, and counting every 1013th letter from left to right spells "Jesus the Creator" *Yeshua yotzar* ישׁוע יוצר. Thus, we see that there are many Scriptures from the Tanakh (Old Testament) that give us proof that Yeshua the Messiah is the Creator.

Next, we turn to the seed of the woman and the promised Redeemer. Genesis 3:15 says, "And I will put enmity between thee and the woman, and between thy seed and her Seed; it [Yeshua] shall bruise thy head, and thou shalt bruise His heel." The Lord has encoded the name of the seed of the woman who shall bruise (crush) the head of the serpent. Starting with the third letter in the second word and counting every sixty-ninth letter from left to right spells *Yeshua* ישׁוע "Jesus." This Genesis passage is confirmed in the New Testament in Hebrews.

> Forasmuch then as the children are partakers of flesh and blood, He [Yeshua] also Himself likewise took part of the same; that through death He might destroy him [the serpent] that had the power of death, that is, the devil.   (Hebrews 2:14)

> And having spoiled principalities and powers, He made a shew of them openly, triumphing over them in it.   (Colossians 2:15)

He that committeth sin is of the devil; for the devil

sinneth from the beginning. For this purpose the Son of God [Yeshua] was manifested, that He might destroy the works of the devil.   (1 John 3:8)

When Jesus was arrested and crucified, He "opened not His mouth" because the purpose of His coming was to completely destroy the works of the Devil and all sin. Had Jesus been combative or had He resisted in any way, God's purpose for sending Him would have been in vain. Isaiah 53:7 reflects this prophecy: "He [Jesus] was oppressed, and He was afflicted, yet He opened not His mouth: He is brought as a lamb to the slaughter, and as a sheep before her shearers is dumb [אלם], so He openeth not His mouth." This was a prophecy concerning the Messiah Who would be as a silent lamb in order to fulfill the complete work of redemption for fallen humanity. Upon the crucifixion of God's Messiah, Satan actually believed that he had circumvented the plan of God by destroying the only solution to sin. The Devil, however, was defeated by the very weapon he used to try to thwart God's plan of salvation — the Cross (tree).

In Genesis 3:6, we see the fall of all humanity in the disobedient act of Adam and Eve, but God had worked out a solution to the problem long before sin entered into this world. God, who is omniscient (all-knowing), had previously anticipated the Fall as He developed a final and complete plan of salvation for His creation.

> And I beheld, and, lo, in the midst of the throne and of the four beasts, and in the midst of the elders, stood a Lamb [Jesus] as it had been slain, having seven horns and seven eyes, which are the seven Spirits of God sent forth into all the earth.
>
> (Revelation 5:6)

And all that dwell upon the earth shall worship him

[antichrist], whose names are not written in the book of life of the Lamb slain from the foundation of the world. (Revelation 13:8)

Forasmuch as ye know that ye were not redeemed with corruptible things, as silver and gold, from your vain conversation received by tradition from your fathers; But with the precious blood of Christ [Messiah], as of a lamb without blemish and without spot: Who verily was foreordained before the foundation of the world, but was manifest in these last times for you, Who by Him do believe in God, that raised Him up from the dead, and gave Him glory; that your faith and hope might be in God.

(1 Peter 1:18–21)

The fall of Adam and Eve was instant and to the point. Satan, by his arrogance and self-deception, thought that his plan would defeat God's wonderful creation. The accuser (Satan) really does believe his own lies. God, however, placed within the Scripture that depicts the fall of Adam and Eve encoded messages that reveal the awesome prophecy concerning the seed of the woman, the Messiah, as can be demonstrated in Genesis 3:6: "And when the woman saw that the tree was good for food, and that it was pleasant to the eyes, and a tree to be desired to make one wise, she took of the fruit thereof, and did eat, and gave also unto her husband with her; and he did eat." Starting with the third letter of the ninth word and counting every twentieth letter, from right to left, gives us four words, *ailem haMashiach me'ged qeri* אלם המשיח מגר קרי, which translates "dumb (silent)," "the eminent Messiah," "a hostile encounter."

This is exactly what happened when they arrested Jesus and crucified Him on the tree. Notice that the weapon (the tree) that the serpent used to deceive Eve was the method by which God brings humanity back from its hopeless condition. Also, encoded within the twenty-letter count are three very important words that give additional credence to the ELS method of analysis: (1) *Jehovah* יהוה; (2) *chanukkah* חנכה; (3) *kippah* כיפה. *Jehovah* is the name of our ineffable God; *chanukkah* means "dedication"; and *kippah* means "a covering (cap)."

Jesus, God's Son, was sent from heaven, and He dedicated Himself so that His blood could be a complete covering for our sins. The first two letters in the Hebrew word "dedication" *chanukkah* חנכה spell grace *chan* חן. Every time I hear the Hebrew for *chanukkah*, this Scripture rings out in my heart and mind with joy unspeakable: "Then he answered and spake unto me, saying, This is the word of the Lord unto Zerubbabel, saying, Not by might, nor by power, but by My Spirit, saith the Lord of hosts. Who art thou, O great mountain? before Zerubbabel thou shalt become a plain: and He shall bring forth the headstone thereof with shoutings, crying, Grace חן, Grace חן unto it." (Zechariah 4:6–7)

"For by grace [*chan* חן] are ye saved through faith; and that not of yourselves: it is the gift of God: not of works, lest any man should boast. For we are His workmanship, created in Christ Jesus unto good works, which God hath before ordained that we should walk in them. (Ephesians 2:8–10)

Exodus שמות, The Passover Lamb and Deliverer of God's People

The story of the Exodus and the first Passover has a greater meaning than simply the deliverance of a nation from the hand of slavery. The far-reaching effects and the meaning of the book of Exodus can bring deliverance and salvation to every person in all generations because of the new covenant (New Testament), which was ratified by Yeshua HaMashiach (Jesus the Messiah). His death, burial, and resurrection fulfills the meaning of the first Passover to the letter.

The entire house of Israel was in complete bondage to the Egyptians. It took the hand of God to deliver the children of Israel from the power of Egypt. God had a threefold plan for His chosen nation. Part one of the threefold plan was to introduce the Israelites to the first Passover, which was prophetic in nature. The second part of God's plan was the complete deliverance of the children of Israel from slavery and the destruction of their oppressors. The third part of His plan was to bring the children of Israel into the Promised Land. There were seven things that they had to do to qualify for the great deliverance:

1. Kill a lamb without spot or blemish on the fourteenth of the first month on the sacred calendar.

2. Put the blood of the lamb on the two side posts and the upper post of the house.

3. Roast and eat the lamb.

4. Eat unleavened bread for seven days.

5. Eat the bitter herbs.

6. Stay in their houses all night until the judgment passed.

7. Worship the God of Abraham, Isaac, and Jacob.

No stranger could participate in the Passover unless the males of the household submitted to circumcision and the keeping of the commandments of the Lord. All these commandments were necessary for their immediate deliverance from the bondage of the Egyptians and their gods. We see, however, a greater picture unfolding, based on all the qualifying commandments that they had to fulfill. This was merely the first Passover, which would be followed by many more until He, the Lamb of God, would come to fulfill all that this feast represents.

Jesus, our Passover Lamb, was sacrificed so that we could be delivered from our sins and the world. Our life is hidden in Jesus; we are shut in with God. His precious blood was applied to the doorpost of our hearts. The call goes out to every creature from every nation to accept the Son of God as the Passover Lamb. When we call upon Him for our salvation from the present wrath and the wrath that is to come, He automatically circumcises our hearts, thereby qualifying us for eternal salvation through Him. Jesus is spoken of as Passover Lamb in many passages:

> The next day John seeth Jesus coming unto him, and saith, Behold the Lamb of God, which taketh away the sin of the world. (John 1:29)

> Purge out therefore the old leaven, that ye may be a new lump, as ye are unleavened. For even Christ [Messiah] our Passover is sacrificed for us.
> (1 Corinthians 5:7)

> Giving thanks unto the Father, which hath made us meet to be partakers of the inheritance of the saints in light: Who hath delivered us from the power of darkness, and hath translated us into the kingdom of His dear Son: In whom we have redemption through His blood, even the forgiveness of sins.
> (Colossians 1:12–14)

Exodus 12:27 says, "That ye shall say, It is the sacrifice of the Lord's passover, who passed over the houses of the children of Israel in Egypt, when He smote the Egyptians, and delivered our houses. And the people bowed the head and worshipped."

> ואמרתם זבח-פסח הוא ליהוה אשר פסח על-בתי בני-ישראל במצרים
> That ye shall say, It is the sacrifice of the Lord's passover, who passed over the houses of the children of Israel in Egypt.

The above portion of Hebrew Scripture reveals some very interesting insights concerning the Passover Lamb. Starting with the last letter of the fifth word from the right and taking the last letter of each word spells *ha'rachel* הרחל, which means "the lamb." This is the same word used in Isaiah 53 when referring to Yeshua HaMashiach as a lamb led to the slaughter. Starting with the second-to-the-last mem (מ) from the far left and counting every fifth letter from left to right spells "Messiah" משׁיח. Starting from the ayin (ע) from the above and counting every 777th letter from right to left spells *Yeshua* ישׁוע. From this Scripture we have, the *Lamb, Messiah*, and *Yeshua* (Jesus). God has placed these remarkable finds here to prove beyond a shadow of a doubt that Jesus is the Messiah, the Lamb of God.

Other passages also refer to Jesus in light of the Passover. For example, in Exodus 12:5, starting with the second letter in the tenth word and counting every thirty-second letter from left to right spells the "burden of Messiah" משׂא משׁיח. The theme of Passover is Jesus the Messiah, and the burden of alleviating our sins was upon Him.

In the books of Leviticus and Deuteronomy, we find some very interesting encoded messages concerning the Lamb of God. For example, in Leviticus 21:15, starting with the second letter in the fifth word and counting every 548th letter from right to left spells "Lord Jesus, the Lamb" יה ישׁוע השׁה. In Deuteronomy 18:22, starting with the first letter in the sixteenth word and counting every 626th letter from right to left spells "Jesus, the Lamb" ישׁוע השׂה. Also, in a 626-letter sequence in this area, we find the Hebrew word for "the sin offering" *ha'ahshahm* האשׁם, twice.

In Exodus 14:31 we read, "And Israel saw that great work which the Lord did upon the Egyptians: and the people feared the Lord, and believed the Lord, and His servant Moses." Starting with the first letter in the eighth word, which is יהוה, and counting every second letter from left to right spells *Yisrael* יִשְׂרָאֵל. Starting with the first letter in the seventh word and counting every twenty-eighth letter from right to left spells *Yeshua* יֵשׁוּעַ. This combination extends into the fifteenth chapter where Moses and the children of Israel sing the song of deliverance. These combinations give the name of the nation that was saved and the name of the deliverer (Jesus). Truly, He is the Savior of Israel and the world.

Another combination that adds credence to our Lord Jesus is found in Exodus 14:30, starting with the second letter in the first word, which is "and saved" וַיּוֹשַׁע, and counting every thirty-first letter from right to left spells "He will save" יוֹשִׁיעַ. This gives us a future-tense picture of when our Lord will complete His salvation for all who believe in Him. We who have accepted Yeshua as our Lord and Savior are saved from the penalty of sin and are being saved from the power of sin in our daily lives. One day soon, we shall be saved from the very presence of sin.

Leviticus וַיִּקְרָא, Yeshua the High Priest

That by two immutable things, in which it was impossible for God to lie, we might have a strong consolation, who have fled for refuge to lay hold upon the hope set before us: Which hope we have as an anchor of the soul, both sure and stedfast, and which entereth into that within the veil; Whither the forerunner is for us entered, even Jesus, made an High Priest for ever after the order of Melchizedek.

(Hebrews 6:18–20)

The priestly order of Melchizedek is different from that of the Levitical priesthood, which was for Israel only. But the High Priest after the order of Melchizedek has entered into the Holy Place in heaven, and with His own spotless blood, he represents all people of every nation and all generations. God, however, has given us a prophetic picture of the High Priest after the order of Melchizedek, which is partly taken from the function of the order of the Levitical high priest in Psalm 110:4: "The Lord hath sworn, and will not repent, Thou art a Priest forever after the order of Melchizedek." Starting with the first letter in the second word, which is the yod (י) in *Jehovah* יהוה, and counting every 156th letter from right to left spells *Yeshua* ישוע. Also, starting with the last heh (ה) in יהוה and counting every twenty-second letter from left to right spells "the dedication" החנוך. This also is the name of Enoch.

Genesis 14:18 also speaks of Melchizedek: "And Melchizedek king of Salem brought forth bread and wine: and He was the priest of the most high God." Starting with the first letter of the eighteenth word and counting every thousandth letter from right to left spells *Yeshua* ישוע. The adjacent letters to the left of each letter in Yeshua's name spell *Melluki* מלוכי, which means "regnant (ruling, the greatest of power)." This one thousand letter count may represent the one thousand years of the messianic kingdom. The meaning of this title gives us a picture of the reign of our coming King, Yeshua, who is a Priest forever after the order of Melchisedek.

In Grant Jeffrey's new book, *The Handwriting of God*, Grant gives an expert analysis on this subject from the Dead Sea Scrolls. The writers of the scrolls mentioned Jesus the Messiah (*Yeshua HaMashiach*) as being none other than God אלהים and Melchizedek. Grant has completed a detailed study of this heavenly Melchizadek scroll that has been hidden for almost two thousand years. Truly, ours is the day of great revelation!

Aaron, the brother of Moses, was the first high priest of the Levitical order. He was Moses' spokesman when they stood before Pharoah. There are numerous prophetic typologies of Jesus portrayed in Aaron's duties as the high priest. For example, in Leviticus 9:2–3 we read, "And he said unto Aaron, Take thee a young calf for a sin offering, and a ram for a burnt offering, without blemish, and offer them before the Lord. And unto the children of Israel thou shalt speak, saying, Take ye a kid of the goats for a sin offering; and a calf and a lamb, both of the first year, without blemish, for a burnt offering."

Leviticus 9:3 is written out below in Hebrew script.

ואל-בני ישראל תדבר לאמר קחו שעיר-עזים
לחטאת ועגל וכבש בני-שנה תמימם לעלה

Every third letter beginning with the last yod (י) spells "Lord Jesus God" *Yah Yeshua El* יה ישוע אל. We see by this combination that Jesus, Lord, and God are one and the same. The word of God teaches us that the Lord God Himself took our infirmities and forgave our sins. Also, in the same area of Scripture we find "Messiah" משיח at both forty-two-letter intervals and at forty-eight-letter intervals.

In Numbers 1:1, starting with the first letter in the third word and counting every 1271st letter from right to left spells *ephod Yeshua Jehovah* אפד ישוע יהוה, which translates "the ephod (gird or girdle) Jesus Jehovah." Only the high priest could wear the ephod, which was a part of the garments attributed to his office. Since Jesus is the High Priest, He alone has the qualifications for the garments of this heavenly position. Revelation 1:13b says, "and girt about the paps with a golden girdle" (a garment of the high priest). In this series of the 1,271-letter count, we also find the words "peace" שלום and "holy" קרש.

> And God said unto Jacob, Arise, go up to Bethel, and dwell there: and make there an altar unto God, that appeared unto thee when thou fleddest from the face of Esau thy brother. Then Jacob said unto his household, and to all that were with him, Put away the strange gods that are among you, and be clean,

and change your garments: And let us arise, and go up to Bethel [the House of God]; and I will make there an altar unto God, who answered me in the day of my distress, and was with me in the way which I went. And they gave unto Jacob all the strange gods which were in their hand, and all their earrings which were in their ears; and Jacob hid them under the oak which was by Shechem.

(Genesis 35:1–4)

Encoded within these Scriptures are some very interesting insights that show us additional truths concerning Yeshua. His office was fourfold, which we will discuss in another chapter.

Notice the Hebrew of Genesis 35:4–5a:

ויתנו אל יעקב את כל אלהי הבכר אשר בידם
ואת הנזמים אשר באזניהם ויטמן אתם יעקב תחת
האלה אשר עם שכם: ויסעו ויהי חתת אלהים על

Starting with the third letter in the seventh word and counting every twelfth letter from right to left spells *Kohain Yeshua* כהן ישוע, which means "Priest Jesus." The adjacent letters that spell "Priest Jesus" are *Roi neer* רעי נר, which means "my shepherd lamp." Here, we find Jesus as shepherd, lamp, and priest. The center lamp of the menorah represents Yeshua the Messiah, as seen in Revelation 1:12–13: "And I turned to see the voice that spake with me. And being turned, I saw seven golden candlesticks [Menorah]; And in the midst [center] of the seven candlesticks one like unto the Son of man [Jesus], clothed with a garment down to the foot, and girt about the paps with a golden girdle."

In Deuteronomy 9:12, starting with the second letter of the first word and counting every 555th letter from right to left spells *Yeshua ha'cohain* ישוע הכהן, which translates "Jesus, the Priest."

Numbers במדבר, The Pillar of Cloud, Fire, and the Manna from on High

And they will tell it to the inhabitants of this land: for they have heard that thou Lord art among this people, that thou Lord art seen face to face, and that thy cloud standeth over them, and that thou goest before them, by day time in a pillar of a cloud, and in a pillar of fire by night. (Numbers 14:14)

Starting with the second letter in the first word and counting every 198th letter from right to left spells *Yeshua* ישׁוע. We again find the pillar in Exodus 13:21–22: "And the Lord went before them by day in a pillar of a cloud, to lead them the way; and by night in a pillar of fire, to give them light; to go by day and night: He took not away the pillar of the cloud by day, nor the pillar of fire by night, from before the people."

Exodus 14:1-2a says, "And the Lord spake unto Moses, saying, Speak unto the children of Israel, that they turn and encamp."

ולילה: לא-ימיש עמוד הענן יומם ועמוד האשׁ לילה לפני העם:
וידבר יהוה אל-משׁה לאמר: דבר אל-בני ישׂראל וישׁבו ויחנו

Starting with the second yod (י) from the far right and counting every third letter from right to left spells *Yeshua yemahmah* ישׁוע ימָמה, which means "Jesus twenty-four hours" — the whole day. The indication is that the glory of God was present every minute of the day. Did not the Lord promise that He would always be with us, even to the ends of the earth? Also, starting with the first yod (י) to the far right and counting every thirteenth letter from right to left spells *Yah HaMashiach* יה המשׁיח, which means "Lord, the Messiah." Isaiah 4:5 is a prophecy about the cloud by day and the pillar of fire by night. We will look at this Scripture when we discuss Joshua, the leader of Israel.

We also see Yeshua as the manna in the book of Numbers.

> And the manna was as coriander seed, and the colour thereof as the colour of bdellium. And the people went about, and gathered it, and ground it in mills, or beat it in a mortar, and baked it in pans, and made cakes of it: and the taste of it was as the taste of fresh oil. And when the dew fell upon the camp in the night, the manna fell upon it.
>
> (Numbers 11:7–9)

From the ayin (ע) in the Hebrew word "cakes" עֻגוֹת, taking the first letter of every thirty-fourth word, and counting in reverse spells *Yeshua* יֵשׁוע, which tells us that Yeshua is the Bread of Life that came down from heaven.

There are many more insights within this eleventh chapter of Numbers that relate directly to Yeshua the Messiah, Jerusalem, and Israel. In Numbers 11:1, starting with the second letter in the seventeenth word and counting every sixth letter from right to left spells "to find Yeshua" ישׁוע. In essence, the children of Israel were looking for the Messiah, but they were not aware of this fact. They complained about the simplicity of the manna and compared it to the spicy food of Egypt. Because they wanted to add to what the Lord had already given them, the Lord became angry and sent fire among them. We should never add anything to what God has given us because He knows best.

Then in Numbers 11:4, starting with the first letter in the tenth word, which is "Israel" יִשׂרָאֵל, and counting every thirtieth letter from left to right spells "Jerusalem" ירושלם. In Numbers 11:2, starting with the first letter in the eighth word, which is *Jehovah* יהוה, and counting every 139th letter from right to left spells "Yeshua Lord" ישׁוע יה. The encoded message seems to echo through the centuries with reference to another group of the sons of Israel who complained about the personified Manna who came down from heaven, as seen in the book of John.

> The Jews then murmured at Him, because He said, I am the Bread which came down from heaven. And they said, Is not this Jesus, the son of Joseph, whose father and mother we know? how is it then that He saith, I came down from heaven?   (John 6:41–42)

> Verily, verily, I say unto you, He that believeth on Me hath everlasting life. I am that Bread of Life. Your fathers did eat manna in the wilderness, and are dead. This is the Bread which cometh down from heaven, that a man may eat thereof, and not die. I am the Living Bread which came down from heaven: if any man eat of this Bread, he shall live for ever: and the Bread that I will give is My flesh, which I will give for the life of the world.   (John 6:47–51)

While in the wilderness, the children of Israel complained to Moses about their hunger and the fact that he had brought them into the desert to die. The Lord had a solution to their problem, as seen in Exodus 16:4, as He always does for all our problems: "Then said the Lord unto Moses, Behold, I will rain bread from heaven for you; and the people shall go out and gather a certain rate every day, that I may prove them, whether they will walk in My law, or no."

The Bible goes on to speak about bread in Exodus 16:29a: "See, for that the Lord hath given you the Sabbath, therefore He giveth you on the sixth day the bread of two days;"

ראו כי יהוה נתן לכם השבת על-כן
הוא נתן לכם ביום הששי לחם

Starting with the last chet (ח), every second letter left to right spells "life, heaven" חִי שָׁמַיִם. Starting with the second-to-the-last mem (מ) and counting every other letter from right to left spells "Messiah" *Mashiach* מָשִׁיח. Truly, the Messiah came from heaven, and He is the Bread of Life for all who would partake of Him. From the same mem (מ) where we found the word "Messiah," counting every 396th letter from right to left gives us the awesome encoded phrase "Messiah Adonai" *Mashiach Jehovah* מָשִׁיח יהוה. I am awestruck when uncovering such magnificent insights that give glory to God! If we do not give Him the praise and glory, the discovery of such beautiful encoded messages would not be to any advantage except to prove that God wrote the Bible by His Holy Spirit when He moved upon holy men who were obedient to the call.

> And when the dew that lay was gone up, behold, upon the face of the wilderness there lay a small round thing, as small as the hoar frost on the ground. And when the children of Israel saw it, they said one to another, It is manna: for they wist not what it was. And Moses said unto them, This is the bread which the Lord hath given you to eat. (Exodus 16:14–15)

The original Hebrew from the Masoretic text says, "Each man to his brother, What is that?" *ish el achiav mahn hu* אִישׁ אֶל אָחִיו מָן הוּא. Starting with the chet (ח) in the phrase "his brother" and counting every seven hundredth letter from right to left spells "Messiah" מָשִׁיח. The seven hundred-letter count may refer to the messianic kingdom when we come into the final Sabbath.

The Hebrew word for "the Manna" *ha'mahn* הַמָּן, means "What is it?" or "What is that?" Jesus answered this question fifteen hundred years later in John 6 when He said, "I am the Bread that cometh down from heaven."

Deuteronomy הדברים, Yeshua, a Prophet Like unto Moses

> The Lord thy God will raise up unto thee a Prophet from the midst of thee, of thy brethren, like unto me; unto Him ye shall hearken; . . . I will raise them up a Prophet from among their brethren, like unto thee, and will put My words in His mouth; and He shall speak unto them all that I shall command Him.
>
> (Deuteronomy 18:15, 18)

> And there arose not a prophet since in Israel like unto Moses, whom the Lord knew face to face.
>
> (Deuteronomy 34:10)

The name of Yeshua appears at least six times in this area of Scripture at various equally spaced letter intervals. One example is found in Deuteronomy 34:12, starting with the second letter in the third word and counting every seventy-second letter from left to right spells "life Yeshua" חי ישוע.

The New Testament, in Matthew 21:9–11, bears witness to the fact that Yeshua is the prophet about whom Moses foretold.

> And the multitudes that went before, and that followed, cried, saying, Hosanna to the Son of David: Blessed is He that cometh in the Name of the Lord; Hosanna in the highest. And when He was come into Jerusalem, all the city was moved, saying, Who is this? And the multitude said, This is Jesus the Prophet of Nazareth of Galilee.   (Matthew 21:9–11)

The Hebrew phrase "Blessed is He that cometh in the name of the Lord" was a prophecy from Psalms 118:26. In this Psalm is encoded the words *Yeshua* ישוע at 433-letter intervals and *Messiah* משיח at 169-letter intervals. Also, there is another sequence that must to be examined in Psalm 118:12. Starting with the second letter in the eighth word and counting every 173rd letter from left to right spells "Lord Jesus" יה ישוע. This insight overlaps into Psalms 117 and 116. We find verification of this in John and Revelation.

> They say unto the blind man again, What sayest thou of Him, that He hath opened thine eyes? He said, He is a prophet. (John 9:17)

> And I fell at his feet to worship him, And he said unto me, See thou do it not: I am thy fellowservant, and of thy brethren that have the testimony of Jesus: worship God: for the testimony of Jesus is the spirit of prophecy. (Revelation 19:10)

Since Jesus is the true Prophet of God, He is the source of all prophecy, and He is the Prophet of prophets.

> When all Israel is come to appear before the Lord thy God in the place which He shall choose, thou shalt read this law [Torah] before all Israel in their hearing. (Deuteronomy 31:11)

במקום אשר יבחר

in the place which He shall choose

Every other letter in the Hebrew text above spells *Mashiach* משיח. The place about which the Lord is speaking is Jerusalem — the place where His name is forever imprinted. Continuing on in Deuteronomy 31 gives us more information concerning the place that the Lord chose for His name, His city, and His people.

> Gather the people together, men, and women, and children, and thy stranger that is within thy gates, that they may hear, and that they may learn, and fear the Lord your God, and observe to do all the words

of this law [Torah]: And that their children, which have not known any thing, may hear, and learn to fear the Lord your God, as long as ye live in the land whither ye go over Jordan to possess it.

(Deuteronomy 31:12–13)

Encoded within these Scriptures is the name of the Messiah. Starting with the first letter in the ninth word in verse 13, and counting every 130th letter from right to left spells *Yeshua* ישוע. In the same 130-letter count, starting with the fourth letter in the seventeenth word of verse 19 from right to left spells *Torah* תורה. Here, we see Jesus directly associated with the Torah in relation to Israel. He is the prophet about whom Moses spoke. There are many other insights throughout the five books of Moses that are directly linked to Yeshua and the Torah.

In Deuteronomy 31:17, starting with the sixth letter in the sixth word and counting every 125th letter from right to left spells *Yeshua* ישוע. Starting with the yod (י) in *Yeshua* ישוע and counting every 375th letter (3 × 125), from left to right spells *Jehovah* יהוה. What are the probabilities of these combinations happening by chance?

Jesus took upon Himself four major roles for our complete salvation and joint heirship with Him: (1) Prophet, (2) Priest, (3) King, (4) Servant. The encoded messages as well as the surface reading reveal to us for all time each of these positions that Jesus came to fulfill for our benefit. Many times an insight will be found in one book and the remainder of that message may be found in another book, both of which may be written many centuries apart from one another.

In Jonah 4:7, starting with the fourth letter in the second word and counting every 243rd letter from left to right spells "the prophet" *ha'navee* הנביא. The adjacent letters and counting every 243rd letter from left to right spell *le'choshen kain Yeshua* עושׁי כן לחשׁן, which translates "the breastplate or office of Jesus, to set upright, honest, truthful." Only the high priest could wear the breastplate, which contained the twelve gems, the names of the tribes of Israel, and the Urim and Thummim. Also, in this insight, we have the word for prophet directly associated with Jesus. These encoded jewels reveal two very important positions of Jesus — one is as the High Priest and the other the Prophet.

8

Joshua, Judges, and Ruth: The Judges
Joshua יהושע The Captain of Our Salvation

The name "Joshua" יהושע means "the Lord of my salvation." This is another name for Jesus, who is our High Priest and Savior.

Joshua was the son of Nun of the tribe of Ephraim. In Numbers 13:16, God changed his name from *Hoshea* הושע, which means "deliverer or salvation," to "Joshua" *Yehoshua*, which translates "the Lord of my salvation" or "salvation of the Lord." The name "Joshua" is associated with several major events and messianic terms throughout the Bible. The first event is when Joshua brought the whole house of Israel to the Promised Land. This is also a prophetic picture of the messianic age. Joshua is directly associated with the terms *king*, *priest*, *prophet*, *branch*, and *servant*. These are titles for Jesus the Messiah, who is our King, Priest, Prophet, Branch, and Servant. He will bring forth the complete fulfillment of each of His titles.

Zechariah 3:8 says, "Hear now, O Joshua the High Priest, thou, and thy fellows that sit before thee: for they are men wondered at: for, behold, I will bring forth My Servant the BRANCH." The Hebrew word for "branch" צמח is a messianic word that refers to Jesus the Messiah. Yeshua, the Branch, took upon Himself all our leaven (sin). When you reverse the letters in the Hebrew word *tzamach* צמח "branch," it spells "leaven" *chamatz* חמץ. Isaiah 4:2, 5 says, "In that day shall the Branch of the Lord be beautiful and glorious, and the fruit of the earth shall be excellent and comely for them that are escaped of Israel. . . . And the Lord will create upon every dwelling place of mount Zion, and upon her assemblies, a cloud and smoke by day, and the shining of a flaming fire by night: for upon all the glory shall be a defence." In verse five, the phrase "and smoke" is ועשן. Counting every 136th letter from the ayin (ע), from left to right spells "the lamp Yeshua" נר ישוע. Jesus is the fire that will bring protection, and the smoke from that fire is the glory of God that will fill all the land of Israel. This is the same pillar of cloud and fire from which God protected Israel during their trek in the wilderness. This is, however, a prophecy concerning the messianic kingdom. In Jeremiah 23:5 we read, "Behold, the days come, saith the Lord, that I will raise unto David a righteous Branch, and a King shall reign and prosper, and shall execute judgment and justice in the earth." Within this chapter, the name of the king and branch are encoded beneath the surface reading of the Scripture.

In Jeremiah 23:9, starting with the fifth letter in the first word and counting every ninety-sixth letter from left to right spells "Jesus Lord" *Yeshua Yah* ישוע יה. It is so astounding to find such magnificent insights directly associated with Jesus, our Lord and Savior.

Joshua was the captain of Israel's great army when they went into battle with the pagan nations that occupied the territory of Israel that was promised to Abraham, Isaac, and Jacob. One of the most difficult obstacles that Israel encountered was the walls of Jericho and the city's mighty men of valor, but God had a plan to deliver Jericho into the hands of Joshua. He commanded all the children of Israel to participate in the fall of this feared, pagan nation.

> And seven priests shall bear before the ark seven trumpets of rams' horns: and the seventh day ye shall compass the city seven times, and the priests shall blow with the trumpets. And it shall come to pass, that when they make a long blast with the ram's horn, and when ye hear the sound of the trumpet, all the people shall shout with a great shout; and the wall of the city shall fall down flat, and the people shall ascend up every man straight before him. (Joshua 6:4–5)

In Joshua 6:4, starting with the sixth letter in the sixteenth word and counting every twentieth letter from right to left spells *Yeshuati Yah* יה ישועתי, which means "my Jesus, Lord" or "my Lord Jesus." From this simple analysis, we have found the leader of the army of Israel, who was working behind the scenes on behalf of God's people. Truly, He is the captain of our salvation, as seen in the book of Hebrews.

> Thou hast put all things in subjection under His feet. For in that He put all in subjection under Him, He left nothing that is not put under Him. But now we see not yet all things put under Him. But we see Jesus, who was made a little lower than the angels for the suffering of death, crowned with glory and honor; that He by the grace of God should taste death for every man. For it became Him, for whom

are all things, and by whom are all things, in bringing many sons unto glory, to make the Captain of their Salvation perfect through sufferings. For both He that sanctifieth and they who are sanctified are all of one: for which cause He is not ashamed to call them brethren, Saying, I will declare Thy name unto My brethren, in the midst of the church [assembly] will I sing praise unto Thee.　　　　　(Hebrews 2:8–11)

The walls of Jericho were an awesome picture of the walls that separate us from God because of our sinful nature. But God, who is full of grace, broke the walls down and flattened them so that we may come boldly to the throne room of grace in time of need.

A remarkable discovery has been made in the 1930s excavation of the walls of Jericho. In 1996, Grant Jeffrey authored the book *The Signature of God* in which he described the archeological discovery by Dr. John Garstang concerning the walls of Jericho. He gives proof in his book that the walls fell down and tumbled outward, precisely as the Bible recorded thousands of years ago in the words of Moses.

Judges שׁופטים, The Judge and Law-Giver and the Sword of Gideon

Fifteen judges ruled the land of Israel between the time of Joshua and the coronation of King Saul. Deborah was the fourth and Samuel was the fifteenth and last judge of Israel. Deborah was also a prophetess whom God anointed to judge Israel and deliver them from their enemies, as seen in Judges 4:4: "And Deborah, a prophetess, the wife of Lapidoth, she judged Israel at that time. And she dwelt under the palm tree of Deborah between Ramah and Bethel in mount Ephraim: and the children of Israel came up to her for judgment."

Our Lord is always in the background, directing events

by His Spirit. As Deborah judged Israel and prophesied, so we, who are believers, must judge spiritual matters in this life. But the day is coming when we shall judge the world in concert with our Lord and Savior, Jesus the Messiah. Jesus will judge the nations who came against His people when He returns to set up His kingdom.

In Judges 4:3, starting with the third letter in the fifteenth word and counting every forty-second letter from right to left spells "Lord Jesus" יה ישוע. The adjacent letters spell "king" מלך. The office of the king functions in judgment, with both negative and positive results.

The Song of Deborah

They that are delivered from the noise of archers in the places of drawing water, there shall they rehearse the righteous acts of the Lord, even the righteous acts toward the inhabitants of his villages in Israel: then shall the people of the Lord go down to the gates. Awake, awake, Deborah: awake, awake, utter a song: arise, Barak, and lead thy captivity captive, thou son of Abinoam.

(Judges 5:11–12)

This is a messianic song that reveals several insights. The gates were opened and Barak led the captivity captive. Barak means "thunder (shine)." His father's name, Abinoam, means "gracious (pleasant) father." These terms allude to Jesus, who led captivity captive and gave gifts unto men. He shall open the gates of heaven some day soon to deliver us from the fiery arrows (darts) of the Devil. We have drawn water from the wells of salvation (Yeshua).

מקול מחצצים בין משאבים שם יתנו צדקות יהוה צדקת
פרזונו בישראל אז ירדו לשערים עם-יהוה: עורי עורי דבורה
עורי עורי דברי-שיר קום ברק ושבה שביך בן אבינעם:

(Judges 5:11–12)

In Judges 5:11, starting with the first letter in the sixth word and counting every twelfth letter from right to left spells "Lord Jesus" יה ישוע. Starting with the first chet (ח) to the far upper right and counting every twelfth letter from right to left spells "Torah, life, the breach mended (repaired)" *chai Torah badak* חי תורה ברק. Also, from the ayin (ע) in Yeshua's name and counting every twenty-first letter in both directions spells "elevated Yeshua" ישוע ירמי. To have all three of these insights in relationship to the subject matter is quite phenomenal.

Isaiah 58:12 says, "And they that shall be of thee shall build the old waste places: thou shalt raise up the foundations of many generations; and thou shalt be called, the repairer of the breach, the restorer of paths to dwell in." This is a messianic prophecy that refers to the time of Jesus' death, burial, and resurrection. Also, this refers to the messianic kingdom age when the Lord Jesus returns again to build up the Tabernacle of David that has fallen down. Encoded within this Scripture is the name of the one who shall repair the breach. Starting with the second letter of the fifteenth word in Isaiah 58:12 and counting every thirteenth letter from right to left spells "Prince Jesus" *Sar Yeshua* שר ישוע.

In the Torah, there are several encoded combinations that reveal the titles "the Judge Jesus" and "Jesus the Judge." In Numbers 23:12, starting with the second letter in the sixth word and counting every 549th letter from right to left spells "Judge Jesus" *Shophaht Yeshua* שפט ישע. In Leviticus 14:10, starting with the third letter in the fourth word and counting every 570th letter from right to left spells "Jesus the Judge" *Yeshua din* ישוע דין. This Hebrew word *din* דין, means "to judge, advocate, rule, to minister justice," as seen in Psalm 7:8–10: "The Lord shall judge the people: judge me, O Lord, according to my righteousness, and according to mine integrity that is in me. Oh let the wickedness of the wicked come to an end; but establish the just: for the righteous God trieth the hearts and reins. My defence is of God, which saveth the upright in heart."

Verses 9, 10, and 11 of Psalm 7 are printed below in Hebrew from the Masoretic text:

יהוה ידין עמים שפטני יהוה כצדקי וכתמי עלי:
יגמר-נא רע רשעים ותכונן צדיק ובחן לבות וכליות
אלהים צדיק: מגני על-אלהים מושיע ישרי-לב:

This Psalm and many others tell us that the Lord will judge not only the righteous but the wicked as well. The encoded message gives us the name of the judge before whom all must stand. In Psalm 7:9, starting with the first letter of the fifth word, which is *Jehovah* יהוה and counting every twenty-sixth letter from right to left spells *Yeshua* ישוע. In Psalm 7:10, starting with the fifth letter in the tenth word and counting every thirty-second letter from right to left spells "Messiah" משיח. The insights in these Scripture verses have revealed to us that Yeshua the Messiah is the person who shall judge. Second Timothy 4:1–2a speaks of this judgment: "I charge thee therefore before God, and the Lord Jesus Christ, Who shall judge the quick and the dead at His appearing and His kingdom. Preach the word." We also see this judgment in Revelation 19:11: "And I saw Heaven opened, and behold a white horse; and He that sat upon him was called faithful and true, and in righteousness He doth judge and make war."

Ruth רות, The Kinsman-Redeemer

I say the truth in Christ [Messiah], I lie not, my conscience also bearing me witness in the Holy Ghost, that I have great heaviness and continual sorrow in my heart. For I could wish that myself were accursed from Christ for my brethren, my kinsmen according to the flesh: Who are Israelites; to whom pertaineth the adoption, and the glory, and the covenants, and the giving of the law [Torah], and the service of God, and the promises; Whose are the fathers, and of whom as concerning the flesh Christ came, Who is over all, God blessed for ever. Amen.

(Romans 9:1–5)

The book of Ruth is messianic from the beginning to the end. Boaz, a type of the Messiah, is the principal character in this book, and was called a kinsman-redeemer because he married Ruth, the Moabite, thus bestowing on her the royal parental lineage that would eventually bring forth the Messiah. Ruth was grafted into the commonwealth of Israel when she adopted the laws of God, the Torah, and became the bride of Boaz.

Ruth is also a picture of the believing Gentile nations that form part of the body of Messiah. Boaz and Ruth were great-grandparents of King David, who also was a type of the Messiah. There is an insight in the Hebrew that provides a glimpse of Ruth's destiny. In many places throughout the book of Ruth, her name is preceded by the aleph and the tav, *et-Ruth* את-רות. If you read this in reverse, it spells "the laws" תרות. Her life became centered around the Torah from the time her first husband died. Ruth's mother in-law, Naomi, until the day she died, was a great influence on Ruth.

Boaz took Ruth to be his bride in accordance with the old tradition of kinsman-redeemer. Their marriage took place in what was to become David's ancestral home, Bethlehem, Ephratah of Judah, the same town in which Jesus was to be born. Ruth 1:1 reads, "Now it came to pass in the days when the judges ruled, that there was a famine in the land."

ויהי בימי שפט השפטים ויהי רעב בארץ

Encoded within this first verse of the book of Ruth is the name of the Messiah, *Yeshua* יֵשׁוּעַ "Jesus." Starting with the fourth yod (י) to the far right and counting every fifth letter from right to left spells "Yeshua" יֵשׁוּעַ. This is an amazing discovery that sets a precedence throughout the book of Ruth. With the insights that are directly related to the genealogy of Boaz, Ruth, and Yeshua the Messiah, one would have to be very foolish or completely deceived not to accept Him as Lord and Savior.

In Ruth 1:1, starting with the ayin (עַ) in the name of Yeshua from the above insight and counting every seventy-seventh letter from right to left spells *Yeshua* יֵשׁוּעַ. From the same ayin and counting every fifteenth letter from right to left spells *Oshiah* אוֹשִׁיעַ, which means "He will save." How amazing and enlightening the Word of God is — that He would reveal unto us these astonishing parallels, giving us absolute proof that God wrote the Bible!

Boaz was a judge and a type of king, as well a kinsman-redeemer in his own right. He was from the tribe of Judah and was a great leader in his day. There are many things that Boaz did in his lifetime that reflect the Messiah in many ways. There is not enough space or time, however, to bring all of these wonderful insights forward in this book.

In Ruth 1:8, starting with the fourth letter in the first word and counting every twelfth letter from left to right spells "Melek Yeshua" מֶלֶךְ יֵשׁוּעַ, which means "King Yeshua."

In the book of Genesis, the first book of the Torah, there are encoded combinations that astonish all those who examine this evidence. Genesis 37:28 says, "Then there passed by Midianites merchantmen; and they drew and lifted up Joseph out of the pit, and sold Joseph to the Ishmaelites for twenty pieces of silver: And they brought Joseph into Egypt." In the phrase "and they sold Joseph" *va'yim'kru et Yoseph* וַיִּמְכְּרוּ אֶת-יוֹסֵף, starting with the first yod (י) to the far right and counting every forty-ninth letter from right to left spells "Yeshua" יֵשׁוּעַ. This insight helps us to understand the typeology that Joseph portrayed. Yeshua was betrayed by His own friend and disciple for thirty pieces of silver, making it possible for Him to be a kinsman-redeemer.

Following the insight in Genesis 37:28, where we located the word *Yeshua*, the complete genealogy of Boaz was found to the fourth generation. In Genesis 38:11, starting with the second bet (ב) and counting every forty-ninth letter from left to right, spells *Boaz* בֹּעַז. In the same verse, starting with the second to last resh (ר) and counting every forty-ninth letter from left to right spells "Ruth" רוּת, the wife of Boaz. In Genesis 38:20, starting with the last ayin (ע) and counting every forty-ninth letter from left to right spells "Obed" עֹבֵד, the son of Boaz and Ruth. In Genesis 38:25, starting with the second to last yod (י) and counting every forty-ninthth letter from left to right spells "Jesse" יִשַׁי, the son of Obed. In Genesis 38:26, starting with the first dalet (ד) and counting every forty-ninth letter from left to right spells "David" דָּוִד, who was the son of Jesse. In Genesis 38:14, starting with the fourth letter in the sixteenth word and counting every seventy-seventh letter from left to right spells "the Messiah" הַמָּשִׁיחַ. The area where the Messiah is encoded is in the same passage where we found the following names of every significant ancestor of King David encoded at forty-nine letter intervals: Yeshua, Boaz, Ruth, Obed, Jesse, and David. This is the same letter-count in the first chapter of Ruth, where we also found Yeshua at seventy-seven-letter intervals.

In Ruth 4:14–15, the women of Israel prophesy to Naomi concerning her daughter-in-law, Ruth. They told her that through Obed, Ruth's baby boy, and his descendants, there would come a famous kinsman (alluding to King David, selected by God through the prophet Samuel). They also told Naomi that because of Ruth's genuine love and respect for her mother-in-law, Naomi would consider Ruth as the equivalent of seven sons.

> And the women said unto Naomi, Blessed be the Lord, which hath not left thee this day without a kinsman, that his name may be famous in Israel. And he shall be unto thee a restorer of thy life, and a nourisher of thine old age: for thy daughter-in-law, which loveth thee, which is better to thee than seven sons, hath born him. (Ruth 4:14–15)

David, the eighth and youngest son of Jesse, was a type of the Messiah; he was the best choice of his seven brothers to become the king of Israel. From Ruth to the fourth generation came forth the one who was better than the seven other sons of Jesse and was to be the shepherd and ruler of all Israel.

In Ruth 4:4, starting with the fourth mem (מ) and counting every 371st letter from left to right spells "Messiah" מָשִׁיחַ. The adjacent letters to the left of each of the letters that form "Messiah" spell "from Israel" מִישְׂרָאֵל. It would be impossible for men, gifted with the greatest of intelligence and using the most advanced super-computers, to compose such a stunning array of codes that span over four hundred years? Moses wrote the book of Genesis about four centuries before the book of Ruth was written. The authors of both books had no earthly way of knowing what the other would write. We must conclude, in light of the evidence presented in this text, that a supernatural mind that is so superior to the combined knowledge and wisdom of all mankind authored the Bible through the inspiration of His divine Spirit.

9

Samuel, Kings, and Chronicles: The Matters of Kings and Prophets

Samuel, born of Levitical parents, was considered to be one of the noblest and purest of characters in biblical history. His father's name was Elkanah אלקנה, which means "God has obtained." His mother's name was Hannah חנה, which means "grace, gracious, merciful." Samuel's name means "his name is God" שמואל. At Samuel's birth, his mother dedicated him to the Lord. Samuel became one of the greatest prophets in the Scriptures, serving as a priest, prophet, and judge. He anointed the first two kings of Israel, Saul and David, and continued to give spiritual advice to the leaders and people of the land of Israel until the day he died. The meaning of Samuel's name and those of his parents seem to reflect his life in an unusual way. His accurate prophecies and his dedication to the Lord won him a position as Israel's faithful prophet. Samuel was also a picture of the coming Messiah. The coming Messiah would be called Faithful and True, as seen in Revelation 19:11: "And I saw Heaven opened, and behold a white horse; and He that sat upon him was called Faithful and True, and in righteousness He doth judge and make war."

> But unto Hannah he gave a worthy portion; for he loved Hannah: but the Lord had shut up her womb.
> (1 Samuel 1:5)

> And they rose up in the morning early, and worshipped before the Lord, and returned, and came to their house to Ramah: and Elkanah knew Hannah his wife; and the Lord remembered her. Wherefore it came to pass, when the time was come about after Hannah had conceived, that she bore a son, and called his name Samuel, saying, Because I have asked him of the Lord.   (1 Samuel 1:19–20)

Samuel's conception and birth was a miracle; however, Jesus' conception and birth was the greater miracle because Mary was a virgin. Nevertheless, there are many similarities in the typology of Samuel to Jesus. In 1 Samuel 1:2, starting with the second letter in the fourteenth word and counting every sixty-first letter from right to left spells *Yeshua bekahtuvo* בכתבו ישוע, which translates "his writing (recording) of Yeshua." Samuel had a revelation of Yeshua the Messiah that transcends most of the types who portrayed their roles as the Messiah.

> The Lord killeth, and maketh alive: He bringeth down to the grave [hades שאול], and bringeth up. The Lord maketh poor, and maketh rich: He bringeth low, and lifteth up. He raiseth up the poor out of the dust, and lifteth up the beggar from the dunghill, to set them among princes, and to make them inherit the throne of glory: for the pillars of the earth are the Lord's, and He hath set the world upon them. He

will keep the feet of His saints, and the wicked shall be silent in darkness; for by strength shall no man prevail. The adversaries of the Lord shall be broken to pieces; out of Heaven shall He thunder upon them: the Lord shall judge the ends of the earth; and He shall give strength unto His king, and exalt the horn of His anointed [Messiah].   (1 Samuel 2:6–10)

Within the above Scripture, there are several prophetic pictures of Jesus as Maker, Giver of Life, Resurrection, Messiah, and Judge:

1. He killeth and maketh alive.
2. He resurrects from the grave.
3. He prospers His people.
4. He sets us among the princes.
5. He causes us to inherit the throne of His glory.
6. He keeps the feet of His saints.
7. He destroys His enemies.
8. He judges the ends of the earth.
9. He gives strength to His king.
10. He exalts the horn of His Messiah.

Also, there are several insights that reveal the name of the Messiah. In 1 Samuel 2:8, starting with the second letter in the seventeenth word and counting every thirty-second letter from right to left spells *Yeshua* ישׁוע. In 1 Samuel 1:28, starting with the fourth letter in the second word and counting every twenty-second letter spells *Yeshua* ישׁוע. The adjacent letters spell "lampstand" *menorah* מנרה.

עלו בשׁמים ירעם

Out of heaven He shall thunder upon [against] them.

Starting with the ayin (ע) to the far right, every second letter in reverse spells *Yeshua* ישׁוע.

Samuel was anointed by God to function as the

interceding priest on behalf of Israel and her sin. This is yet another portrait of Yeshua.

> Wherefore the sin of the young men was very great before the Lord: for men abhorred the offering of the Lord. But Samuel ministered before the Lord, being a child, girded with a linen ephod [the garment of the high priest]. Moreover his mother made him a little coat [mantle], and brought it to him from year to year, when she came up with her husband to offer the yearly sacrifice. (1 Samuel 2:17–19)

In 1 Samuel 2:18, starting with the first letter in the seventh word, which is "girded" חגור, and counting every ninth word from right to left, reading only the first letter of each word spells "chalah Yeshua Yah" חלהישׁועיה, which means "punctured bread, Yeshua Lord." This is a picture of the sacrificial Lamb of God, the Bread who came down from heaven and who was pierced for us.

Samuel's crowning achievement was his anointing of David as king of Israel; it was also a direct edict from the Lord of heaven. This was a prophetic picture of the anointing of God's Messiah, Yeshua. The insights in 1 Samuel 16:13 reflect this truth: "Then Samuel took the horn of oil, and anointed him in the midst of his brethren: and the Spirit of the Lord came upon David from that day forward. So Samuel rose up, and went to Ramah."

רוח-יהוה אל-דוד
The Spirit of the Lord on David

Starting with the yod (י) in "the Lord" *Jehovah* יהוה, taking the first letter of each tenth word from left to right, spells *Yeshua* ישׁוע. What is so interesting about this insight is that the shin (שׁ) that is used in Yeshua's name is also used in two other encoded words that spell the name *Yeshua* ישׁוע. One is at twenty-nine-letter intervals and the other at sixty-one-letter intervals. Throughout this text, the names of Jesus and Messiah are marvelously encoded at least six times.

Samuel was the founder of the first religious school of higher learning that was concerned with the laws and concepts of God, that had disciples תלמדים, and that had a system of learning that set a standard for the other prophets. Yeshua chose His disciples, setting a standard that paralleled that of Samuel. Samuel's institution of learning, however, was a picture of the heavenly standard that Jesus also set for all believers.

Do we have any doubts at all about who the author of the Bible is? Only God could have divinely inserted each letter in its proper place so as to reveal to us His magnificent signature in His Word. There are many other thoughts on Samuel that could fill volumes — too many to bring forth at this time.

David was a shepherd and a reigning king. David's name means "beloved" דוד. His love for his father's sheep won him a place with the great shepherds of all time. He had protected the fold with his sling and stone when he killed the lion and bear. David was willing to give his life, if necessary, for his father's flock. Jesse, David's father, loved him. This, of course, is a picture of our Lord Jesus, who is the good, great, and faithful Shepherd of His sheep, as seen in John 10:14–16: "Jesus said, I Am the Good Shepherd, and know My sheep, and am known of Mine. As the Father knoweth Me, even so know I the Father: and I lay down My life for the sheep. And other sheep I have which are not of this fold: them also I must bring, and they shall hear My voice; and there shall be one fold, and one Shepherd."

After Samuel anointed him to be king of all Israel, David met and killed Goliath, the Philistine, on the battlefield. With one stroke of the expert's weapon, David slew and beheaded the enemy of Israel. He had a great love for Israel and a disdain for the Philistines because they defied the Lord God and His people.

> And David said to Saul, Let no man's heart fail because of him; thy servant will go and fight with this Philistine. . . . So David prevailed over the Philistine with a sling and with a stone, and smote the Philistine, and slew him; but there was no sword in the hand of David. Therefore David ran, and stood upon the Philistine, and took his sword, and drew it out of the sheath thereof, and slew him, and cut off his head therewith. And when the Philistines saw their champion was dead, they fled.
>
> (1 Samuel 17:32, 50–51)

In 1 Samuel 17:32, starting with the yod (י) of the phrase "your (thy) servant will go" *avedka yailek* עבדך ילך, counting every twelfth word from left to right, and reading the first letter of each word spells *Yeshua* ישוע. Continue counting, taking the first letter of every twelfth word to the right, and you will have the sentence *lu mush ohav hu Yeshua* לוא מוש אהב הוא ישוע. This means "I pray thee, feel the love; He is Jesus." Perhaps the interval of twelve has something to do with the twelve tribes of Israel.

David was the king's servant who faced the enemy in a fight to the death. Jesus faced our enemy, Satan, and was victorious when He crushed the head of the serpent. The sword, the weapon that Goliath was going to use against David, became the very weapon that David used to cut off Goliath's head. So it was with Jesus — the weapon that Satan used to kill our Messiah became the instrument that destroyed the Serpent, putting to flight his army of demons. The nails that pierced Jesus' hands and feet did not keep Him on the cross; it was His love for you and me that caused Him to endure to the end.

David was anointed (crowned) king three times in his

lifetime. The first time was when Samuel anointed him in the house of Jesse, his father. The second time was when David became king over the house of Judah, reigning for seven years and six months. The third time was when David became king of all Israel, reigning for thirty-three years. Every time David was anointed king, it was as though he was being crowned anew. We see a parallel in the crowning of Jesus. The first time Jesus was crowned was with thorns that pierced Him through His skull. The second time will be when all believers crown Him King of Kings in heaven. According to my understanding of prophecy, we shall be with Him at least seven years before the final coronation. The third and last time that Jesus will be crowned will be in Jerusalem, where Israel will crown Him the King of all the twelve tribes of Israel, as well as the world.

When David came face-to-face with the Philistine Goliath, he had no doubt in his mind as to who would be the winner of the contest of life. Encoded within this text is the name of the person whom David was portraying. In 1 Samuel 17:51, starting with the fifth letter in the seventeenth word and counting every twenty-third letter from right to left spells Yeshua יֵשׁוּעַ.

Hebrews 12:2 says, "Looking unto Jesus the Author and Finisher of our faith; Who for the joy that was set before Him endured the cross, despising the shame, and is set down at the right hand of the throne of God." We have a sure foundation in our God. Jesus is the chief cornerstone, and we are His lively stones. Satan was defeated from before the foundation of the world. The problem that Satan had, however, is that he believed his own lies. He thought he could eliminate God's Messiah by the method of execution on the cross, but it became not only Satan's demise but also the salvation of all who would believe and receive Jesus as their substitute. Colossians 2:14–15 says, "Blotting out the handwriting of ordinances that was against us, which was contrary to us, and took it out of the way, nailing it to His cross; And having spoiled principalities and powers, He made a shew of them openly, triumphing over them in it [in Himself.]"

The prophecy that King David would sit on the throne of Israel forever must be understood from a messianic point of view.

> Behold, the days come, saith the Lord, that I will perform that good thing which I have promised unto the house of Israel and to the house of Judah. In those days, and at that time, will I cause the Branch of Righteousness [Messiah] to grow up unto David; and He shall execute judgment and righteousness in the land. In those days shall Judah be saved, and Jerusalem shall dwell safely: and this is the name wherewith she shall be called, The Lord our Righteouness. For thus saith the Lord; David shall never want [cut off] a man to sit upon the throne of the house of Israel. (Jeremiah 33:14–17)

In verse 17, starting with the first letter in the sixth word and counting every forty-second letter from left to right spells *Yeshua* ישוע. In verse 16, starting with the last letter in the seventh word and reading the last letter of every seventh word from right to left spells "Messiah" *Mashiach* משיח.

> The book of the generation of Jesus Christ, the son of David, the son of Abraham . . . So all the generations from Abraham to David are fourteen generations; and from David until the carrying away unto Babylon are fourteen generations; and from the carrying away into Babylon unto Christ are fourteen generations. (Matthew 1:1, 17)

When you count the generations from Abraham to

Messiah, the total is forty-two. This is the same count as the count we used to find "Jesus" in the above Scripture. Not a mere coincidence, I would say. Encoded within this area of Scripture, we have the Messiah and His name (Jesus). Also, the names "Jesus" and "Messiah" show up at least seven other times in the same area.

In Jeremiah 32:41, starting with the seventh letter in the fifth word and counting every twenty-third letter from left to right spells "Messiah" מׁשׁיח. Also, in Jeremiah 33:12, starting with the third letter in the sixteenth word and counting every twenty-third letter from right to left spells *Yeshua* יׁשׁוע. Now we have the names *Jesus* and *Messiah* encoded at the twenty-three-letter intervals. Fascinating!

This passsage in Jeremiah is one of many prophecies concerning David and his throne. In one place, the Bible states that David will sit on his own throne, and in another place it states that his seed will occupy his throne forever. Jesus, the Son of David, will sit on the throne in Jerusalem when He returns to earth.

One of the greatest prophecies concerning the Church (believers) and the return of Jesus for His people, Israel, is found in the new covenant. Acts 15:14–16 states, "Simeon hath declared how God at the first did visit the Gentiles, to take out of them a people for His name. And to this agree the words of the prophets; as it is written, After this I will return [Second Coming], and will build again the tabernacle of David, which is fallen down; and I will build again the ruins thereof, and I will set it up." In these few Scriptures we have five very interesting statements:

1. God will visit the Gentiles to take a people for His name.

2. God will return when the body of Christ is complete.

3. God will again build the Tabernacle of David.

4. God will build again the ruins thereof.

5. God Himself will set it up.

This Scripture passage informs us of some very important data concerning the time and manner in which the Millennial Temple will be built. The Lord will build it after His body is complete, and not before. There will be, however, a Third Temple during the Tribulation period that will be defiled by the false messiah, the Antichrist, but this is not the Temple to which He is referring in the above Scriptures. The Millennial Temple will be the Fourth Temple, built by the Messiah, following the Tribulation period when Jesus returns to establish His Kingdom forever.

At the end of this age, the Lord Jesus will return and claim His throne in Israel. In the Scripture passage below, we see Him as King reigning over the whole House of Israel.

> And David My servant shall be king over them; and they all shall have One Shepherd: they shall also walk in My judgments, and observe My statutes, and do them. And they shall dwell in the land that I have given unto Jacob My servant, wherein your fathers have dwelt; and they shall dwell therein, even they, and their children, and their children's children for ever: and My servant David shall be their prince for ever. Moreover I will make a covenant of peace with them; it shall be an everlasting covenant with them: and I will place them, and multipy them, and will set My Sanctuary in the midst of them for evermore. My tabernacle also shall be with them: yea, I will be their God, and they shall be My people.   (Ezekiel 37:24–27)

It is quite obvious from this Scripture that Israel will be in the land forevermore and that David's Tabernacle will be erected once more. The Lord will return to shepherd His flock and will reign over them as King. Mysteriously, the name of the shepherd and king is recorded throughout this section of Scripture.

In Ezekiel 37:18, starting with the first letter in the seventh word and counting every twenty-eighth letter from right to left spells "the Messiah" *HaMashach* הַמָשִׁיחַ. Also, in verse 19, starting with the third letter in the twenty-first word and counting every thirteenth letter from right to left spells "Yeshua" יֵשׁוּעַ.

> And speak unto him, saying, Thus speaketh the Lord of hosts, saying, Behold the Man Whose name is The BRANCH; and He shall grow up out of His place, and He shall build the temple of the Lord: Even He shall build the temple of the Lord; and He shall bear the glory, and shall sit and rule upon His throne; and He shall be a priest upon His throne: and the counsel of peace shall be between them both [King and Priest].   (Zechariah 6:12–13)

The words "priest and king" refer to Yeshua, who is after the order of Melchizedek מַלְכִּיעֶדֶק, the King of Righteousness. Several times, the names "Yeshua" and "Messiah" emerge from the insights in Zechariah, chapter six. Verse 15 states, "And they that are far off [distant ones] shall come and build in the temple of the Lord, and ye shall know that the Lord of hosts hath sent Me [Yeshua] unto you. And this shall come to pass, if ye will diligently obey the voice of the Lord your God." Starting with the third letter in the tenth word and counting every seventh letter from left to right spells *Yeshua* יֵשׁוּעַ. There is an interesting combination of words where each letter forms the name *Yeshua* יֵשׁוּעַ. The first word is וִירַעְתֶּם, meaning "and you shall know." The second word is יֵהוָה *Jehovah*. The third is שְׁלָחַנִי, meaning "has sent me." The fourth is אֲלֵיכֶם, meaning "to you." Put them all together and we have "And you shall know Jehovah has sent me to you."

In the messianic prophecy of Zechariah 2, we have a combination similar to the above insight.

> For thus saith the Lord of hosts; After the glory hath he sent me unto the nations which spoiled you: for he that toucheth you toucheth the apple of his eye. For, behold, I will shake mine hand upon them, and they shall be a spoil to their servants: and ye shall know that the Lord of hosts hath sent me. Sing and rejoice, O daughter of Zion: for, lo, I come, and I will dwell in the midst of thee, saith the Lord.
>
> (Zechariah 2:8–10)

The above Scripture is from the King James Version. In the Masoretic text, however, it is Zechariah 2:12–14. Starting with the third letter in the first word and counting in reverse every seventh letter spells *Yeshua* ישׁוע. The four words in this insight where His name is found are quite similar to the above combination of the seven-letter count in Zechariah 6:15. The words are רני, meaning "sing"; שׁלחני, meaning "has sent me"; יהוה, meaning "Jehovah"; and וידעתם, meaning "and you shall know." Better stated it reads, "Sing, you shall know Jehovah has sent me." We see a beautiful fulfillment of these insights in John 17:25: "O righteous Father, the world hath not known thee: but I have known thee, and these have known that thou hast sent me."

Many Jewish people from around the world are receiving Yeshua as their Messiah. The eyes of Israel, as a nation, will be opened at a future date. The exact date is not revealed to us in a clear manner; the time of this great event is known only by the Lord.

The disciples came to Jesus and asked a very important question pertaining to the time element of the messianic kingdom. Jesus, however, did not give them the answer that they expected to hear. This is recorded in Acts 1:6: "When they therefore were come together, they asked of Him, saying, Lord, wilt Thou at this time restore again the kingdom to Israel?" Israel had been in bondage to the iron fist of Rome. They anticipated deliverance from the Messiah, which they received, but not in the way they expected. The gospel of the kingdom must first be preached unto all the world; then the messianic kingdom will come: "And this gospel of the kingdom shall be preached in all the world for a witness unto all nations; and then shall the end come" (Matthew 24:14).

1 Kings א מלכים, The Reigning King and Temple Builder

Solomon *Shlomo* שלמה means "peaceful, His peace, the peaceful one." He was the son of David and successor to the throne of Israel. Solomon was considered to be the wisest man in the world. God gave him this heavenly wisdom because he was to build the first Temple where God would dwell, and he would judge Israel with godlike wisdom and integrity. Solomon, at his best, was a picture of the coming King (Yeshua) and Temple Builder, who would rule not only Israel but also the whole world with justice and wisdom. Both the Tabernacle and Temple were pictures of the coming Redeemer and His divine character.

David's kingship gives a messianic picture of our coming King and Savior. In spite of his sins and rebellion against the Lord, David was a man after the heart of God. David knew how to repent. Solomon, his son, was born in David's old age. He was not only the king of Israel, but, like his father, he was an author. By the Holy Spirit he wrote wonderfully inspired psalms that are part of God's divine Word. The book of Proverbs (*Mishlai* מֹשלי), which was written by Solomon, is a book of great wisdom that has set a standard for the godly character of God's people. The Torah, written by Moses, gives us Levitical laws and is the foundation stone of all the other books of the Bible.

Regardless of Solomon's greatness of character and wisdom, his life was a portrait of one greater — the coming King and Temple Builder. Each, intricate part of the Temple, as well as the Tabernacle in the Wilderness, is a manuscript and picture of our Lord Jesus, the Messiah. In Matthew 12:42b we read, "Behold, a greater than Solomon is here. Jesus was speaking of Himself when He was talking to the scribes and Pharisees."

David's desire was to build the Temple, but God had other plans. The Lord reserved that privilege for David' son, who was Solomon, a type of the Messiah, who would build the eternal Temple, the body of believers in Yeshua the Messiah, but the Son of David through the Virgin Birth.

The Temple, a magnificent structure with all its gorgeous furnishings, is a picture and type of Jesus the Messiah. Whenever the Bible describes any part of the Temple or Tabernacle, the name "Jesus" *Yeshua* ישוע is hidden somewhere within that Scripture. Only by the leading of the Holy Spirit can one find Him in relationship to the true revelation of our Lord and Savior. First Kings 8:19–20 is a prophetic Scripture referring to God's Messiah and David's Son who came forth from his loins: "Nevertheless, thou shalt not build the house; but thy son [Yeshua] that shall come forth out of thy loins, he shall build the house unto My Name. and the Lord hath performed His Word that He spake, and I am risen up in the room of David my father, and sit on the throne of Israel, as the Lord promised, and have built an house for the Name of the Lord God of Israel."

There is another insight that is relevant to the subject under discussion. Starting with the first letter in the fourteenth word of verse 20, counting every fifth word, and reading the first letter of each word from right to left spells "Joshua" *Yehoshua* יהושע. Continue counting every fifth word, and you will find *Yo'av* יואב, which means "Jehovah Fathered." Jesus the Messiah is the Son of the virgin Mary

(*Miryam*) and the Son of God. Another verse related to this insight is Zechariah 3:9: "For behold the stone that I have laid before Joshua; upon one stone shall be seven eyes: behold, I will engrave the graving thereof, saith the Lord of hosts, and I will remove the iniquity of that land in one day." This Scripture is messianic because Jesus the High Priest will remove the sin from Israel in one day and lay the foundation stone for the messianic temple, which He will build with His companions.

In Zechariah 3:8, starting with the second letter in the fourteenth word and counting every 232nd letter from left to right spells *Yeshua* ישוע. This is the same count in Genesis where we found *Israel* and *Yeshua* at 232-letter increments. Also, in this same area, we will find the words "virgin" עלמה and "Mary" *Miryam* מרים. In these insights, we have *Jehovah fathered, Yeshua, Yehoshua, virgin*, and *Miryam* (Mary). This is not a coincidence, but the result of God's hand working through the writers of His precious Word. The book of Zechariah was written at least one thousand years after the Torah.

We know that Jesus, the suffering Messiah, has a legal claim to the Throne of David as the legal, adopted son of Joseph. Jesus is also, therefore, the Son of David, the conquering Messiah. Judah was the son of Leah, and he became the leader of the tribe of Judah. David was the son of Jesse, who also was the natural ancestor of Jesus the Messiah. We must remember that all the Word of God is linked together like a great network of letters and books. You cannot separate His Word from the Author, who is God, nor treat His Word independently of any other portion of the Holy Scriptures. How many times have we been in the dark about a statement in the Bible, only to find the answer — to our amazement — in another location? God always answers our questions by His Holy Word through His Holy Spirit.

While studying His precious Word in the book of
Zechariah, I came across another set of interesting insights
that are relative to our study. In Zechariah 2:13, starting with
the third letter in the tenth word and counting every
seventy-seventh letter from right to left spells "David" דוד.
This is not a very unusual find, but when we consider the
adjoining words, it raises the odds considerably. In this
same area of Scripture, where we found the word "David"
דוד, I located the words "Jesse" ישי, "Leah" לאה, "the
prophet" הנביא, the "stone" האבן, the "ram" האיל
(twice), "my tree" עצי (cross), and "the manna" המן — all
at seventy-seven-letter increments. I believe that the
Tabernacle and Temple are a picture of the Lord Jesus and
His Body.

In 1 Kings 8:20, starting with the second letter in the
fourteenth word, which is the same word where we arrived
at the name "Yeshua" from the above insight, and counting
every fifty-ninth letter from right to left spells *Shmi Yeshua*
שמי ישוע, which means "My name is Jesus." The adjacent
letters to Yeshua spell "creator" *borai* בורא.

First Kings 8:23 states, "And he said, Lord God of Israel,
there is no God like Thee, in heaven above, or on earth
beneath, Who keepest covenant and mercy [grace] with Thy
servants that walk before Thee with all their heart." Solomon
said that God has a covenant of mercy (grace) for all who
will walk in His way. We are both saved and kept by His
wonderful grace through Jesus the Messiah.

After Solomon dedicated the Temple and the people
rejoiced unto the Lord, they offered themselves and their
sacrifices unto the Lord God of Israel.

And so return unto Thee with all their heart, and
with all their soul, in the land of their enemies, which
led them away captive, and pray unto Thee toward
their land, which Thou gavest unto their fathers, the

city which Thou hast chosen, and the house which I have built for Thy name: Then hear Thou their prayer and their supplication in heaven Thy dwelling place, and maintain their cause, And forgive Thy people that have sinned against Thee, and all their transgressions wherein they have transgressed against Thee, and give them compassion before them who carried them captive, that they may have compassion on them.   (1 Kings 8:48–50)

There is an insight in the Hebrew text that escapes the English translations.

העיר אשר בחרת והבית אשרבנית לשמך: ושמעת השמים
מכון שבתך את — תפלתם ואת — תחנתם ועשית משפטם:

Starting with the third yod (י) from the right and counting every third letter from right to left spells *Yeshua shmo* ישוע שמו, which means "Jesus is His name." Who is the one who will answer our prayers? The answer is given without any question — Jesus, our mediator and High Priest.

Seeing then that we have a Great High Priest, that is passed into the heavens, Jesus the Son of God, let us hold fast our profession. For we have not an high priest which cannot be touched with the feeling of our infirmities; but was in all points tempted like as we are, yet without sin. Let us therefore come boldly unto the throne of Grace, that we may obtain Mercy, and find Grace to help in time of need.
                (Hebrews 4:14–16)

The Scripture says that whosoever shall call upon the name of the Lord shall be saved. There are volumes of books that could be written about Solomon and his wisdom. One example of that wisdom is found in Proverbs 31:10–31. This is one of the songs we sing on Shabbat every week. It is about the woman of valor, the virtuous woman. This chapter is packed with information that is normally overlooked by the less-than-serious reader. The Bible student without a background in Hebrew is often unaware that the Hebrew aleph-bet, the aleph through the tav, forms an acrostic in the book of Proverbs. The first letter of the first word in each verse of the book of Proverbs spells out the Hebrew aleph-bet in sequential order. The Hebrew aleph-bet is how God, by His Spirit, revealed His wisdom to Solomon. "If any of you lack wisdom, let him ask of God, that giveth to all men liberally, and upbraideth not; and it shall be given him" (James 1:5).

2 Kings 2 מלכים, The Power in Elijah's Mantle and the Miracle Worker

"Elijah" *Eliyahu* אליהו means "the Lord is my God." This is a very powerful name, and it seems that Elijah fulfilled, in measure, the meaning of his name. Many of our biblical fathers, in ages past, had names that reflected the glory of God in one way or another. When we think of Elijah, we generally associate him with the Passover Feast and the miracles that he performed in the name of the God of Israel. The prophecy in Malachi about Elijah directly refers to the Lord Jesus when He will come to bring justice upon the earth. Malachi 4:5–6 says, "Behold, I will send you Elijah the prophet before the coming of the great and dreadful day of the Lord. And He shall turn the heart of the fathers to the children, and the heart of the children to their fathers, lest I come and smite the earth with a curse." Notice that the Word says, "lest I come and smite the earth with a curse." This is a conditional prophecy. If Jesus had been totally rejected when He came the first time, the Lord would have smitten the earth with a curse. However, many received

Him as the Messiah, thereby holding back the curse that surely would have come.

Isaiah 61:1–2 gives us a prophecy concerning the Messiah and the ministry He would have. Verse 2 says, "To proclaim the acceptable year of the Lord, and the day of vengeance of our God; to comfort all that mourn." In Luke 4:18–19 the Lord Jesus quoted Isaiah 61:1, but He did not quote verse 2. The reason He did not quote the whole Scripture is because He did not come the first time to smite the earth with a curse, but He came to bring deliverance to all who would accept Him. The portion of Scripture in Isaiah 61 that refers to the day of vengeance will be fulfilled during the time of Jacob's trouble (the Tribulation).

> And his disciples asked Him, saying, Why then say the scribes that Elias [Elijah] must first come? And Jesus answered and said unto them, Elias truly shall first come, and restore all things. But I say unto you, That Elias is come already, and they knew him not, but have done unto him whatsoever they listed. Likewise shall also the Son of man suffer of them. Then the disciples understood that he spake unto them of John the Baptist.   (Matthew 17:10–13)

Yochanan the Immerser (John the Baptist) had the same fiery spirit that Elijah had. For example, Elijah appeared before Ahab, king of Israel, and his wife Jezebel, who was a Phoenician princess, and denounced them for their sin against God and Israel. Also, we see John the Baptist denouncing the self-proclaimed king of Israel, Herod, and his wife, Herodias, for sins against God and Israel. The parallels of Elijah and John the Baptist are quite astounding. Elijah wore a leather mantle as did John. Tradition tells us that the mantle of leather that John had was the same mantle that was handed down from Elijah to Elisha, from generation to generation. Elijah's hair was long and so was

John's. Both of these prophets were completely dedicated to fulfilling their prophetic calling from the Lord God of Israel. Elijah performed many miracles, whereas John was a "voice crying in the wilderness."

> And as they departed, Jesus began to say unto the multitudes concerning John, What went ye out into the wilderness to see? A reed shaken with the wind? But what went ye out for to see? A man clothed in soft raiment? behold, they that wear soft clothing are in kings' houses. But what went ye out for to see? A prophet? yea, I say unto you. and more than a prophet. For this is he, of whom it is written, Behold, I send my messenger before thy face, which shall prepare thy way before thee.   (Matthew 11:7–10)

When we have our Passover every year, I do not save a chair for Elijah, nor pour his cup at our seder table, as Jewish tradition teaches us, should he show up to announce the coming of the Messiah. The Messiah has already come and gone. It would be hypocritical for us who are believers in Yeshua to await Elijah when we know that he also has come and gone. John, in the spirit of Elijah, announced the Lamb of God and His Messiah, as it was prophesied according to the First Covenant (Old Testament) prophets. As a matter of fact, John the Baptist earned this title from believers because he baptized Jesus and many others in the River Jordan.

Many people connect Elijah with the two witnesses who will testify during the Great Tribulation in Revelation 11. They suggest Elijah because of the prophecy in Malachi. If we are to believe that John the Baptist fulfilled this prophecy, as Jesus Himself said he did, why are we trying to name Elijah as one of these witnesses who will announce the coming Messiah in Revelation 11? That is like setting a place for Elijah at the Passover Seder when we that know Elijah and John the Baptist have come and gone. I believe that one of the witnesses in Revelation will have the same dynamic spirit that Elijah and John had, and the other will have the same powerful clarity of the commandments that Moses had. Moses died, but Elijah was caught up by God with horses and a chariot of fire. The argument for Elijah being one of the prophets in Revelation 11 is that Elijah did not die; therefore, he must return to die like everyone else. What about the Rapture, when we who are alive shall be caught up? Must we all come back and fulfill the same standard that some think Elijah will fulfill? "And they of the people and kindreds and tongues and nations shall see their dead bodies three days and an half, and shall not suffer their dead bodies to be put in graves" (Revelation 11:9).

Elijah's last great miracle before he was caught up was to divide the River Jordan by striking the waters with his mantle. Moses' last miracle just before the wilderness experience was to strike the water of the Red Sea. Striking the water was the first miracle Elisha did after Elijah was transported to heaven. "Elisha" אֱלִישָׁע means "my God is salvation" (Jesus). Elisha asked for a double portion of Elijah's anointing, which he received when he took Elijah's mantle by faith.

> And Elijah took his mantle, and wrapped it together, and smote the waters, and they were divided hither and thither, so that they two went over on dry ground . . . He took up also the mantle of Elijah that fell from him, and went back, and stood by the bank of the Jordan; And he took the mantle of Elijah that fell from him, and smote the waters, and said, Where is the Lord God of Elijah? and when he also had smitten the waters, they parted hither and thither, and Elisha went over. (2 Kings 2:8, 13–14)

2 Kings 2:13

וירם את אדרת אליהו אשר נפלה
מעליו וישב ויעמד על שפת הירדן:

Starting with the second letter in the ninth word and counting every third letter from left to right spells *Yeshua* ישוע. Also, the last letter of each word, starting with the third word spells *Torah* תורה. Jesus is the absolute fulfillment of the Torah and the prophets. All that they had written about the coming Messiah was fulfilled in Jesus. He was the manna that came down from heaven, and on the day of Shavuot (Pentecost) the believers received a double portion, just as Elisha had when he took up the mantle of Elijah. Have you received your double portion since you believed?

> Verily, verily, I say unto you, He that believeth on Me, the works that I do shall he do also; and greater works than these shall he do; because I go unto My Father. (John 14:12)

> And, behold, I send the promise of My Father upon you: but tarry ye in the city of Jerusalem, until ye be endued with power from on high. (Luke 24:49)

Yeshua spoke to the believers who were present before He ascended into heaven, but the promise in Luke 24:49 is to all people in every generation to those who have been born of the Spirit. In 2 Kings 2:16, starting with the yod (י) in the phrase "the Spirit of Jehovah" רוח יהוה and counting every sixty-first letter from right to left spells *Yeshua* ישוע. John 16:7 says, "Nevertheless I tell you the truth; It is expedient for you that I go away: for if I go not away, the Comforter [Holy Spirit] will not come unto you; but if I depart, I will send Him unto you." It was also expedient for Elijah to depart because Elisha, who was the follower of Elijah, never would have received the mantle (his double portion, representing the anointing of the Spirit of God) otherwise. We who are followers of Yeshua will receive our double portion of His Spirit if we diligently seek Him.

Elijah was caught up by the horses and chariot of fire, a small demonstration of the glory of God. This echos the new covenant's promise of the baptism of fire that we, who are transformed by the wonderful, saving grace of our Lord, should receive. "John the Baptist said, I indeed baptize you with water unto repentance: but He that cometh after me is mightier than I, Whose shoes I am not worthy to bear: He shall baptize you with the Holy Ghost [*Ruach haKodesh*] and with fire" (Matthew 3:11).

> And when the day of Pentecost [*Shavuot*] was fully come, they were all with one accord in one place. And suddenly there came a sound from Heaven as of a rushing mighty wind, and it filled all the house where they were sitting. And there appeared unto them cloven tongues like as of fire, and it sat upon each of them. And they were all filled with the Holy Ghost [*Ruach haKodesh*], and began to speak with other tongues, as the Spirit gave them utterance.
>
> (Acts 2:1–4)

The Pentecost event was the fulfillment of the prophecy, the promise of the Father. We should desire everything that God promises us.

There is a portion of 2 Kings 2:14 that reveals an astonishing insight concerning the above study. After Elisha received Elijah's mantle, he asked a question for which he had the answer. Elisha spoke in an assertive tone, asking, "Where is Jehovah, God of Elijah?" איה יהוה אלהי אליהו. Starting with the first yod (י) and counting every sixtieth letter from left to right spells "Yeshua the Lord" ישועיהו. In the sixty-letter count, adjacent to the above, we will find

"God" אלהי and "Lord God" אליה. Nothing could be more pronounced and obvious than that Jesus is Lord יהוה and that He is the rewarder of them who diligently seek Him?

It would take a lifetime for us to cover all the exploits of Elijah and Elisha. We may have to wait until we are caught up into glory before we can fully understand all that God has for us.

The Chronicles דברי הימים,
The Matters of the Days: The Shekinah Glory of God in the Temple

The first book of Chronicles is the history of the genealogy from Adam to David, and the second book is the basic history of the kings of Judah, excluding the kings of Israel. Also, the second book of Chronicles covers some of the history of the returning Jews from the Babylonian and Persian captivities. In this section, however, we will deal with Solomon's Temple, which was destroyed by the Babylonians on the ninth of Av, about 586 B.C.

Second Chronicles 6:41 states, "Now therefore arise, O Lord God, into Thy resting place, Thou, and the ark of Thy strength; let Thy priests, O Lord God, be clothed with Salvation, and let Thy saints rejoice in goodness."

ועתה קומה יהוה אלהים לנוחך אתה וארון עזך
כהניך יהוה אלהים ילבשו תשועה וחסידיך ישמחו בטוב:

This Scripture is one of the most outstanding in the books of Chronicles because it reveals our Messiah, the Lord Jesus. Solomon was praying that God would come and dwell in the Holy of Holies in the Temple that he completed for the glory of God. There is a larger picture developing within this text that uncovers astounding information that is missed in the common reading. Starting with the fourth letter in the fourteenth word and counting every tenth letter from left to right spells *Yeshua* ישוע. Also, starting with the second letter in the tenth word and counting every seventh letter from right to left spells "the Messiah" המשיח. There is another interesting combination that reflects one of the purposes for which the Messiah came to a sinful world. Starting with the fourth letter in the thirteenth word and counting every seventh letter from left to right spells *olah ha'rachel* עלה הרחל, which means "burnt offering of the lamb." This represents the Lamb of God, Yeshua, who came from glory to dwell with us. But before He could tabernacle in us, He first had to cleanse us of all our sins. God will not dwell in a temple that is unclean. Starting with the mem (מ) in the word "rise" *qumah* קומה, which is the second word in verse 41 and counting every 111th letter from left to right spells "Messiah" משיח. "Know ye not that ye are the temple of God, and that the Spirit of God dwelleth in you? If any man defile the temple of God, him shall God destroy; for the temple of God is holy, which temple ye are" (1 Corinthians 3:16–17).

When Solomon dedicated the Temple, there were 120 trumpeters and 4,000 musicians, not counting the priests of the Temple and the doorkeepers. This was the greatest event in Solomon's life. The presence of God came in the cloud of His Shekinah Glory in such a fulness that the priests could not administer their rituals. These wonderful people were dying to themselves and giving glory to God; they could do nothing but stand in awe and praise the Holy One, the Lord God of Israel!

> It came even to pass, as the trumpeters and singers were as one, to make one sound to be heard in praising and thanking the Lord; and when they lifted up their voice with the trumpets and cymbals and instruments of musick, and praised the Lord, saying, For He is good; for His mercy endureth for ever: that then the house was filled with a cloud, even the

house of the Lord; So that the priests could not stand to minister by reason of the cloud: for the glory of the Lord had filled the house of God.

(2 Chronicles 5:13–14)

In Acts 2, there was another body of believers meeting in one accord in one place and praising God. There were 120 people present on that special day. They did not sound the trumpets of silver, but they gave resounding praises with the trumpet of their voices unto the Lord of glory. All of a sudden the cloud of glory filled them and the house in which they were sitting to such an extent that they could not speak their own languages but spoke, instead, with tongues of fire as the Spirit gave them utterance. Unlike the day when Moses came down from the mountain and found rebellion in the camp, which caused God to strike three thousand dead; on this great day of Pentecost (Shavuot), the 120 spoke the word of God with boldness, giving witness to the power of God, and three thousand souls died spiritually to themselves and were reborn to new spiritual life in Jesus Christ by the power of God. Just as Jesus had performed an outstanding miracle when He fed the five thousand men who had not eaten in three days, shortly after the day of Pentecost, the resurrected Jesus sent forth the Heavenly Manna and another five thousand men and women were added to the Kingdom of God. They received the same blessing as Peter and the others had on the Day of Pentecost. The Bible declares that all these promises are for us today: "For the promise is unto you, and to your children, and to all that are afar off, even as many as the Lord our God shall call" (Acts 2:39).

10

Ezra, Nehemiah, and Esther: Israel's Dispersion and Return

Ezra עֶזְרָא, The Faithful Scribe

The name "Ezra" means "help." Ezra was a priest of the tribe of Levi and he was a scribe. Ezra arrived in Jerusalem in the fifth month, which was in the seventh year of king Artaxerxes. God had given Ezra a commission to teach the commandments of the Lord that were written in the Torah. Before Ezra went to Israel, however, God moved the heart of King Cyrus of Persia, God's chosen ruler, as we see in the book of Ezra.

> Now in the first year of Cyrus king of Pesia, that the Word of the Lord by the mouth of Jeremiah might be fulfilled, the Lord stirred up the spirit of Cyrus king of Persia, that he made a proclamation throughout all his kingdom, and put it also in writing, saying,

> Thus saith Cyrus king of Persia, The Lord God of
> Heaven hath given me all the kingdoms of the earth;
> and he hath charged me to build him an house at
> Jerusalem, which is in Judah. Who is there among
> you of all his people? his God be with him, and let
> him go up to Jerusalem, which is in Judah, and build
> the house of the Lord God of Israel, (He is the God,)
> which is in Jerusalem.   (Ezra 1:1–3)

There is encoded here an awesome insight that reveals
the wonderful Name of our Lord. In Ezra 1:3, begin in the
Hebrew phrase "He is God, Who is in Jerusalem" *hu
haElohim asher beYerushalayim* הוא האלהים אשר בירושלם
and count every twenty-sixth letter from right to left,
starting with the yod (י) in Jerusalem ירושלם. This spells
Yehu Yeshua יהו ישוע, which means "Lord Jesus." From
this insight, we can see the power that was behind the
commandment of King Cyrus.

Because of their time in captivity, Israel needed to be
reminded of the oracles and statutes of the Torah. God
anointed Ezra to be the teacher and scribe who would bring
Israel back to the foundation of her faith in God and His
written Word before the foundation stone could be laid for
the Temple. Zerubbabel, however, was the one who
engineered the Temple project. Nevertheless, we see a
wonderful and precious picture unfolding in Ezra's life. His
desire to obey the Lord to the letter was an example to all of
the Jews who had returned to Israel from captivity. When
Yeshua (Jesus) came to earth, He explained the meaning of
the Torah to those who had lost the true meaning of Moses'
writings. Since all the Word of God is a picture of Yeshua,
He who *is* the Word of God scribed His Words within the
hearts and minds of all who would believe and receive Him.
When Yeshua the Messiah returns to Jerusalem at the
Second Coming, He will write His laws on the hearts and
minds of the whole house of Israel.

> This Ezra went up from Babylon; and he was a ready scribe in the law of Moses, which the Lord God of Israel had given: and the king granted him all his request, according to the hand of the Lord his God upon him. . . . For Ezra had prepared his heart to seek the law of the Lord, and to do it, and to teach in Israel statutes and judgments.　　　(Ezra 7:6, 10)

We begin in Ezra 7:6 with the Hebrew phrase "and he was a ready [skilled] scribe in the laws of Moses" *vehu soh'per mah'hir be'torat moshe* וְהוּא-סֹפֵר מָהִיר בְּתוֹרַת מֹשֶׁה. Starting with the first mem (מ) to the right and counting every seventy-fourth letter from right to left spells "Messiah" מָשִׁיחַ. In Ezra 7:11, begin with the phrase "Ezra the priest" *Ezra hakohain* עֶזְרָא הַכֹּהֵן. Starting with the ayin (ע) and counting every 142nd letter from right to left spells *Yeshua* יֵשׁוּעַ. Also, in this same count we will find the phrase "the ark" הַתֵּבָה, which is a type of Noah's ark. Encoded in the passage about the scribe Ezra are the words for *Yeshua, Messiah, ark, truly, Jesus is our Messiah, ark of rescue*, and *our faithful Scribe.*

Nehemiah נְחֶמְיָה, The Wall Builder and Restorer of Jerusalem

The name Nehemiah means "comforted of the Lord." While in captivity, Nehemiah was a cupbearer for King Artaxerxes of Persia. He asked the king's permission to go to Jerusalem to better both the conditions of the city and "his brothers." The king appointed him governor of Judah, with the promise that Nehemiah would return to Persia within a given time. God gave Nehemiah the awesome responsibility of restoring the city of Jerusalem and the walls. We see a greater meaning to this task when viewed as a picture of Yeshua when He returns to complete the restoration not only of Jerusalem but also of all Israel. Yeshua will govern from Jerusalem and oversee the rebuilding of a broken nation. The rebuilding of the walls and the Temple will be the greatest engineering feat of all time. After all, Jesus is the Master Builder and restorer of all things.

> The words of Nehemiah the son of Hachaliah. And it came to pass in the month Chisleu, in the twentieth year, as I was in Shushan the palace, That Hanani, one of my brethren, came, he and certain men of Judah; and I asked them concerning the Jews that had escaped, which were left of the captivity, and concerning Jerusalem. And they said unto me, The remnant that are left of the captivity there in the province are in great affliction and reproach: the wall of Jerusalem also is broken down, and the gates thereof are burned with fire.   (Nehemiah 1:1–3)

Begin in verse one with the phrase "and it was in the month of Kisleu, in the twentieth year" *vayehi bechodesh kisleu shenat esrim* ויהי בחדש כסלו שנת עשׂרים. Starting with the second yod (י) to the right and counting every fourth letter from right to left spells "Yeshua" ישׁוע. The ninth month, Kisleu, is also the month of the Feast of Chanukkah (Dedication). One of Nehemiah's priorities was to oversee the rebuilding of Jerusalem, the walls, and the Temple. Everyone participated in the reconstruction of Israel, except the Samaritans, who viciously opposed the work.

In Nehemiah 4:6 we read, "So built we the wall; and all the wall was joined together unto the half thereof: for the people had a mind to work." Starting with the mem (מ) in "wall" *hachomah* החומה and counting every fortieth letter from right to left spells "Messiah" משׁיח.

In Nehemiah 12:5, starting with the third letter in the first word and counting every twelfth letter from right to left spells "Messiah" משׁיח. In Nehemiah 12:16, starting with the fifth letter in the second word, which is "Zechariah"

זכריה and counting every twenty-fourth letter from right to left spells "the Messiah" המשיח. Zechariah was a type of messiah but not the Messiah. As with others who were types of the Messiah, Zechariah could only fulfill in part the role of the Messiah to come who would fulfill all things.

All of our biblical forefathers were given names that are derivitives of the words "God" and "Lord." The names had special meanings. For example, Nehemiah's name means "comforted of the Lord." We must remember that the Word of the Lord, the Bible, is an expression of His holiness and beauty.

Esther אסתר

The book of Esther is one of the most unusual books of the entire Bible. The complete scroll of Esther, which is part Persian, part Chaldaic, and part original Hebrew, is read during the Feast of Purim with joy, shouting, hissing, and stomping of the feet. The Jews' deliverance from Haman and his cohorts is the reason for the joy, even today. The hissing and stomping of feet is to symbolically drown out Haman and his sons' names while the scroll is being read.

There are some very remarkable insights that add flavor to the experiences of Esther and Mordecai. Regardless of whether this book is in Persian, Chaldaic, or original Hebrew, it is nevertheless inspired of God. He has put His hand of approval on it by inserting encoded messages so as to add credence to it and to prove its authority. It has been said, and perhaps you have said it yourself, that the words "Adonai" *Jehovah* יהוה, "God" *Elohim* אלהים, "God Almighty" *El Shaddai* אל שדי are not found in the book of Esther and that, therefore, the book may not be inspired and should not have a place in the Canon of Scripture. I totally disagree with this argument! While His name does not appear on the surface reading, the name of God does appear encoded in equidistant-letter spacing many times throughout this wonderful book. One must look carefully in order to find His name and the name of the Messiah in this inspired book of the Holy Scriptures.

The name "Esther" אסתר means "star." Previously, she had been known as "Hadasah" הדסה, which means "myrtle (tree)." Esther, of the tribe of Benjamin, was an orphan, but Mordecai, her cousin, raised her from childhood. He, too, was one of the principal characters in the deliverance of the Jews from Haman's power and hate while they were in captivity in Persia. Haman has been likened to our century's Adolph Hitler, a type of the Antimessiah (Antichrist), who will persecute God's people in the end time.

Mordecai מרדכי means "warrior." He was a type of the Messiah who would come to the rescue of Messiah's people. The most stirring statement made by him was to Esther and is found in the book of Esther.

> Then Mordecai commanded to answer Esther, Think not with thyself that thou shalt escape in the king's house, more than all the Jews. For if thou altogether holdest thy peace at this time, then shall there enlargement and deliverance arise to the Jews from another place; but thou and thy father's house shall be destroyed: and who knoweth whether thou art come to the kingdom for such a time as this?
>
> (Esther 4:13–14)

Esther stood before the king on behalf of her people, who were being persecuted by the tyrant Haman. To enter the king's presence without approval could have meant instant death; so, for a year in advance, Esther prepared herself with prayer, fasting, and beauty treatments before she presented herself to the king.

> Then Esther bade them return Mordecai this answer, Go, gather together all the Jews that are present in

Shushan, and fast ye for me, and neither eat nor drink three days, night or day: I also and my maidens will fast likewise; and so will I go in unto the king which is not according to the law: and if I perish, I perish. So Mordecai went his way, and did according to all that Esther had commanded him.

(Esther 4:15–17)

The king, Esther's husband, loved her more than he loved anyone in all his domain. King Ahasuerus was delighted with her beauty and boldness and was ready to grant her every request.

In Esther 4:15–17, however, we see the real power that was working behind the scenes on behalf of Esther, Mordecai, and the Jews who were in Persia. In Esther 4:17, beginning with the third letter in the first word and counting every eighth letter from right to left spells *Shilo Yeshua* שלה ישוע, which means "Shiloh Jesus." "Shiloh" is another name for the Messiah, as recorded in Genesis 49:10; and here the word is directly associated with the heavenly lawgiver, Yeshua. When we understand the power that was behind the power of the throne of Persia, there can be no doubt as to the outcome of the Jews' precarious situation. The odds of the words "Shiloh Jesus" appearing by chance are simply astronomical.

Haman came to an ignominious end, as did his ten sons. He had prepared a gallows (tree) for Mordecai, but, instead, Haman was hanged on this gallows until he was dead. The strange, but miraculous, events that transpired during this crisis are fascinating. The very weapon that Haman had intended for Mordecai became his own doom. Before Haman's destruction, however, the king had him honor Mordecai by parading him through the streets of the city and announcing Mordecai's name publicly. "Then took Haman the apparel and the horse, and arrayed Mordecai, and brought him on horseback through the street of the city, and proclaimed before him, Thus shall it be done unto the man whom the king delighteth to honor" (Esther 6:11).

Esther had a place next to the king because she was the queen of Persia; Mordecai, also, was exalted to a position next to the king. These wonderful portraits of God's beloved people and the Messiah are reflected in the very last verse in the book of Esther. "For Mordecai the Jew was next unto king Ahasuerus, and great among the Jews, and accepted of the multitude of his brethren, seeking the wealth of his people, and speaking peace to all his seed" (Esther 10:3).

In his new position, Mordecai spoke peace to all his kinsmen and sought their benefit. This is an awesome, prophetic picture of the Messiah, when He returns to earth. Believers will not only be seated next to Him in His glory, but we will also be exalted as heirs of God and joint heirs with Jesus Christ.

Before Mordecai could be exalted, however, he had to suffer many afflictions for his people, the Jews. We see, in Mordecai, a greater fulfillment in type of the Messiah whom he portrayed. The book of Isaiah is one of the most detailed descriptions of the suffering Messiah in all the Bible. Yeshua was the Lamb who took away our repoach. Mordecai was the man used by Messiah to take away the reproach of his people.

In Esther 6:3, starting with the second letter in the twelfth word and counting every one-hundredth letter forward spells "from the soul of Yeshua my sin offering" מנפש בישוע אשמי. What better insight could there be to prove that Yeshua was our sin offering? One may ask, Why is this insight found in the Chaldaic Hebrew? We must remember that all the Word of God is gathered together into one unified magnificent expression of His holiness and beauty. His Holy Word demonstrates His love for humanity and His plan for redeeming fallen humanity. The Hebrew word for "sin offering" אָשָׁם is the same word that is used in Isaiah 53:10. The adjacent letters to the word "sin offering" prove to be just as powerful and enlightening in revealing the true nature of Yeshua when He came to this world to save lost sinners.

In Esther 6:3, starting with the first letter in the thirteenth word and counting every one-hundreth letter from right to left spells "the perfect (truthful) Rabbi" *Ravi Tummim* רבי תמים. Yeshua is our perfect teacher who explains the meaning of the Law of Moses and the Prophets.

> And one of the scribes came, and having heard them reasoning together, and perceiving that He had answered them well, asked Him, Which is the first commandment of all? And Jesus answered him, The first of all the commandments is, Hear O Israel; The Lord our God is one Lord, [*Shma Israel, Adonai Elohainu Adonai echad*
> שמע ישראל יהוה אלהינו יהוה אחד]: And thou shalt love the Lord thy God with all thy heart, and with all thy soul, and with all thy mind, and with all thy strength: this is the first commandment. And the second is like, namely this, Thou shalt love thy neighbour as thyself. There is none other commandment greater than these. And the scribe said unto Him, Well, Master [Rabbi], thou hast said the truth: for there is one God; and there is none other but He.   (Mark 12:28–32)

There are various combinations dispersed throughout the book of Esther that form the names *El Shaddai, Lord, God, Yeshua,* and *Messiah.* They blend together in a composed, prearranged order. These encoded names are arranged in a stunning array of God's manifestation of His resplendent heavenly grandeur, quite beyond man's capability to have produced such an arrangement.

In Esther 4:2, starting from the aleph (א) in the Hebrew phrase "the gate of the king" אל-שׁער המלך and counting every seventh letter from right to left spells "El Shaddai" אל שׁדי, which means "God Almighty." The gate of heaven is truly the Lord's gate where, one day, we shall enter and stand before the Lord God Almighty.

The insight in Esther 9:22 reflects the messianic kingdom, when our Lord will nourish His people and turn their sorrow into gladness. "As the days wherein the Jews rested from their enemies, and the month which was turned unto them from sorrow to joy, and from mourning into a good day: that they should make them days of feasting and joy, and of sending portions one to another, and gifts to the poor." Starting with the first letter in the twenty-fourth word and counting every eighth letter in reverse spells *Lachem Mashiach* לחם משׁיח, which means "bread (of) Messiah." This brings to mind the image of Yeshua the Messiah feeding the five thousand and then the four thousand men, not counting the women and the children. But of course, we see a greater fulfillment of all three of these thoughts in the Kingdom of Heaven on earth.

In the phrase "and the king extended the golden scepter" ויושׁט המלך לאסתראת שׁרביט (Esther 5:2), taking every third letter in reverse, starting with the yod (י) to the far right, spells "Israel" ישׂראל. Phenomenal! In verse 4, starting with the third letter in the fourteenth word and counting every twenty-fourth letter, in reverse, spells *Jehovah* "Adonai" יהוה.

In Esther 9:5, starting with the sixth letter in the second word and counting every twenty-fourth letter from left to right spells "Yeshua" ישׁוע. In verse 30 of this chapter, starting with the third letter in the ninth word and counting every twenty-fourth letter from right to left spells *Elohim* אלהים, which means "God." These insights are but a few of the wonderful gems that God is revealing in these last days.

Who could possibly question the divine arrangement and validity of His sacred word?

His Name Is Jesus

11

Jonah Yonah יונה:
A Type of Israel and Yeshua

The book of Jonah contains 4 chapters, 48 verses, 80 lines, 687 words, and 2700 letters. This book is considered to be the fifth book of the Minor Prophets. There are multiple insights that baffle the mind which are dispersed throughout the book of Jonah. The Hebrew name "Jonah" *Yonah* יונה means "dove." Jonah was the son of Amittai *Ami'tai* אמתי, which means "my truth." Jonah was a prophet from Gittah-hepher (winepress on the hill) in the land of Zebulon, Israel. He was a contemporary of King Jeroboam II of the northern tribes, and lived about 820 B.C. Jonah was commanded of God to go to Nineveh to tell the Ninevites of God's impending judgment on them unless they repented of their wickedness.

One of the commandments to Israel was that they were to be a light to the Gentiles. Jonah, however, shrank from a commission that he felt would surely result in the salvation of an enemy hostile to his own country. This is one of the signs of Jonah to which Yeshua referred in the Scriptures when He said that salvation would also be for the pagan nations. This fact is reflected in both Isaiah and Mark:

> I the Lord have called thee in righteousness, and will hold thine hand, and will keep thee and give thee for a covenant of the people, for a light of the Gentiles. To open the blind eyes, to bring out the prisoners from the prison, and them that sit in darkness out of the prison house. (Isaiah 42:6–7)

> And he said unto them, Go ye into all the world, and preach the gospel [Good News] to every creature.
> (Mark 16:15)

The initial sign of Jonah's being three days and three nights in the fish's belly was fulfilled by Jesus when He was three days and three nights in the heart of the earth. There are other signs in Jonah that are clustered around his experiences when he was called to be a witness to the Gentiles. His running from God and man, however, proved to be futile in the end.

At the end of the book, God had compassion on Jonah and caused a nauseating gourd to grow for his protection from the sun. Then, no sooner was Jonah comfortable than God appointed a worm (*tola'at* תולעת) to consume the plant of protection, thus teaching Jonah another lesson. The crimson (scarlet) dye used for the Tabernacle and both Temples came from the *tola'at* worm. The crimson color represents the redemptive power of the blood that would ultimately be applied on the Ark of the Covenant for the salvation of all who would believe and receive the atoning blood of Yeshua, the Lamb of God. Jonah understood the significance of the *tola'at* worm and was displeased to think that the heathen Gentiles could also be the recipients of God's redemptive plan. The blood of Jesus (of which the *tola'at* worm was a type) is the only means by which man may obtain this great salvation. All our works are nauseating to the Lord and will be rejected because without the shedding of blood, there is no remission of sins.

It would take a lifetime to explore all the truths and mountains of prophecies that are found in the story of Jonah. Jonah's experience was and is being fulfilled by Yeshua HaMashiach, Israel, and the nations. There are many direct parallels and contrasts in the book of Jonah concerning Yeshua HaMashiach, Jonah, Israel, and the nations. The time during which Jonah received the command from the Lord to go to Nineveh and warn them of impending disaster is believed to have been at the beginning of the twelfth month, *Elul* אלול, on the Hebrew civil calendar or the sixth month on the sacred calendar. Generally, this month comes around August or early September on the Gregorian calendar. From the beginning of the month of Elul to Yom Kippur is the time of return (repentance) *T'shuvah* תשובה to the Lord. There are insights in the book of Jonah alluding to that time, and we shall analyze them later in this study. The forty days of God's warning gives us a picture of the coming judgment or salvation of all nations, kindreds, and tongues. From the first of Elul to the tenth of Tishri תשרי, the Day of Atonement or Yom Kippur יום כפר, is forty days. It is believed that this is the time when all nations will be judged by Yeshua HaMashiach, and the gates of heaven will be closed on a future Yom Kippur.

> When the Son of man shall come in His Glory, and all the holy angels [messengers] with Him, then shall He sit upon the throne of His glory: And before Him shall be gathered all nations: and He shall separate them one from another, as a shepherd divides his sheep from the goats: And He shall set the sheep on His right hand, but the goats on the left. Then shall the King say unto them on His right hand, Come, ye

blessed of My Father, inherit the kingdom prepared for you from the foundation of the world.

(Matthew 25:31–34)

And Enoch also, the seventh from Adam, prophesied of these, saying, Behold, the Lord cometh with ten thousands of His saints, to execute judgment upon all, and to convince all that are ungodly among them of all their ungodly deeds which they have ungodly committed, and of all their hard speeches which ungodly sinners have spoken against Him. (Jude 14–15)

In Matthew 25, the Scripture says that the Son of Man is returning to judge the nations, but in Jude 14, the Scripture says that Jehovah יהוה is coming to judge the nations with the saints of glory. To better understand these Scriptures, we need to look at the books of Zechariah and Acts.

Behold, the day of the Lord cometh, and your spoil shall be divided in the midst of thee. For I will gather all nations against Jerusalem to battle; and the city shall be taken, and the houses rifled, and the women ravished; and half of the city shall go forth into captivity, and the residue of the people shall not be cut off from the city. Then shall the Lord [Jehovah] go forth, and fight against those nations, as when He fought in the day of battle. And His [Yeshua's] feet shall stand in that day upon the Mount of Olives, which is before Jerusalem on the east, and the Mount of Olives shall cleave in the midst thereof toward the east and toward the west, and there shall be a very great valley; and half of the mountain shall remove toward the north, and half of it toward the south.

(Zechariah 14:1–4)

But ye shall receive power, after that the Holy Spirit

is come upon you: and ye shall be witnesses unto me
both in Jerusalem, and in all Judaea, and in Samaria,
and unto the uttermost part of the earth. And when
He had spoken these things, while they beheld, He
was taken up; and a cloud received Him out of their
sight. And while they looked steadfastly toward
heaven as He went up, behold, two men stood by
them in white apparel; Which also said, Ye men of
Galilee, why stand you gazing up into heaven? This
same Jesus *Yeshua* which is taken up from you into
heaven, shall so come in like manner as ye have seen
Him go into heaven. Then returned they unto
Jerusalem from the mount called Olivet, which is
from Jerusalem a sabbath day's journey.

(Acts 1:8–12)

We can see by these Scriptures that Jesus, the Son of
Man *Yeshua Ben A'dam* ישוע בן אדם, and Jehovah יהוה are
one and the same person. Allow me to elaborate a little
more on this thought from the Zechariah passage.

In that day shall the Lord defend the inhabitants of
Jerusalem; and he that is feeble among them at that
day shall be as David; and the house of David shall
be as God, as the angel [messenger] of the Lord
before them. And it shall come to pass in that day,
that I will seek to destroy all the nations that come
against Jerusalem. And I will pour upon the house of
David, and upon the inhabitants of Jerusaslem, the
spirit of grace and of supplications: and they shall
look upon Me [Jesus], whom they have pierced, and
they shall mourn for Him, as one mourns for his only
son, and shall be in bitterness for him, as one that is
in bitterness for his firstborn.   (Zechariah 12:8–10)

The phrase "they shall look upon Me" is a statement *of*

the first person, and the phrase "they shall mourn for Him" is a statement *to* the second person. It is difficult for anyone to understand this terminology unless he or she knows that both persons referred to here are one and the same person — God. This type of phraseology is common in the Scriptures and may confuse the reader unless he or she is aware of the triune nature or trinity in which the Lord clothed Himself in order to demonstrate His wonderful grace. Many times the Lord has taken the first-person position (Me), and then in midstream, so to speak, He takes the second-person position (Him). If this seems to befuddle you, I will give you an example so as to clear your mind of any confusion that may occur concerning the first and second positions that the Lord has taken for Himself throughout the Scriptures. Remember, the Father, Son, and Holy Spirit are one (*echad* אחד).

The first example of the first and second parties being the same person is when Jacob wrestled all night with a man. When dawn came, however, he found that he was wrestling with God. Did Jacob know that he was wrestling with God at first? No, because God had changed His appearance to conceal His true identity at the beginning of the wrestling match. Is there any doubt as to who was going to win this contest? No. God allows us to contend with Him within limits to drive home a spiritual lesson in our lives. In the final analysis, God always wins and has His way. This was the case with Jacob because God was in the process of changing Jacob to Israel. A mortal man could not change Jacob's name to Israel; only God could do this. So, we must conclude that it was the Lord who was wrestling with Jacob all along. Perhaps you have wrestled with God and thought it was man you were fighting, only to realize in hindsight that you were battling God all along.

And Jacob was left alone; and there wrestled a man

with him until the breaking of the day. And when He saw that He prevailed not against him, He touched the hollow of his thigh; and the hollow of Jacob's thigh was out of joint, as he wrestled with Him. And He said, let Me go, for the day breaketh. And he said, I will not let Thee go, except Thou bless me. And He said unto him, what is your name? And he said, Jacob. And He said, Your name shall be called no more Jacob, but Israel: for as a prince hast thou power with God and with men, and hast prevailed. And Jacob asked Him, and said, Tell me, I pray Thee, thy name. And He said, Wherefore is it that thou do ask after My name? And He blessed him there. And Jacob called the name of the place Peniel: for I have seen God face to face, and my life is preserved. And as he passed over Penuel the sun rose upon him, and he halted upon his thigh [hip-socket]. Therefore the children of Israel eat not of the sinew which shrank, which is upon the hollow of the thigh, unto this day: because He touched the hollow of Jacob's thigh [*gid hanasheh* גיד הנשה] in the sinew that shrank. (Genesis 32:24–32)

The sinew of the thigh (*gid hanasheh* גיד הנשה) is the section of the animal's body where the sciatic nerve is located, and it is very rich in blood. According to the Torah, the Jews were forbidden to eat it. Jacob's sciatic nerve was pinched, so to speak, and it caused him to walk differently from that day forward.

We find the name of Yeshua at least five times throughout the insights in the context of this story of Jacob. In the Hebrew Tanakh, starting with the last ayin (ע) in verse 25 and counting every fifty-third letter from right to left spells *koph l'Yeshua* כף לישוע, which means "the palm (or hand) of Yeshua." Who was the person wrestling with Jacob, dislocating his hip *koph*? Could it have been Yeshua before He became a Son of Israel and a man? The count of fifty-three is unique because it is the positional value of Yeshua's name. Let me explain. There are twenty-two letters in the Hebrew aleph-bet, and each letter has its rightful position; that is, the first letter is the aleph (א), the second is the bet (ב), and so forth. The four letters that compose the name of Yeshua are the yod (י), which is the tenth letter, the shin (ש), which is the twenty-first letter, the vav (ו), which is the sixth letter, and, finally, the ayin (ע), which is the sixteenth letter. Adding these together gives us a sum of fifty-three. This is considered a very unusual find and should cause us to realize that the Word of God is divinely structured, both mathematically and geometrically. It is very interesting to find the koph associated with Yeshua in such a way as to suggest the possibility that God divinely arranged His Word to reflect His physical manifestation.

If we begin with the same ayin (ע) where we found *Yeshua* and count every thirty-eighth letter from left to right, we also find *Yeshua* the second time. Why does Yeshua show up so often in these insights? Because His name is called the Word of God, and His written Word reveals Him from the beginning through to the end.

When Jacob's name was changed to Israel after he wrestled with the Lord, he asked the question, "What is your name?" The Lord responded with another question, "Why do you ask My name?" Then Jacob said, "I have seen God face-to-face." Jacob called the place where he received his blessing *Peniel* פניאל, which means "the face of God." This was an exhilarating experience for a man who was a rebel at heart, but God changed his name and his walk. Many of us are like Jacob, but God can transform and bless us if we seek Him with our whole heart.

In the book of Judges we have a wonderful story about a man named Manoah, whose wife was barren. Like Jacob, he asked the ultimate question, "What is your name?" The messenger (angel) of the Lord appeared to his wife and told her that she would conceive and bear a son, and that the son would be a Nazarite. Later, the angel appeared to both of them. In Judges 13:17–18 we read, "And Manoah said unto the angel of the Lord, What is thy name, that when thy sayings come to pass we may do thee honor? And the angel of the Lord said unto him, Why askest thou thus after My name, seeing it is secret [פלאי wonderful]."

The Hebrew word for "secret" in this text means "wonderful" פלאי. Perhaps you have wondered why Manoah received the name of the messenger, even though the Lord refused Jacob's request for His name. Possibly, it has something to do with progressive revelation of the Word of the Lord. The names "Savior" מורשיע, "Messiah" משיח, "Adonai" *Jehovah* יהוה, and "Jesus" *Yeshua* ישוע are also encoded within these texts at variable equidistant-letter sequences. In Judges 13:13, starting with the first letter in the fifth word and counting every 119th letter from right to left spells "Savior" מורשיע. The adjacent letters spell *Jehovah* יהוה. Both of the hehs (ה) are taken from the name *Jehovah* יהוה in the common reading of this text. In Judges 13:6, starting with the second letter in the twenty-second word and counting every 140th letter from right to left spells *mohail Mashiach* מורהל שמיח, which means "Messiah the circumcizer." In Judges 13:15, starting with the second letter in the sixth word and counting forward every 455th letter spells *Yeshua* ישוע.

> And Manoah said unto his wife, We shall surely die, because we have seen God. But his wife said unto him, If the Lord were pleased to kill us, he would not have received a burnt offering and a meat offering at our hands, neither would he have shewed us all these things, nor would as at this time have told us

such things as these. And the woman bore a son, and called his name Samson: and the child grew, and the Lord blessed him. (Judges 13:22–24)

In Isaiah 9:6, we have a direct prophecy concerning the name of the Blesser: "For unto us a Child is born, unto us a Son is given: and the government shall be upon His shoulder: and His name shall be called Wonderful פלא, Counsellor, the mighty God, the everlasting Father, the Prince of Peace." There is an insight in the Hebrew phrase "everlasting Father" *Avi ad* אבי עד that gives us the name of our Savior, whose name is "Wonderful" and "Everlasting Father." Starting with the ayin (ע) and counting every seventy-fifth letter in reverse spells *Yeshua* ישוע. This is a powerful revelation and messianic prophecy that was fulfilled in Yeshua the Messiah.

We can better understand the Scriptures that refer to the Lord in the first and second persons, where seemingly He speaks of Himself in the first person and then, suddenly, in the middle of the verse, he speaks of Himself in the second person.

The numerical value of *Yeshua* ישוע is 386, but His positional value is fifty-three. In Genesis 23:16, starting with the last yod (י) and counting every 386th letter from right to left spells *Yeshua* ישוע. The adjacent letters to each letter in Yeshua's name spell *rinnah Yonah* רנה יונה, which means "Jonah cried out (in joy or grief)." Jonah, the prophet of this book, is tied to Yeshua in the insights hundreds of years before either one came on the scene.

Then Jonah prayed unto the Lord his God out of the fish's belly, And said, I cried by reason of mine affliction unto the Lord, and He heard me; out of the belly of hell cried I, and Thou heardest my voice. (Jonah 2:1–2)

In the Hebrew Bible, the above verses are two and three, but in the King James Version, they are one and two. Starting with the sixth letter in the seventh word of verse three in the Hebrew Bible, the yod (י), and counting every 241st letter from left to right spells *Yeshua* ישרע. The adjacent letters spell *liphnai ahr* לפני ער, which means "before the face of the enemy." To completely grasp the significance of this combination, we need to understand what and who Yeshua faced while He was in the grave for the three days and nights. He came face-to-face with death, hell, and the grave, the Enemy of all mankind. He defeated Satan and made a show of him openly, conquering death, hell, and the grave with His resurrection. Notice, that Jonah cried from the belly of *she'ol* (hell).

Jonah 2:5, starting with the first mem (מ) and counting every sixty-ninth letter from left to right spells *Mashiach yam ahr* משיח ים ער. This combination means "the Messiah, the sea, and the enemy."

We read in Matthew 12:40, "For as Jonas [Jonah] was three days and three nights in the whale's belly; so shall the Son of man be three days and three nights in the heart of the earth." This event took place on Passover, when Yeshua was executed on the tree, placed in the tomb, and then resurrected after three days and three nights. Yeshua went to the heart of she'ol and defeated death, hell, and the grave for you and me.

> And when I saw Him, I fell at His feet as dead. And He laid His right hand upon me, saying unto me, Fear not; I Am the First and the Last: I Am He that liveth, and was dead; and, behold, I am alive for evermore, Amen; and have the keys of hell and of death. (Revelation 1:17–18)

Jonah 1:17 says, "Now the Lord had prepared a great fish to swallow up Jonah. And Jonah was in the belly of the fish three days and three nights." In the Hebrew Bible, this Scripture is Jonah 2:1. Beginning with the last yod (י) in Jonah 2:1, and counting every twelfth letter from left to right spells *Yeshua* ישוע, whom Jonah was portraying about eight hundred years before His birth.

The central theme of the book of Haggai is repentance and the rebuilding of the Temple of the Lord, which was destroyed by the Babylonians at least seventy years prior to the writings of the prophet Haggai. Though the Passover Feast is not mentioned, it is, however, alluded to in the insights, which relate to the book of Jonah and the new covenant in some measure. There is a span of about three hundred years from the prophet Jonah to the prophet Haggai. We must understand this one major truth: the Bible, as a whole, is interwoven throughout to give balance where balance is needed. Sometimes the Lord will give us a portion of truth in one book, and then, in another book, He will elaborate on the same subject matter with more clarity. Haggai was written about 516 years before the birth of Yeshua the Messiah. It focuses on the theme of the Feast of Dedication, along with important encoded messages concerning the coming Messiah, Yeshua.

Beginning in Haggai 1:15, there are some very interesting combinations that deserve a deeper analysis. Starting with the first shin (ש) and counting every thirteenth letter from right to left, gives us thirteen letters which compose four very important words: גּעשׁ אביב לילה שׁשׁ. At another location, five additional words that add more information to our study appear at thirteen-letter intervals: העץ השׂה האיל הכהן חשׁךְ. These nine words are defined as follows:

1. *Shaish* שׁשׁ means "six."
2. *Lilah* לילה means "night."
3. *Aviv* אביב is the first month of the Hebrew sacred

calendar, March or April, when the Feast of Passover is observed.

4. *Gah'ash* נעש means "to shake, quake violently, storm."

5. *Choshek* חשך means "to withhold light (darkness)."

6. *Ha'kohain* הכהן means "the priest."

7. *Ha'ayil* האיל means "the ram and leader of the flock."

8. *Ha'seh* השה means "the Lamb."

9. *Ha'aitz* העץ means "the tree (cross)."

Notice that the last letter of the third, fourth, fifth, and sixth words spell "in the presence (glory)" *be' shekan* בשכן. This is a reference to the presence of Yeshua the Messiah in the Temple.

1. Yeshua hung upon the cross six (שש) hours before His death. Mark 15:25, "And it was the third hour, and they crucified him."

2. For three hours it was as though it was night (לילה). Luke 23:44: "And it was about the sixth hour, and there was darkness over all the earth until the ninth hour."

3. This prophetic event took place on the fourteenth of Aviv אביב. Luke 22:1–2: "Now the feast of unleavened bread drew nigh, which is called the Passover. And the chief priests and scribes sought how they might kill Him; for they feared the people."

4. There was a great earthquake (*gah'ash* נעש). Matthew 27:50–54: "Jesus, when He had cried again with a loud voice, yielded up the ghost [spirit]. And, behold, the veil of the temple was rent in twain from the top to the bottom; and the earth did quake, and the rocks rent; And the graves were opened; and many bodies of the saints which slept arose, And came out of the graves after His resurrection, and went into the holy city, and appeared unto many. Now when the centurion, and they that were with him, watching Jesus, saw the earthquake, and those things that were done, they feared greatly, saying, Truly this was the Son of God."

5. The sun became darkened and withheld its light (*choshek* חשך). Luke 23:45: "And the sun was darkened, and the veil of the temple was rent in the midst."

6. Jesus was the High Priest (*Kohain* הכהן). Hebrews 7:17: "For he testifieth, Thou art a priest for ever after the order of Melchisedech."

7. Yeshua was the Ram (*ha'ayil* האיל) of God and the leader of the flock, because He is the Shepherd. Leviticus 19:22: "And the priest shall make an atonement for him with the ram [*ayil* איל] of the trespass offering before the Lord for his sin which he hath done: and the sin which he hath done shall be forgiven him.

8. Jesus was the Lamb (*haseh* השה) of God that was led to the slaughter for our sakes. John 1:29: "Behold the Lamb of God, which taketh away the sins of the world."

9. Jesus was hanged on a tree (*ha'aitz* העץ). Acts 5:30: "The God of our fathers raised up Jesus, whom ye slew and hanged on a tree."

The Feast of Pesach and Yom Kippur are separated by six months and have a great deal in common. Both these feasts represent atonement, salvation, and judgment. The flower of Egypt, the best the country had (firstborns, gods, Pharaoh, and so forth) was judged and destroyed during the first Passover, and correspondingly, the nations will be judged on a feast of Yom Kippur during Armageddon, introducing the messianic kingdom. The first Passover lamb was sacrificed, and the blood was applied to the lintel and doorpost. The blood of the sacrifice on Yom Kippur was taken by the high priest into the last room of the Tabernacle (*Mishkan* משכן), the most Holy of Holies (*kodesh hakadashim* קדש הקדשים) and applied on the Ark of the Covenant of the Lord (*Aron brit Jehovah* ארון ברית-יהוה) in the Holy of Holies to atone for the sins of the high priest, his family, Israel, and the nations. Yeshua did not need to atone for Himself because He was sinless, but He did atone for all the sins of the world, including yours. In the Holy of Holies, an inscription is engraved on the gold plate that covers the holy Ark of the Covenant: "Holiness to the Lord" *Kodesh le'Adonai* קדש ליהוה. It was there, where the High Priest (Yeshua) applied His blood after His resurrection — not on the earthly Ark of the Covenant, but on the holy Ark of the Covenant, which is in the heavenly Holy of Holies. One day soon, we shall see the altar where Yeshua applied His blood. Exodus 28:36 says, "And thou shalt make a plate of pure gold, and grave upon it, like the engravings of a signet HOLINESS TO THE LORD *(KODESH L'ADONAI* קדש ליהוה*)."* Starting with the shin (שׁ) in Kodesh קדשׁ and counting in both directions, every thirty-eighth letter spells *Yeshua* ישׁוע. The adjacent letters to Yeshua spell *a'dam* אדם, which means "the man."

In Zechariah 14:17 we find a combination reflecting the above insight that opens our understanding to the importance of Yeshua, the man: "And it shall be, that whoso will not come up of all the families of the earth unto Jerusalem to worship the King [Yeshua], the Lord of hosts, even upon them shall be no rain." We can see by this Scripture that there will be order and discipline during the messianic kingdom. "For as the lightning cometh out of the east, and shineth even unto the west; so shall also the coming of the Son of man [Jesus] be" (Matthew 24:27).

In Zechariah 14:17, starting with the second-to-the-last yod (י) and counting every twenty-sixth letter from left to right spells "Yeshua, the man" ישׁוע אדם. His name, which was engraved on the golden plate on the ark in the Holy of Holies, will be on the bells of the horses, as described in Zechariah 14:20. We also find His name in Exodus 28:36. Taking the last letter of each word, beginning with the last word, spells *haShem yo'ter* השׁם יותר, which means "the name is superior, above, over, to exceed." At the name of Lord Yeshua, every knee shall bow. Isaiah 45:22–23 says,

"Look unto Me, and be ye saved, all the ends of the earth: for I Am God, and there is none else. I have sworn by Myself, the Word is gone out of My mouth in righteousness, and shall not return, That unto Me every knee shall bow, every tongue shall swear [confess]." The same statement was made about Jesus. Some people have a difficult time understanding that the Lord was speaking of Himself and Jesus as one person. Hebrews 12:2 says, "Looking unto Jesus the Author and Finisher of our faith; Who for the joy that was set before Him endured the cross, despising the shame, and is set down at the right hand of the throne of God."

Isaiah 45:25 states, "In the Lord shall all the seed of Israel be justified, and shall glory." The phrase in verse 25 "seed of Israel" *zera Israel* זרע ישראל, gives us the exalted name of Jesus. Starting with the ayin (ע) and counting every sixtieth letter from right to left spells "Jesus" *Yeshua* ישוע.

> Hearken unto Me, O house of Jacob, and all the remnant of the house of Israel, which are borne by Me from the belly, which are carried from the womb: And even to your old age I am He awh yna; and even to hoar [gray] hairs will I carry you: I have made, and I will bear; even I will carry, and will deliver you.
>
> (Isaiah 46:3-4)

שמעו אלי בית יעקב וכל-שארית בית
ישראל העמסים מני-בטן הנשאים מני-רחם.
ועד-זקנה אני הוא ועד-שיבה אני אסבל
אני עשיתי ואני אשא ואני אסבל ואמלט.

The Holy Spirit has placed the name of the person who watches over Jacob (Israel) within the above Scripture. Also, in the Scripture we find Jacob's Creator, Yeshua ישוע, at five-letter intervals and at three-letter intervals. The combination, however, truly identifying Him as the Creator and protector of Jacob, is at twelve-letter intervals. Starting with the third letter in the first word and counting every twelfth letter from right to left spells "I (Myself) Am Jesus" *Ani Yeshua* אני ישוע. Many times, the Lord will say, "I Am He," or, "I Am the Lord your God," but here, we have an awesome statement by the Lord Himself: "I Am Jesus." Since the Lord is saving people out of every nation, He certainly will save Israel as well.

In Isaiah 46:4, the Hebrew phrase "I have made" *ani ahsiti* אני עשׂיתי gives us another combination relative to the above and also to Jonah. Starting with the first yod (י) in the word "made" עשׂיתי and counting every sixty letter from left to right spells *Yeshua hayeled* ישׁוע הילד, which means "Jesus, the Manchild (Son)." The Hebrew word *yeled* ילד is also used in Isaiah 9:5: "For unto us a Child (ילד) is born, unto us a Son is given: and the government shall be upon His shoulder: and His name shall be called Wonderful, Counsellor, the mighty God, the everlasting Father, the Prince of Peace." The adjacent letters, spell "Jonah" יונה, which means "dove." The Spirit of God rested upon Jesus in the form of a dove when He was baptized, yet another sign of Jonah for Israel.

Without question, Jesus is the Son and the Creator. Scripture shows that Yeshua came from the seed of Israel and is also their Creator. This can only be understood from the Holy Word of God. Jesus (Yeshua) is the root and offspring of David; the Progenitor and Son. "I Jesus have sent Mine angel to testify unto you these things in the churches. I Am the root [progenitor] and the offspring [Son] of David, and the Bright and Morning Star" (Revelation 22:16).

> Wherefore God also hath highly exalted Him, and given Him a name which is above every name: That at the name of Jesus every knee should bow, of things in heaven, and things in earth, and things

under the earth; And that every tongue should confess that Jesus Christ is Lord, to the glory of God the Father. (Philippians 2:9–11)

The month of Elul אלול is the time of repentance to the Lord and occurs forty days before Yom Kippur. The awesome trials of Jonah began in the month of Elul, when he rebelled against God and was cast into the deep. But God had compassion on Jonah and prepared a great fish for him. In the final analysis, Jonah repented in measure and ran to Nineveh.

In Jonah 2:2, the last word is *ha'dagah* הדגה, which means "the fish." Taking the first letter of each word from right to left spells *miqveh* מקוה, which means "baptized in water." Jonah surely had his *miqveh* and came forth a different person. In Jonah 2:4, starting with the first shin (שׁ) and counting every fifth letter from left to right spells *sus shanan ha'atzar Jehovah elul* שׁרשׁ שׁנן האחר יהוה אלול, which means "rejoice, teach (sharpen, point, prepare for judgment) the treasure of Adonai (in the month of) Elul." In Deuteronomy 6:7 the Hebrew word *shanan* שׁנן is used in the *shma* שׁמע which means "to teach the concepts (both positive and negative) of the Torah (Law)." Jonah repented in the fish's belly. "When my soul fainted within me I remembered the Lord; and my prayer came in unto Thee, into Thine holy temple" (Jonah 2:7).

Jonah made a three-day journey in one day after the fish spewed him out. Can you imagine, for a moment, the conditions in the fish's belly? Jonah may have been bleached from the enzymes of the fish's belly. I can picture him as a white streak running through the desert toward Nineveh. One would think that Jonah would make full repentance, given his attitude toward the Ninevites and the consequences of a rebellious heart. But something was not yet complete (perfect) in Jonah's heart. He did not care at all for Gentiles, but God had not yet finished His work in Jonah. Jonah 3:4 says, "And Jonah began to enter into the city a day's journey, and he cried and said, 'Yet forty days, and Nineveh shall be overthrown.'"

Starting with the last shin (שׁ) in Jonah 3:10 and counting every seventh letter from left to right spells *shalav* שׁלב, which means "equidistant-sequence." The adjacent letters, spell *oht* אות, which means "letter" or "a sign." In this series of the seven-letter spacing, we will come across different words and phrases.

1. *l'shanah moreh* לשׁנה מורה, which means "the year of Moreh (the teacher of righteousness, and the early rain)," which is the first month (Tishri) on the civil calendar.

2. Wife *ishah* אשׁה.

3. Moses *Moshe* משׁה.

4. heaven *shamayim* שׁמים.

All these terms are God-related, proving the divinely inspired Word of God. The people of Nineveh believed Jonah and repented. "So the people of Nineveh believed God, and proclaimed a fast, and put on sackcloth, from the greatest of them even to the least of them. . . . And God saw their works, that they turned from their evil way; and God repented of the evil, that He had said that He would do unto them; and He did it not" (Jonah 3:5, 10).

God had given a conditional prophecy concerning Nineveh. If they repented, He would not judge them in severity, but if they did not repent, sore judgment was sure to come. This type of prophecy refers to all humankind. Jonah makes a *sukkah* (booth) [prior to the Feast of Sukkot]. "So Jonah went out of the city, and sat on the east side of the city, and there made him a booth, and sat under it in the shadow, till he might see what would become of the city" (Jonah 4:5).

In Jonah 4:7, starting with the first lamed (ל) and counting every 243rd letter from left to right spells *l'choshen kain Yeshua* לחשן כן ישוע, which means "a breastplate for upright (honest) Yeshua." Only the high priest was permitted to wear the breastplate. The adjacent letters spell *ha'navai* הנביא, which means "the prophet." Yeshua is our prophet, high priest, and king. These insights show us that Yeshua is in the position of High Priest in the heavenlies, ready to make intercession for us according to the will of God. Apparently, the Lord looked forward to the Atonement and applied the finished work of His sacrifice, spanning the ages to bring temporary deliverance to a sinful city. Though their cleansing was not yet ratified in reality by the blood of the Lamb of God, God, in His grace, leaped over the dispensation of the "age of the curse" and brought salvation to the Gentiles of that city. Nineveh's repentance reminds me of King David. David knew how to repent, and God honored his repentance because He foresaw that David would one day have his place in glory, but not until the Son of David became his substitute for sin and rejection.

When Jonah's prayer entered into the Holy of Holies of the throne room (Temple) of the Lord in heaven, his request was received by the High Priest. Who was interceding for Jonah? Could it have been our Lord and Savior, Yeshua, our High Priest? We must remember that the earthly building of God is a pattern of the heavenly.

> Who serve unto the example and shadow of heavenly things, as Moses was admonished of God when he was about to make the tabernacle: for, See, saith He, that thou make all things according to the pattern showed to thee in the mount.
>
> (Hebrews 8:5)

> But Christ being come an High Priest of good things to come, by a greater and more perfect tabernacle, not made with hands, that is to say, not of this [earthly] building.   (Hebrews 9:11)

In spite of Jonah's rebellion, God's purpose was fulfilled in Jonah's mission. However, Jonah was still angry at God for sparing the people of Nineveh, and he was provoked to jealousy. "But I say, Did not Israel know? First Moses saith, I will provoke you to jealousy by them that are no people, and by a foolish nation I will anger you" (Romans 10:19). The apostle Paul posed the question, "I say then, Have they stumbled that they should fall? God forbid: but rather through their fall salvation[Yeshua] is come unto the Gentiles, for to provoke them to jealousy" (Romans 11:11).

We see, in type, these Scriptures reflected in Jonah's dislike and jealousy of the Gentiles — Nineveh. In Nehemiah we learn some of the names of the Jews who were responsible for the rebuilding of the wall and the Second Temple, which were destroyed by the Babylonians. It is quite interesting that certain other names and events are also encoded within these few Scriptures.

> Mattaniah, and Bakbukiah, Obadiah, Meshullam, Talmon, Akkub, were porters keeping the ward at the thresholds of the gates. These were in the days of Joiakim the son of Jeshua, the son of Jozadak, and in the days of Nehemiah the governor, and of Ezra the priest, the scribe. And at the dedication of the wall of Jerusalem they sought the Levites. . . .
> (Nehemiah 12:25–27b)

מתניה ובקבקיה עבדיה משלם טלמון עקוב שמרים
שוערים משמר באספי השערים: אלה בימי יויקים בן-
ישוע בן-יוצדק ובימי נחמיה הפחה ועזרא הכהן הסופר:
ובחנכת חומת ירושלם בקשו את הלוים

In Nehemiah 12:25 the last letter of the last four words spell *Miryam* מרים, which means "bitter waters." The first letter of each word in verse 26, beginning with the first word spells *avivi beYonah* אביבי ביונה, which means "My Aviv, in Jonah." The phrase "My Aviv" refers to the month when Yeshua was crucified. In the book of Jonah, this month is linked to the three days and three nights that Yeshua was in the grave. In verse 27, starting with the fifth letter in the sixth word and counting every eighth letter in reverse spells "our Messiah" מְשִׁיחֵנוּ. This was the time when they were dedicating the walls of Jerusalem after the Jews came back from captivity. This same Temple under construction was the Temple where Jesus taught the people and where He made the famous statement in the gospel of John: "Jesus answered and said unto them, Destroy this temple, and in three days I will raise it up. Then said the Jews, forty and six years was this temple in building, and wilt Thou rear it up in three days? But He spake of the temple of His Body." (John 2:19–21)

In Jonah 2:9, starting with the fourth letter in the second word and counting every ninth letter from right to left spells "Jacob" *Ya'akov* יעקב. In this same count of nine, using the qof (ק) in *Ya'akov* and counting every seventy-second letter in both directions spells יעקב the second time. Also, in this nine-letter count we find *Jehovah* יהוה. Jacob is referred to as Israel. When God was speaking of the Tribulation, He said that it was the time of Jacob's trouble. We see a tremendous connection between Jonah's trouble and the time of Jacob's trouble, the Tribulation, yet another sign of Jonah. In this same verse, starting with the fifth letter in the first word and counting every 194th letter from right to left spells "Joseph" יוסף. Also, from the same vav (ו) in "Joseph" and counting every 309th letter in both directions spells *Yoseph* יוסף the second time. It is no wonder that the name of Joseph would show up in these passages. It was Yeshua ben Joseph ישוע בן יוסף, the suffering Messiah from Israel (*Ya'akov*), Who fulfilled the prophetic picture portrayed by Jonah. Still another sign of Jonah.

In Jonah 2:6, starting with the third letter in the seventh

word and counting every 153rd letter from left to right spells *hapenah* הפנה, which means "the (chief) corner." This could refer to the Chief Cornerstone, Yeshua. The adjacent letters spell "Elul" אלול, the sixth month, or the month of returning and repenting before the Lord.

In Jonah 2:4, starting with the first letter in the sixth word and counting every 153rd letter from left to right spells *Jehovah* יהוהי; from left to right and from right to left. The adjacent letters spell *kur Hadasah* כור הרסה, which means "tender myrtle tree." This was also Esther's name before it was changed. Queen Esther was in the right place at the right time to help bring about complete deliverance to the Jewish captives in Persia. This wonderful story of deliverance is a picture of Mordecai as the Messiah, and Esther as the Bride, coming to the rescue of Israel in its tribulation.

In Jonah 2:8, starting with the second letter in the third word and counting every 153rd letter from right to left spells "to distinguish, set apart" *palah* פלה, and counting in the opposite way, every 153rd letter spells *Roiyah* רעיה, which means "the Shepherd Lord." The adjacent letters at 459-letter intervals spells אור and יונה, which mean "Jonah" and "light." Jonah's commission was to bring the light of the glorious Good News to the Gentiles. The 153-letter count reminds me of the Scripture in John 21:11: "Simon Peter went up, and drew the net to land full of great fishes, an hundred and fifty and three: and for all there were so many, yet was not the net broken." This is a picture of God's people who have been rescued from the troubled waters of the world and captivated by His love and Spirit. Notice that not one was lost. Neither shall we be lost if we are in His holy net of redemption.

The experiences of Jonah in Nineveh was and still is a scenario of God's purpose for all His people, regardless of whether they are Jew or Gentile. If Jonah had had a willing heart full of love for the doomed Ninevites, he would have had a better time of it all. It is doubtful, however, if Jonah will receive a full reward for his efforts. First Corinthians 13:1 reflects this thought: "Though I speak with the tongues of men and of angels, and have not charity [love], I am become as sounding brass, or a tinkling cymbal."

This Scripture does not say that others will not benefit from such a person's ministry, but that the person is like sounding brass to the Lord and to himself. Why? Because he does not minister with love. Many people have been blessed by the words of ministers, but that does not mean that the minister delivered his message with love. It would be much better for him if he had. Jonah was God's spokesperson for Nineveh; it was God who was speaking through him. Had it been left up to Jonah, he might still be on that ship to Tarshish, running from God and shunning his spiritual responsibility at a time of impending disaster for a sinful nation.

> So shall My word be that goeth forth out of My mouth: it shall not return unto Me void, but it shall accomplish that which I please, and it shall prosper in the thing whereto I sent it. (Isaiah 55:11)

Starting with the second letter in the second word and counting forward every thirty-second letter spells "the Messiah" *HaMashiach* המשיח. How many times have we quoted this Scripture from memory? Each time you say His Word, somewhere within the context of the words that you speak, there is a message so powerful that heaven sings praises unto Him with reverberating beauty. We may not always understand His Word; it is not visible nor is it audible. Nevertheless, His name is being resounded and echoed from our hearts throughout the chambers of glory, so that even our precious Lord and Savior joins with us in perfect harmony — a praise that is forever recorded in His annals of the great deeds of humankind.

ORDER FORM

Quantity	Code	Description	Price	Total
		Softback Books		
	BK-3	Messiah – War in the Middle East & The Road to Armageddon	$12.99	
	BK-4	Apocalypse – The Coming Judgment of the Nations	$12.99	
	BK-5	Prince of Darkness – Antichrist and the New World Order	$13.99	
	BK-6	Final Warning – Economic Collapse and Coming World Government	$13.99	
	BK-7	Heaven – The Mystery of Angels	$12.95	
	BK-8	The Signature of God – Astonishing Biblical Discoveries	$13.95	
	BK-9	Yeshua – The Name of Jesus Revealed in the Old Testament	$11.95	
	BK-10	Armageddon – Appointment With Destiny	$12.99	
	BK-11	His Name is Jesus – The Mysterious Yeshua Codes	$12.99	
	BK-12	The Handwriting of God – Sacred Mysteries of the Bible	$13.99	
		ANY THREE BOOKS OR MORE **EACH**	$11.00	
		Videos		
	V-1	Rebuilding the Temple and Its Treasures	$19.99	
	V-2	The Ark of the Covenant and The Red Heifer	$19.99	
	V-3	The Coming Russian Invasion and Armageddon	$19.99	
	V-4	Russia's Secret Agenda	$19.99	
	V-5	The Rebirth of Israel and The Messiah	$19.99	
	V-6	The Antichrist and The Mark of The Beast	$19.99	
	V-7	The Rapture and Heaven's Glory	$19.99	
	V-8	The Coming Millennial Kingdom	$19.99	
	V-9	The Search for The Messiah	$19.99	
	V-10	The European Superstate and The Tribulation	$19.99	
	V-12	Financial Strategies and Assault on Our Freedom	$19.99	
	V-13	Archeological Discoveries: Exploring Beneath the Temple Mount	$19.99	
	V-14	Prince of Darkness and The Final Inquisition	$19.99	
	V-15	Agenda of The New World Order and The Tribulation	$19.99	
	V-16	Rush to Armageddon	$19.99	
		ANY TWO VIDEOS OR MORE **EACH**	$17.00	
ORDER THE ENTIRE FRONTIER RESEARCH LIBRARY		(All of the above items)	$339.99	
		Total this page (to be carried forward)		

continued overleaf

ORDER FORM

Quantity	Code	Description	Price	Total
		Total from previous page		
		Hardcover Books		
	HC-H	Heaven – The Mystery of Angels	$19.95	
	HC-S/G	The Signature of God – Astonishing Biblical Discoveries	$19.95	
		Double-length Videos		
	V-17	The Signature of God – Astonishing Biblical Discoveries	$34.95	
	V-18	Mysterious Bible Codes	$29.99	
	VP-1	Final Warning, Big Brother Government	$29.99	
		Audio Cassettes		
	AB-14	The Signature of God – The Audio Album (2 tapes)	$15.99	
	AB-15	Mysterious Bible Codes – The Audio Album (2 tapes)	$15.99	
	AP-01	Super Money Management for Christians (6 tapes)	$39.99	
		Computer Programs		
	IBM-1	Torah Codes (educational software for IBM-compatible computers)	$call	
	MAC-1	Torah Codes (educational software for Macintosh computers)	$call	
	IBM-2	Bible Scholar (educational software in Hebrew and English)	$call	
	MAC-2	Bible Scholar (educational software in Hebrew and English)	$call	
	PIB	**Product Brochure**	No charge	
		News Updates		
		Destiny Dateline Tape of the Month (12 tapes)	$89.99	
		Oklahoma residents add 7.5% sales tax		
		Canadian residents add 7% G.S.T.		
		One low shipping and handling fee (per order) for U.S. and Canada	$4.95	$4.95

Additional shipping charges will apply to orders outside North America

Grand Total

U.S. orders: mail along with your check or money order to:
Frontier Research Publications • P.O. Box 470470 • Tulsa, OK 74147-0470

U.S. credit card orders: call 1-800-883-1812

Canadian orders: remit payment to:
Frontier Research Publications • P.O. Box 129, Station "U" • Toronto, Ontario M8Z 5M4

Canadian VISA card orders: call 1-800-853-1423

Prices effective July 1, 1997